Jon E. Lewis is the editor ... series, including *The Autobiography of ...* book! 5 stars,' *Sunday Express*), *England: The Autobiography* and *London: The Autobiography*. His father served with a Seafire – the Spitfire – squadron during the Second World War.

Also by Jon E. Lewis

London: The Autobiography
World War II: The Autobiography
Rome: The Autobiography
The Autobiography of the British Soldier
England: The Autobiography

SPITFIRE

The Autobiography

Edited by Jon E. Lewis

Constable & Robinson Ltd
3 The Lanchesters
162 Fulham Palace Road
London W6 9ER

www.constablerobinson.com

First published in the UK by Robinson,
an imprint of Constable & Robinson Ltd, 2010

A copy of the British Library Cataloguing in Publication

Data is available from the British Library

ISBN: 978-1-84901-392-5

Printed and bound in the UK

1 3 5 7 9 10 8 6 4 2

Contents

I should like an outfit of Spitfires.
Hauptmann Adolf Galland, Luftwaffe, on being asked by
Reichsmarschall Hermann Göring what he needed for his
squadron during the Battle of Britain.

*On taking over 64 Squadron, one of the first things I impressed
on my pilots was that you did not 'strap yourself in', you
'buckled the Spitfire on', like girding on armour in days of old. I
knew it was essential: the Spitfire became an integral part and
extension of one's own sensitivity.*
                    Squadron Leader Wilfrid Duncan Smith, RAF

INTRODUCTION

Taking Wing – The Birth of the Spitfire

'The Supermarine Shrew.' Such was R.J. Mitchell's preferred name for his invention answering to Air Ministry specification F37/34. Sir Robert McLean, the chairman of Vickers; the company that had bought out the Supermarine Aviation Works, instead named the aeroplane after his daughter Ann, whom he considered 'a little spitfire'. R.J. Mitchell persisted in thinking 'Spitfire' to be a 'bloody silly name' for his small but deadly fighter.

Reginald Joseph Mitchell may have lacked an ear for a name but he did not lack an eye for design. The Supermarine Spitfire was Mitchell's most famous aircraft, but it was far from being his only one. Born to husband and wife teachers on 20 May 1895, at 115 Congleton Road, Butt Lane, near Stoke-on-Trent, Mitchell was 'mad about aeroplanes' from an early age and was making gliders with paper and bamboo even before the Wright brothers took to the air with *Kitty Hawk* in 1903. Yet opportunities for work in aviation engineering in Edwardian England were scarce and when Mitchell left school he was apprenticed to the drawing office of the nearby Kerr, Stuart & Co.

locomotive manufacturers, who specialized in the construction of engines for narrow gauge railways.

In 1915 Mitchell volunteered for the Royal Flying Corps but Kerr, Stuart & Co. refused to release him. Still intent on a career in aviation, Mitchell took night school classes at Stoke in mathematics and engineering, with a view to a job in aeroplane manufacturing.

Mitchell's persistence won its reward. At twenty-two he was employed as a draughtsman by the Supermarine Aviation Works at Woolston, Southampton. Founded in 1913 by Hubert Scott-Paine and the adventurous Noel Pemberton-Billing (who, during the Great War, had organized a bombing raid by Royal Navy aircraft on the Zeppelin sheds at Lake Constance), Supermarine specialized in seaplanes. Three years after arriving at the Supermarine works, 'R.J.' became the company's chief engineer and designer, and the range of Supermarine aircraft began to broaden markedly. Aside from flying boats, Supermarine designed light aircraft, bombers and fighters, no less than twenty-four of them coming from Mitchell's own drawing board, but few of them displayed the Spitfire's elegance. The cumbersome Southampton flying boat, the only less slightly lumbering Stranraer flying boat and the Walrus amphibian bi-plane, were workhorses, successful ones, but workhorses nonetheless.

Mitchell's real fascination, however, was speed. He was at the right place, because Supermarine had been involved with the Schneider Trophy since 1919. Named after Jacques Schneider, a French financier and aviation enthusiast, the prize of an art nouveau bronze and silver statue (plus 25,000 French francs) was awarded to the fastest seaplane in the world in an annual race. Schneider's intention had been to entice global progress in civil aviation; instead, the trophy became a ruthless contest between countries. National pride notwithstanding, most gimlet-eyed governments could also see the military advantages from supporting their Schneider teams. In the post-war era planes were seen as the machines that would break the deadlock of any future conflict.

Mitchell and Supermarine won the Schneider Trophy in 1922, and then twice in a row, 1927 and 1928. Alas, Supermarine then flew into a political mountain. in the middle of the Depression, Labour Prime Minister Ramsay MacDonald decided he could not continue with the traditional government sponsorship of the British Schneider effort. Although there was outrage ('Government blunder. Public astounded', headlined the *Daily Mail*), MacDonald took comfort from the view of Sir Hugh Trenchard, Marshal of the RAF, who could see 'nothing of value' in the air race and regarded the Schneider seaplanes as 'freak machines'.

Salvation for Supermarine came from Dame Lucy Houston, a showgirl with a habit of marrying well, who, on declaring that her 'blood boiled' at Labour's lack of patriotic fibre, promptly wrote the company a cheque for £100,000. Dame Lucy's largesse was used to improve the shape and engine of the Supermarine S6; it won the 1931 trophy race with ease. Two weeks later, with Flight Lieutenant George Stainforth in the cockpit, the S6B broke the 400mph barrier with a speed of 407.5mph.

Trenchard was wrong; the Supermarine S6B was not a freak. It was a goddess of the air that influenced British fighter design. One need only look at the sleekness of the S6B monoplane to see its genetic consequences in the Spitfire. The beautiful shape owed much to Mitchell's artistry but also to a revolution in engineering that had occurred across the ocean. Mitchell, like everyone else in aviation, had been seduced by the inline, V-configuration, liquid-cooled engine that had allowed the Americans to win the Schneider Trophy in 1923 at 177.38mph and then again in 1925 at 232.57mph. The traditional air-cooled rotary engine had a large fan front; the inline liquid-cooled engine was long and thin, thus allowing designers to create a more streamlined craft.

The engine in Mitchell's S6B seaplane was a Rolls-Royce R-Type V12, which bore more than a passing resemblance to an American Curtiss D-12 engine disassembled in the Rolls-Royce factory in Derby, by Henry Royce himself. A development of the R-Type by Rolls-Royce engineers R.W. Harvey-Bailey and James Ellor led to a smaller 27-litre V12 engine for sustained high speed flight. Rolls-Royce had the habit of calling their engines after birds of prey and the Griffon, Vulture, Eagle, Kestrel and Peregrine all found their home under the cowlings of RAF aircraft. For the new engine, Rolls chose the name Merlin. There was another connotation to the cognomen 'Merlin'; one of wizardry, for Merlin was King Arthur's sorcerer-in-chief. Not a few pilots of Spitfires believed that the engine that pulled their plane through the sky was a piece of mechanical magic.

Nobody knew it yet, but the pieces of the Spitfire were beginning to assemble in the backroom of history. The engine existed. The basic monoplane shape was there. All that was needed was a moment of design inspiration.

Instead, R.J. Mitchell was in the midst of a design nightmare. In 1930 the Air Ministry issued specification number F7/30 for a fighter plane armed with four .303 machine guns. For four years Mitchell laboured with Type 224, a grotesque monoplane which lacked flaps on the wings – making it nigh on impossible to land safely – and a wretchedly overcomplicated cooling system. Type 224 was so erratic that, in 1935, the RAF chose the old-fashioned Gloster Gladiator bi-plane in its stead. By then Mitchell himself had undergone surgery to remove cancer of the rectum, which had resulted in the re-routing of his severed colon though his abdominal wall, requiring him to wear a colostomy bag. Some would have retired to domesticity with such a disability, but Mitchell went back to work. Needless to say, his legendary temper was not improved.

Perhaps it was the awareness of his own mortality, perhaps it was the pressure of the historical imperative that came with the rise of Nazism and Göring's building of the Luftwaffe in contravention of the Versailles treaty, perhaps it was the insight into flying that came from winning his own wings – whatever, in 1934 Mitchell had the shining idea. There was also the opportunity to develop it. Destined to be remembered as the arch appeaser of Hitler, Neville Chamberlain had a rather different, earlier incarnation as the Chancellor of the Exchequer who, in 1934, pushed through increased spending on RAF fighters, to the delight of Air Vice-Marshal Sir Hugh Dowding, the Air Member for Supply and Research. Dowding was a modernist and on this occasion backed his subordinate, Air Commodore Cave-Brown-Cave, in pressurizing the Air Ministry to offer Mitchell one more chance to design a fast monoplane fighter. As a result, on 5 January 1935, the Air Ministry issued Supermarine a contract for a new fighter, officially designated F37/34.

Within five months Mitchell had a mock-up ready to show the Ministry. At Mitchell's insistence the Spitfire's wings were thin; his Canadian aerodynamicist Beverley Shenstone, who had worked with the Heinkel aircraft manufacturing company in

Germany, responded with an elliptical shape. Shenstone Said later:

> The elliptical wing was decided upon quite early on. Aerodynamically it was the best for our purpose because the induced drag, that caused in producing lift, was lowest when this shape was used; the ellipse was an ideal shape, theoretically a perfection. There were other advantages, so far as we were concerned. To reduce drag we wanted the lowest possible wing thickness-to-cord ratio, consistent with the necessary strength . . . Mitchell was an intensely practical man and he liked practical solutions to problems. I remember once discussing the wing shape with him and he commented: 'I don't give a b—— whether it's elliptical or not, as long as it covers the guns!' The ellipse was simply the shape that allowed us the thinnest possible wing with sufficient room inside it to carry the necessary structure and the things we wanted to cram in.

Mitchell and Shenstone wanted to 'cram in' the wheels and eight .303 Browning machine guns. Squadron Leader Ralph Sorley of the Operational Requirements section at the Air Ministry had calculated that in combat the pilot of an F37/34 would likely only manage a two second burst against the metal, fast high-flying bombers of Nazi Germany. And Nazi Germany was likely to be the enemy. About his involvement with the Spitfire, Sorley recollected:

> Like so many others, I had spent many years trying to hit targets with one, two, or even four machine guns, with, I confess, singularly poor results. Others were so much better,

but I estimated that, if one could hold the sight on for longer than two seconds, that was better than average. We were now going to have to hold it on at appreciably higher speeds, so the average might be even less than two seconds . . . By 1934 a new Browning gun was at last being tested in Britain which offered a higher rate of fire. After much arithmetic and burning of midnight oil, I reached the answer of eight guns as being the number required to give a lethal dose in two seconds of fire . . . to obtain confirmation I arranged with a Major Thompson, who had helped me so much over the Browning gun data, that we would obtain an obsolete aircraft, set it up on a range, mount eight guns at 400 yards, fire bursts of two seconds with solid and explosive ammunition, and assess what happened. This we did on the ranges at Shoebury, and to my joy the effect was all I imagined. The structure was cut through in so many vulnerable places that one could safely count on two seconds as being the necessary lethal dose.

A two second 'squirt' from eight .303 Brownings, firing at the rate of eighteen rounds a second, would put 288 bullets into an enemy aircraft. However, with eight Brownings spread out along the elliptical wings of the F37/34, there was no room for aviation fuel, which was stored in a small tank between the engine and the cockpit. Fred Meredith's neatly efficient radiator and the adoption of ethylene glycol as the coolant for the Merlin (now improved to produce 990hp) enabled Mitchell to design a very slim nose for the fighter, which went under the factory code of Supermarine Type 300.

In February 1936 an unpainted prototype of Supermarine Type 300, K5054, was wheeled out from behind its tarpaulin screen in the corner of the Woolston works near Southampton. After a number of engineering tests, carried out at night to prevent prying from German mail planes who docked nearby, the aircraft was dismantled and taken to the Supermarine hangar at Eastleigh to await its first test flight.

At 4.35 a.m. on 6 March 1936, Vickers' chief test pilot, Flying Officer Joseph 'Mutt' Summers, took K5054 to the air for eight minutes. Among the small group watching was Summers' assistant, Jeffrey Quill, a twenty-three-year-old former RAF pilot. Soon Quill was to take over the testing of the Spitfire, yet of all his recollections of the Spitfire that maiden flight remained strongest:

There was a light wind blowing across the aerodrome which meant that 'Mutt' had to take the short run, and he taxied towards one of the four large Chance lights which (in those days) were situated round the perimeter, turned into the wind and opened the throttle. The aeroplane was airborne after a very short run and climbed away comfortably. 'Mutt' did not retract the undercarriage on that first flight – deliberately, of course – but cruised around fairly gently for some minutes, checking the lowering of the flaps and the slow flying and stalling characteristics, and then brought K5054 in to land. Although he had less room than he would probably have liked, he put the aeroplane down on three points without too much 'float', in which he was certainly aided by the fine-pitch setting of the propeller. He taxied towards the hangar and the point where we in the group of Supermarine spectators were standing . . . When 'Mutt' shut down the engine and everybody crowded round the cockpit, with 'RJ' foremost, 'Mutt' pulled off his helmet and said firmly, 'I don't want anything touched.' This was soon destined to become a widely misinterpreted remark. What he meant was that there were no snags which required correction or adjustment before he flew the aircraft again. The remark has crept into folklore implying that the aeroplane was perfect in every respect from the moment of its first flight, an obviously absurd and impracticable idea.

If the Spitfire was not yet perfect it was, as Summers stated in his report after his fourth flight in K5054, 'remarkably good' in its handling.

When the reports of Summers and observers from the RAF reached the Air Ministry there was a sense of relief, even excitement. Now Britain, it seemed, had a modern fighter to counter the Luftwaffe. Among the rejoicing, R.J. Mitchell hid a bitter disappointment. He had expected his machine to excess 350mph, whereas it managed only 335mph, only a fraction faster than the Hurricane fighter being developed by Sidney Camm at Hawker. Mitchell's anxiety dissipated over the coming weeks with a series of improvements including an ultra smooth paint finish and an improved propeller. In the restyled K5054 Jeffrey Quill reached 348mph. 'I think we have something here,' he said on landing.

Flight Lieutenant Humphrey Edwardes-Jones concurred. At RAF Martlesham Heath on 26 May, Edwardes-Jones put the K5054 through its official paces for the Air Ministry. Despite a near disaster when he almost forgot to wind down the retractable undercarriage, he found she 'handled very well'. Edwardes-Jones had been requested to urgently telephone the Air Ministry as soon as he landed to give his opinion of the new plane. When asked by the new Air Member for Research and Development, Sir Wilfrid Freeman (Dowding having been promoted to

Commander-in-Chief Fighter Command), whether young pilots would be able to cope with such 'an advanced aircraft', Edwardes-Jones replied 'Yes, provided they are given adequate instruction in the use of flaps and retracting carriage.'

Satisfied, Freeman ordered 310 Spitfires to be delivered by March 1939. It was the largest ever order given to a British aviation manufacturer. The total price of the contract for 310 was £1,395,000, excluding the engine, radio and guns. The planes were to be built at Supermarine's Southampton plant and a 'shadow' factory at Castle Bromwich in the Midlands. Meanwhile, the Spitfire made its first public appearance at a Vickers open day at Eastleigh on 18 June and within the fortnight, crowds at Hendon, London, for the RAF Pageant, thrilled to 'the world's fastest fighter'. A high climbing one too; when Edwardes-Jones took K5054 up to 34,700 feet he observed vapour trails coming from the exhaust pipes on the nose, the first he had ever seen.

The Spitfire had other novelties. The slender shape of the wings allowed the Spitfire to perform turns so tight and fast that the pilot pulled 'g's (acceleration due to gravity), which might cause blackouts. Yet the selfsame elliptical wings had a forgiving quality; because the wing was thicker near the fuselage, the plane gave a wobble of alarm before stalling in a too tight turn. This made the 'Spit' extremely safe to fly in combat, as a future Spitfire ace, Wilfrid Duncan Smith, noted:

> One of the features of the Spitfire I discovered was how beautifully she behaved at low speeds and at high 'g' close to the stall. With full power in a steep turn and at slow speeds she would judder and shake, rocking to and fro, but as long as she was handled correctly she would not let go

and spin – surely a unique feature for a high performance aeroplane!

It is sometimes mooted that Shenstone 'cribbed' the elliptical wing shape of the Spitfire from the Heinkel 70 transport plane, which he always denied, pointing out that the elliptical wing had been used on other aircraft and that the Spitfire's wing was always much thinner. Shenstone, did admit to one influence of the Heinkel 70 on the Spitfire, however: at the Paris Aero Show he had been greatly impressed by the smoothness of the Heinkel 70's skin. 'I ran my hand over the surface and it was so smooth that I thought it might be constructed of wood,' he recalled later. In a letter exchange with Heinkel he established that the skinning was of metal with countersunk rivets. He adopted much the same method for the Spitfire to allow it to cleave through the air with a clean line.

Throughout 1937 and 1938 the Spitfire was modified. New exhaust pipes increased the top speed to 360mph. When it was discovered that the Brownings seized up with cold at height, engine heat had to be diverted to the armaments. The internal structure of the wing was strengthened, permitting the Spitfire to dive at 470mph. In July 1938, the first production Spitfire rolled out of Supermarine's Woolston works. An issue of the specialist journal the *Aeroplane* carried the first precise public specifications of this Spitfire Mark I:

The Spitfire is of straightforward stressed-skin design. The elliptical cantilever low wing, which tapers in thickness, is built upon a single spar with tubular flanges and a plate web. Forward of the spar, the wing is covered with a heavy gauge light alloy sheet, which forms the torsion box with the spar.

Aft of the spar, the covering is of thinner gauge sheet with light alloy girder ribs. The wing spars are detachable for ease of maintenance and repair. Split flaps are between the ailerons and the fuselage.

The fuselage is an all-metal monocoque, built on four main longerons with transverse frames and a flush riveted light alloy skin. The front frame forms the fireproof bulkhead and is built as an integral part with the centre portion of the main wing spar. To help in maintenance the tail portion of the fuselage with fin and tailplane is detachable.

The tail unit is of the cantilever monoplane type. The fin is integral with the rear fuselage. The tailplane is of metal with smooth metal covering. The elevator and rudders have light alloy frames and fabric covering. There are trimming tabs on elevator and rudder.

The undercarriage is fully retractable outwards into the under surface of the wings. There are two Vickers cantilever oleo-pneumatic shock absorber legs which are retracted hydraulically. An emergency hand system is fitted to lower the wheels should the hydraulic system be damaged. The first Spitfire had a tail skid, but the production models have a fully castoring tail wheel which does not retract.

The Rolls-Royce Merlin II 12-cylinder Vee liquid-cooled motor when operating on 87 octane is rated at 990hp at 12,250 feet, and has a maximum output of 1,030hp at 16,250 feet and for take-off. The forward facing intake effect gives a top speed at a rather greater height. The motor is slung in a steel tube mounting.

The radiator, which is fully ducted to give low drag by low velocity cooling, is in a duct underneath the starboard wing with a hinged flap for temperature control. The oil tank of fifty-five gallons capacity is underneath the engine with its surface forming part of the body contour. There are two fuel tanks with a total of eighty-five imperial gallons capacity in the fuselage in front of the pilot. Feed is direct to the engine through fuel pumps. There is an electric starter and hand turning gear.

The enclosed cockpit is set over the wings with a sliding canopy and hinged panel in the fuselage for entry and exit.

The armament is eight Browning guns mounted in the wings, four on each side of the fuselage. Access to them, for inspection and maintenance, is through doors in the top and bottom surface of the wings. A camera gun is also installed and has proved of use in showing details of fights with enemy aeroplanes. There is full radio installation, electrical, night flying and blind-flying equipment.

For security reasons, the *Aeroplane* did not publish the Spitfire's top speed: It was 362mph at 18,500 feet. The service ceiling was 34,500 feet. The length of the aircraft was 29 feet 11 inches, and the wingspan 36 feet 10 inches.

Mitchell never lived to see the Mark I take to the sky; the cancer returned and claimed his life on 11 June 1937. He was forty-two. At the moment of interment of his ashes in South Stoneham Cemetery, three RAF planes flew past and dipped their wings in salute. In a letter of condolence to his widow, the Air Secretary, Viscount Swinton, wrote of Mitchell: 'His was real genius, a flair of his own and an infinite thoroughness. His work is his memorial.'

The first RAF squadron to be equipped with Mitchell's ultimate memorial, the Spitfire, was 19 Squadron at Duxford on

4 August 1938. Previously, 19 Squadron had been equipped with the Gloster Gauntlet. The arrival of the Spitfire was not a moment too soon for later that summer, when Hitler invaded Czechoslovakia, Europe slid dangerously close to the brink of war; only an humiliating climb down by the British Prime Minister, Neville Chamberlain, averted the sound of guns. Returning from his discussions with 'Herr Hitler' in Munich, Chamberlain claimed to have negotiated 'peace in our time'. Many hoped he was right, but even Chamberlain doubted his own rhetoric. The defence of Britain from Nazi attack became a recurring theme of Cabinet minutes after Munich. And in that defence, the Spitfire was starred to play the leading role.

Almost everyone, on seeing their first Spitfire, was moved to exclamation on its beauty: Richard Hillary, who left school to join 603 Squadron and penned the classic Battle of Britain memoir *The Last Enemy* (1942), wrote:

> Then one day a Spitfire Squadron dropped in. It was our first glimpse of the machine which Peter, Noel, and I eventually hoped to fly. The trim deceptive frailty of their lines fascinated us and we spent much of our spare time climbing on to their wings and inspecting the controls.

Wilfrid Duncan Smith had been inspired to fly by watching an eagle when he was 'still a prep school brat'. During his pilot training his instructor asked him what plane he would like to fly once he had secured his 'wings':

> Without hesitation I told him – Spitfires. It was my natural reaction for the simple reason that I had made up my mind

from the first moment I saw a Spitfire, after it had landed one day at Woodley, that this had to be my aeroplane. It had been a thrilling first meeting, while the sheer beauty of line and the exciting power in flight reminded me of my golden eagle soaring up the mountainside with effortless ease after making his kill.

Lettice Curtis was a pilot with the Air Transport Auxiliary (ATA), whose task was to ferry RAF planes. The 164 women of the ATA were often socialites whose pre-war hobby had been flying. (Early recruits to the ATA included Audrey Sale-Barker, later the Countess of Selkirk, Diana Barnato, daughter of the motor racing champion Woolf Barnato and Margaret Fairweather – the first woman to fly a Spitfire – who was the daughter of Viscount Runciman.) To a woman they were fearless to the point that many men were put to shame. Curtis made explicit the Spitfire's connection to poetry: 'To sit in the cockpit of a Spitfire, barely wider than one's shoulders, with the power of the Merlin at one's fingertips, was a poetry of its own. The long, flat-topped cowling and the pop-popping stub exhausts gave an almost break taking feeling of power'.

Some pilots on seeing their first 'Spits' could find no words, no words at all. Lee Grover, a Californian who flew with the RAF, recorded in his diary in late 1941:

Had my first look at the Spitfire this afternoon. What an airplane! It is much bigger than I thought it would be – over 30 feet long and I can almost stand under the wingtip. I just stood there and looked and couldn't say a word. This is the best fighter in the world and I am going to fly it.

William Ash, an American volunteer, thought the Spitfire had aristocratic breeding, its long nose reminiscent of English nobility and Borzoi dogs. Bill Rolls was posted to a Spitfire squadron in early 1940: 'As we went by the grass mound, we saw a Spitfire only a few yards away. It was fantastic to see one so close. We looked for as long as we could and then hugged each other in sheer joy. We had arrived.'

After the looking, came the first unforgettable flight. In the early days there were no trainer Spitfires and pilots went straight from bi-planes to Spitfires. Pilot Officer James 'Johnnie' Johnson, was luckier than some; he had trained on a monoplane, the Miles Master. Even so, his introduction to the Spitfire was rudimentary and typical. The instructor talked him around the controls – and then left him to it:

The day I flew a Spitfire for the first time was one to remember. To begin with the instructor walked me round the lean fighter plane, drab in its war coat of grey and green camouflage paint, and explained the flight-control system. Afterwards I climbed into the cockpit while he stood on the wing root and explained the functions of the various controls. I was oppressed by the narrow cockpit for I am reasonably wide across the shoulders and when I sat on the parachute each forearm rubbed uncomfortably on the metal sides.

'Bit tight across the shoulders for me?' I inquired.

'You'll soon get used to it,' he replied. 'Surprising how small you can get when one of those yellow-nosed brutes [Messerschmitts] is on your tail. You'll keep your head down then! And get a stiff neck from looking behind. Otherwise you won't last long!' – and with this boost to my morale we pressed on with the lesson. After a further half-hour spent memorizing the various emergency procedures and handling characteristics, the instructor checked my harness straps and watched while I adjusted the leather flying helmet.

'Start her up!'

I carried out the correct drill and the Merlin sprang to life with its usual song of power, a sound no fighter pilot will easily forget.

For all its elegance, however, the Spitfire was a troublesome charge on take-off, as Geoffrey 'Boy' Wellum of 92 Squadron discovered:

As I start to taxi, I remember snippets of advice: view is bad on the ground so when taxiing swing the nose from side to side so you can see what's ahead; don't take too long on the ground; use the brakes very carefully, if you don't they'll tip up on to their nose as soon as look at you; they are bloody nose heavy on the ground. Then of course, there was the warning, the CO's parting shot, the one and only time I spoke to him: 'If you break one there will be merry hell to play.'

We reach the far end of the aerodrome and stop cross-wind. For the third time I do my checks. My God, this is an incredible piece of machinery to be in charge of. The glycol temperature is up to 105 degrees and that is just a shade on the high side. I'd better get cracking. There's no excuse for waiting around here any longer.

With the narrow undercarriage in mind, I make sure I am exactly into wind and, almost with a feeling of resignation, I let off the brakes and slowly open the throttle. The power comes on in a huge surge, deep and smooth. There is a rich throaty growl from the Merlin as I open up still further, purely out of habit. The acceleration is something I have never experienced before and the port wing has dipped down with the terrific torque. Direction is held quite easily on the rudder and with a touch of aileron. We seem to be charging over the ground and I am still opening the throttle when the Spitfire hurls itself into the air, dragging me along with it. I feel I am hanging on to the stick and throttle in order not to be left behind.

The reason why Spitfires overheated when taxiing was that there were so streamlined that the heat from the engines had nowhere to go; the air intakes under the wings were ineffectual. If the Spitfire did not ascend into its natural element, the glycol coolant would boil.

Jim Goodson, an American colonel flying for the RAF from 1941, concurred that, 'the Spit was a little bitch on the ground'. He found landing as trying as take-off because 'the narrow landing gear also made it prone to ground looping'. So did a 20-year-old British pilot with 152 Squadron. Eric Marrs confided to his diary on 2 April 1940:

I have got on to Spitfires at last. I had my first trip on Sunday and it was rather hectic. They are very sensitive and delicate on the controls at low speeds and after the other aeroplanes I have been flying I found myself being very ham-handed with the controls. Apart from this, they are very nice machines. The view forwards and downwards is not so good but otherwise excellent, though when coming into land the approach is made with the nose up, and that makes you very blind. A special curving approach is thus necessary, which only leaves you blind for the final hold off. The speed is not noticeable until you get near the ground. On the whole they are very gentlemanly aircraft and the only really bad habit is a tendency to tip up on to its nose very easily, on the ground. This necessitates great care in using the brakes . . .

There were others cares on take-off. With the early model Spitfires it was necessary to remember to set the airscrew – which controlled the wooden two- or three-bladed propeller – to fine pitch. (Changing pitch is best likened to changing gears in a car; the two-pitch Spitfires required fine pitch for take-off and landing, and coarse pitch otherwise.) Failure to select fine pitch on the runway was disastrous, as the legendary Douglas Bader discovered on 31 March 1940 when his Spitfire refused to leave the ground and instead ploughed across a road, through a hedge and into a field. Bader emerged unscathed, with the exception of his tin legs, which were mangled. His Spitfire, K9858, was a write-off.

There was one more thing the Spitfire pilot had to do as his plane reached for the sky. He had to remember to retract the undercarriage by pumping the long handle on the right of the cockpit. Frequently, he would, in his tyro days, wobble the aircraft around the sky while doing this. Pilot Officer Bobby Oxspring of 66 Squadron:

The next action was one unique to early Spitfires which entailed getting the undercarriage retracted before the airspeed built up too high. This was a manual action whereby the pilot had to lock the throttle in climb power with his left hand, transfer this hand to the control column, at the same time moving his right hand to an undercarriage retraction pump handle – and start pumping. It took time until pilots new to the aircraft got used to these procedures. The energetic pumping motion of the right hand inevitably resulted in an alternate reaction with the left hand which was guiding the aircraft, and this sequence in turn resulted in the most extraordinary flight gyrations on the climb out. Sometimes on formation take-offs it got really hairy, especially at night. After some experience most pilots managed to control it. My method was to dig my left elbow into my groin and hold the stick level with fingers and thumbs until the wheels locked up.

Often the pilot, in the narrow cockpit, would suffer 'Spitfire Knuckle' when he scraped his hand pumping the undercarriage.

Then the Spitfire was properly airborne, sheer speed exhilarating and fearful in equal measure. Sergeant Pilot Pierre Clostermann, his RAF pilot wings and brevet of the Free French 'Armée de l'Air' freshly stitched on his uniform, recalled his first ascent:

Suddenly, holding my breath, and as if by magic, I found myself airborne. The railway line passed by like a flash. I was vaguely aware of some trees and houses, which disappeared indistinctly behind me . . . Phew! Drops of sweat ran down my forehead . . . How light she was on the controls! The slightest pressure with hand or foot and the machine leapt into the sky.

'Good heavens! Where am I?'

The speed was such that the few seconds which had elapsed had been enough to take me half a dozen miles from the airfield.

Clostermann, on landing, found himself overcome. 'At last I had flown a Spitfire,' he thought to himself, and then, 'Softly, as one might caress a woman's cheeks, I ran my hand over the aluminium of her wings, cold and smooth like a mirror, the wings that had borne me.' He decided there and then that he would love his combat Spitfire, when allotted, 'like a faithful friend.'

Perhaps the greatest rapture on flying a Spitfire was felt by Pilot Officer John Gillespie Magee Jr, 412 Squadron Royal Canadian Air Force (RCAF). Gillespie was an American student at Yale who crossed the border into Canada illegally to serve with the RCAF in England. After flying a Spitfire Mark V on 3 September 1941 he wrote 'High Flight', which has been called the first great poem of the Second World War:

> Oh! I have slipped the surly bonds of Earth
> And danced the skies on laughter-silvered wings;
> Sunward I've climbed, and joined the tumbling
>   mirth
> Of sun-split clouds, — and done a hundred things
> You have not dreamed of — wheeled and soared
>   and swung
> High in the sunlit silence. Hov'ring there,
> I've chased the shouting wind along, and flung
> My eager craft through footless halls of air . . .
> Up, up the long, delirious burning blue

I've topped the wind-swept heights with easy
  grace
Where never lark, or ever eagle flew —
And, while with silent, lifting mind I've trod
The high untrespassed sanctity of space,
Put out my hand, and touched the face of God.

Gillespie was killed three months later when his Spitfire V
crashed into an Oxford trainer in a cloud. Although Gillespie
bailed out, his parachute failed to open. His white military
tombstone stands in the country churchyard at Scopwick,
Lincolnshire.

No one who flew a Spitfire doubted its ability. The nagging
doubt was about self. As he took up a Spitfire for the second
time, Richard Hillary reflected:

The flight immediately following our first solo was an
hour's aerobatics. I climbed up to 12,000 feet before
attempting even a slow roll.

  Kilmartin had said 'See if you can make her talk.' That
meant the whole bag of tricks, and I wanted ample room for
mistakes and possible blacking out. With one or two very
sharp movements on the stick I blacked myself out for a few
seconds, but the machine was sweeter to handle than any
other that I had flown. I put it through every manoeuvre
that I knew of and it responded beautifully. I ended in two
flick rolls and turned back for home. I was filled with a
sudden exhilarating confidence. I could fly a Spitfire; in any
position I was its master. It remained to be seen whether I
could fight in one.

PART I

First Light – The Spitfire in Action, September 1939–June 1940

When the Second World War began on 3 September 1939, the RAF had nine fully equipped Spitfire squadrons, based at Duxford, Catterick, Abbotschurch, Church Fenton and Hornchurch. On 6 September 1939, Spitfires from Hornchurch's 74 Squadron, led by Adolph 'Sailor' Malan, a native South African who had joined the RAF in 1936, made the aeroplane's first 'kills', shooting down a brace of aircraft over the River Medway. Tragically, the enemy turned out to be Hurricanes from 56 Squadron. The Spitfire pilots were exonerated; fault, it was determined, lay with the RAF's fighter control system, subsequently remedied by the installation of IFF (Identification Friend or Foe) equipment in every plane, which signalled to ground control that the aircraft was friendly. Still, 'The Battle of Barking Creek' was an ignominious debut for the fighter in time of war.

The Spitfire's reputation was retrieved on 16 October, when 602 (City of Glasgow) and 603 (City of Edinburgh) squadron intercepted Junkers 88s of the Luftwaffe's I/KG30 as they attacked the Royal Navy's Home Fleet at Rosyth on the Firth of Forth. As Hauptmann Helmut Pohle pulled away after bombing the cruiser *Southampton* (which suffered only slight damage), his port engine and then his starboard engine were hit by bullets from Spitfires of 603's Red Section. With the rest of his crew dead, Pohle 'ditched' in the Firth of Forth where he was picked up unconscious by a Scottish trawler.

Another Ju 88 was shot down, while Lieutenant Horst von Riesen had a narrow escape after causing casualties on the *Nohawk*. He later wrote: 'I pushed down the nose and dived for the sea. But it was no good. The Spitfires, as we recognized them to be, had the advantage of speed and height from the start and they soon caught up with us.' There appeared on the water what 'looked like raindrops'; they were Spitfire bullets, and eventually they found their target. The starboard Jumo engine on von Riesen's Junkers went 'phoof' and had to be shut down.

Now far from the coast, the Spitfires gave up the chase. The bomber staggered along on one engine. Von Riesen and his crew had 400 miles to go before reaching their base. They debated whether they should turn back to Rosyth. 'No, no, never!' shouted someone over the intercom. 'If we go back there the Spitfires will certainly get us!' So on they went. Four hours later von Riesen and his crew sighted the home lights of Westerland.

It was a compliment to the Spitfire's ferocity that in its first action, von Riesen and his men preferred to drown in the North Sea than face Spitfires again.

On the following day, Spitfires from 41 Squadron shot down a Heinkel 111 off the coast of Whitby; on 29 November, Spitfires from 602 and 603 Squadrons downed a Heinkel 111 over Lothian.

Such was the type of warfare the Spitfire knew throughout

the so-called 'Phoney War' period; intermittent skirmishing with Luftwaffe reconnaissance planes and bombers. They were days of comfortable victories, for the Germans' principal bombers, the Ju 88 and He 111, were outclassed and their pilots overconfident, while Fighter Command's new box of tricks, the radar, enabled Spitfire pilots to be guided directly to their target. By 1939 almost the entire east and south coasts were covered by radar stations; the Luftwaffe consistently failed to understand the importance of radar even during the Battle of Britain, a year later. Radar enabled nearly every German incursion to be 'seen' and intercepted; moreover, it did away with the need to perform continuous standing patrols of the air, which were tiring on both men and machines.

It was the German invasion of France and the Low Countries on 10 May 1940, however, which brought the Spitfire properly into the maw of the war. Pounded by the 4,000-strong Luftwaffe, the French government appealed to Britain for aid. Newly appointed Prime Minister, Winston Churchill, whose love of France mixed potently with his love for a fight, heeded the request and squadrons of RAF fighters were sent across the Channel. But then Air Chief Marshal Sir Hugh Dowding, head of Fighter Command, dug in his heels. Dowding's personal mantra was that, 'The best defence of the country is the Fear of the Fighter'. The deployment of fighters to France would leave Britain herself unguarded for her own battle with Hitler, which Dowding realized must come. On 18 May Dowding wrote a terse memorandum to the Air Ministry:

Sir
    I have the honour to refer to the very serious calls which have recently been made upon the Home Defence Fighter

Units in an attempt to stem the German invasion on the Continent . . .

2. I hope and believe that our Armies may yet be victorious in France and Belgium, but we have to face the possibility that they may be defeated.

3. In this case I presume that there is no one who will deny that England should fight on, even though the remainder of the Continent of Europe is dominated by the Germans.

4. For this purpose it is necessary to retain some minimum fighter strength in this country and I must request that the Air Council will inform me what they consider the minimum strength to be, in order that I may make my dispositions accordingly.

5. I would remind the Air Council that the last estimate which they made as to the force necessary to defend this country was fifty-two Squadrons, and my strength has now been reduced to the equivalent of thirty-six Squadrons.

6. Once a decision has been reached as to the limit on which the Air Council and the Cabinet are prepared to stake the existence of the country, it should be made clear to the Allied Commanders on the Continent that not a single aeroplane from Fighter Command beyond the limit will be sent across the Channel, no matter how desperate the situation may become.

7. It will, of course, be remembered that the estimate of fifty-two Squadrons was based on the assumption that the attack would come from the eastwards except in so far as the defences might be outflanked in flight. We have now to face the possibility that attacks may come from Spain or even the North coast of France. The result is that our line

is very much extended at the same time as our resources are reduced.

8. I must point out that within the last few days the equivalent of ten Squadrons have been sent to France, that the Hurricane Squadrons remaining in this country are seriously depleted, and that the more squadrons which are sent to France the higher will be the wastage and the more insistent the demand for reinforcements.

9. I must therefore request that as a matter of paramount urgency the Air Ministry will consider and decide what level of strength is to be left to the Fighter Command for the defence of this country, and will assure me that when this level has been reached, not one fighter will be sent across the Channel however urgent and insistent the appeals for help may be.

10. I believe that, if an adequate fighter force is kept in this country, if the fleet remains in being, and if Home Forces are suitably organised to resist invasion, we should be able to carry on the war single-handed for some time, if not indefinitely. But, if the Home Defence Force is drained away in desperate attempts to remedy the situation in France, defeat in France will involve the final, complete and irremediable defeat of this country.

I have the honour to be,

Sir,

Your obedient Servant

Air Chief Marshal

Sir Hugh Dowding

Dowding got his way and his Spitfires, still coming off the production lines painfully slowly at Southampton and Castle

Bromwich, were reserved for the defence of Britain. It was a decision that altered the course of the war.

Hitler's blitzkrieg tore through France and Dowding could not but agree to provide air cover – including from his precious Spitfires – for 'Operation Dynamo', the evacuation of the British Expeditionary Force from Channel port of Dunkirk in the last week of May 1940.

On the morning of 27 May the Luftwaffe went into action at Dunkirk, with Ju 87 'Stukas' dive-bombing the troops gathered around the port and nearby dunes. Messerschmitt 109 pilots strafed the ground, much to the dismay of many pilots: hitherto they had shot at seemingly inanimate objects – airplanes – now they were killing men. One 109 pilot, Paul Temme, said: 'I hated Dunkirk. It was just unadulterated killing. The beaches were jammed full of soldiers. I went up and down at three hundred feet "hose-piping".'

Göring had claimed to Hitler that his Luftwaffe would prevent the evacuation and the German air force did its utmost to bring the boast to pass, as Signaller Sidney Leach of the Royal Signals could testify. On arriving at Dunkirk Leach found a scene reminiscent of Dante's *Inferno*:

A thick black cloud hung like a pall over us, tinged with red from the burning buildings. About seven miles to our left a number of buildings were on fire, and we could hear the whine of shells and the explosions as they found a mark . . . Suddenly a plane dived out of the clouds and dropped a few bombs. The first landed about 10–15 yards away from me. I flattened out in the sand and was lifted two feet in the air. Small pebbles and sand covered me, and there was a rotten smell of cordite . . . After a brief look round I fainted, and it was a few hours before I woke again. I found a chap of my section, Jock Stewart, and we crawled along the beach for a while. Then came down a plane and dropped hundreds of flares, then followed the worst bombardment I had experienced. The planes came down in hundreds, whining and screaming, and I buried down in a bit of a dip and waited for one to get me. But luck was with me, and apart from some shrapnel splinters in my feet and a scratch on my cheek, I was unscathed.

Later, after picking up a stray machine gun round in his leg, Leach joined a queue 'about four or five hundred yards long and about ten deep' for the boats:

For ten hours I waited, and just when it came my turn, the boats started on another queue and I was sent to the end of it. It was getting dark then, and a naval officer came up and asked us if we would care to go to the pier (about 11 miles to our left) and catch a liner, which was docked there. I volunteered, and about 250 of us started out. The beach was being shelled then, and these kept falling around us. Delayed action bombs were going off all over the place. Dead-beat, we went on and on. The chaps were dropping out continually, most of them driven frantic by thirst, others exhausted. We reached the pier, about 4 a.m., and as we were walking up it, a shell burst right in front of us . . . The enemy had a range by now and the shells were pouring into us. Piles of French dead were stacked on the pier . . . About 6 a.m. we boarded a minesweeper and put out to sea. We had not got far when a bomb or shell hit our stern. We made for the boats [life rafts] and boarded another minesweeper and started for home. Planes followed us, about half way, continually bombing and machine-gunning us, but we made it. We landed at Ramsgate at 10 a.m. and were we glad! England at last, and home.

Sidney Leach does not complain about the lack of protection from the RAF at Dunkirk, but many soldiers did; 'Where are the Brylcreem boys [Army slang for fighter pilots]?' they asked. But the RAF *was* at Dunkirk; it was just that many of its operations were either too high or too far inland for the troops to see. And at Dunkirk the Spitfire was committed in numbers for the first time. Pilot Officer Johnny Allen of 54 Squadron:

We kept well together, but of course kept radio silence. We knew every inch of the coastline to which we were heading, but even without that knowledge there was no mistaking it was Dunkirk. Only a few minutes after leaving Britain and at our height, we could see the pillars of smoke arising from the burning town and the villages all the way up from Calais. The horizon was one vast pall. We went right across the city and settled down to patrolling on a 50 mile long beat, but we saw nothing and decided to come downstairs.

At 4,000 feet we were beetling along still looking for trouble when I saw a Hun formation of about sixty machines – twenty bombers and forty fighters – at about 15,000 feet, and cursed the height we had lost. The fighters, mostly Messerschmitts, heeled over and came screaming down at us, and the next second we were in the thick of it. That attack developed, like most dogfights, into individual scraps. It was at about 10,000 feet that I found myself on the tail of my first Hun, a Messerschmitt 110. Most of my instruments, I remember, had gone haywire in the course of the violent manoeuvring. I remember particularly that my giro was spinning crazily, and the artificial horizon had vanished somewhere into the interior of the instrument panel, calmly turning up its bottom and showing me the maker's stamp and the words Air Ministry Mark IV, or something like that.

Down went the Messerschmitt again with me close on his tail. With the great speed of the dive my controls were freezing solid, and I was fighting the stick hard to bring the Hun up into the centre of my sights. When you get there they stick, in fact it's hard to get them out. Once there you can hold them for ever. I thumbed the trigger button just once, twice. I smelt the cordite fumes blowing back from my Brownings as the 1,200 squirts a minute from each of them went into him. I saw the little spurts of flame as the tracers struck. For a fraction of a second I saw the black outline of the pilot's head half-slewed around to see what was after him, before presumably he ceased to know. I saw a burst of flame and smoke from his engine, and the he was going down in a twirling spin of black smoke.

I looked around for the rest, but they were gone. My own scrap had brought me about 30 miles inland, so I turned and headed back, noticing with a shock that my petrol reserve was just enough to get me home, provided that I ran into no more trouble. Dogfighting uses up juice at an enormous rate. About that first fight – when you're going into it you think 'what fun', and when it's over you think 'how bloody dangerous'. Out over the North Sea and on the way back to the station I clicked on the radio and called up the pilots of my squadron one by one: 'How are you? Did you get any?' The first one came bad jubilantly – he had got one. Then the rest – all of them had got one or two. One was funny. When I asked him what he had got, he came back, growling and disgusted, with a 'Graf Zeppelin'. Two didn't answer.

Back at the station we refuelled, reloaded, and were off again in a quarter of an hour. Back over Dunkirk at 10,000 feet we ran into a whole flock of Messerschmitts, which came charging down out of the clouds. They had obviously been sitting upstairs guarding some bombers hidden in the smoke below. They nearly caught us. I saw tracers going past my ears, and actually heard the gun rattle from one on my tail, and then he was gone. I followed him down, banging the throttle open and leaning on my stick, but in the last smoke clouds hanging over Dunkirk I lost him.

Up again, I saw the rest of the squadron at about 6,000. They were in a hell of a mix-up with the Hun fighters and some Junkers 88s, and I climbed up to join them. My radio was open, and as I climbed I could hear a stream of occasionally comic backchat passing backwards and forwards between some of the other members of the squadron, occasionally punctuated with bursts of gunfire as they were popping off at Huns. Once, for instance, I heard a New Zealander calling and saying calmly, 'There's a Messerschmitt on your tail,' and the reply, 'Okay, pal,' and then I was in it too.

I picked out a Junkers 88 whose tail gunner got on to me as soon as I engaged. The tracers of his guns sheered past me, seeming to curve lazily past my clear-vision window. You watch them quite calmly. They never look as though they were going to hit you, even when they are practically dead on.

Again there was that lovely feeling of the gluey controls and the target being slowly hauled into the sights. Then thumb down on the trigger again and the smooth shuddering of the machine as the eight gun blast let go. This time the squirt I gave him must have cut him in two. His tail folded back on his wings and there was a great smoke and flash of flame as he went down. As I spiralled down slowly after him, keeping a lookout for more, I saw one man bail out and his chute open.

The sky was nearly clear of Huns, and I turned round for home again, calling up the squadron as I went. This time we were all there, but our total bag was better than the first show. We had got eleven in all, making nineteen in one morning for our two.

The second day we had a defined objective, but I detached two pilots to do some freelance patrolling, one above the clouds which were at about 12,000 feet over Dunkirk and the other about 2,000 feet below. The rest of us went off toward Calais. About halfway there I heard the one above the clouds calling to the other in a deliberately affected sort of actor's voice, 'O, look what's coming, dearie, hordes and hordes of Messerschmitts. Nasty Messerschmitts.' And the answer back, 'Okay, pal, keep them busy. I'm coming upstairs.'

I didn't know then how they had got on with the Messerschmitt swarm they had got into above Dunkirk, but on the way back the first to answer my radio call said that he had got four. Then he suddenly said, 'Oh, hell, my engine's packed up.' Then, 'I'm on fire.' There was silence for a second or two, and he said, 'Yippee! There's a destroyer downstairs. I'm bailing out.' A second later I heard him mutter, 'But how?'

It is, as a matter of fact, not easy to bail out of a Spitfire. The best way is to turn her over on her back and drop out through the hood – if you can. That, we found out, later, was exactly what he had done. He turned up in the mess three days afterwards wearing a naval sub lieutenant's jacket and bell-bottom trousers, and carrying a sailor's kitbag over his shoulder.

That day, for all its excitement was a poorer bag than we had expected – a total of eleven. The third day we had the biggest show of all because then the evacuation was in full swing, and the Hun was throwing in everything he had in the way of aircraft to smash up the proceedings. We were now starting off at dawn, and on that day we went over Dunkirk and back again twice before breakfast time, and my squadron was in thirty different combats.

On the second occasion my squadron ran into the biggest cloud of fighters that I'd seen so far. They were all Messerschmitt 109s, and there must have been pretty nearly one hundred of them. They seemed like a swarm of bees. We went in, however, and tore off a chunk each. My recollections of that show are a bit hazy because we were fighting upstairs and downstairs between 1,000 and 15,000 feet, and I was blacking out fairly often in the pull outs after diving after a Hun. But I'm certain I got four, and the rest of the squadron wasn't doing too badly because at one time the air seemed to be full of burning aircraft. They were enemy planes all right, because we lost only one machine in that mad half-hour. The pilot of that one had his ailerons blown away, but managed to land on Dunkirk beach. He had a big gash in his forehead, but managed to radio operations room at our station that he had 'landed safely'.

The downed pilot was Al Deere, who had been shot up by the rear gunner of a Dornier 17. After 'pancaking' his Spitfire on the beach, Deere made his way his way to the port at Dunkirk, with the intention of getting the first boat back across the Channel so he could rejoin his squadron. However, the Army major controlling the evacuation from the jetty was decidedly antagonistic and belligerently informed Deere, 'For all the good you chaps seem to be doing over here you might just as well stay on the ground.' Deere's reception on the Royal Navy destroyer taking him home was no warmer:

My identity established, I was escorted below decks to the tiny wardroom, already crowded with Army officers. A stony silence greeted the announcement that I was an RAF officer. This caused me to ask of a young gunner lieutenant nearby, 'Why so friendly, what have the RAF done?'

'That's just it,' he replied, 'What have they done? You are about as popular in this company as a cat in the prize canary's cage.'

So that was it. For two weeks non-stop I had flown my guts out, and this was all the thanks I got. What was the use of trying to explain that the RAF had patrolled further inland, often above cloud, with the insuperable task of covering adequately a patrol line from Ostend to Boulogne?

★

If the army was ignorant of what the RAF had achieved over Dunkirk, Churchill was not. The 'clawing-down rate' of the RAF (which, by its own figures, downed fifty enemy aircraft for the loss of twelve RAF planes on the 27 May alone) provided the Prime Minister with a reason for continued resistance against Hitler, at a time when elements of his Cabinet were wavering towards a truce.

The Luftwaffe also had no doubts about the RAF's record at Dunkirk. The Germans were used to easy kills over Poles, Belgian, Dutch and French pilots, so the resolve of the RAF came as a shock. 'The days of easy victory were over,' Luftwaffe General Werner Kreipe noted in his review of air operation over Dunkirk. 'We had met the RAF head on.' The German airmen were equally impressed with the capability of the RAF's new fighter. The airfleet commander General Albert Kesselring pointed out to his boss Hermann Göring that the modern Spitfires had recently appeared, making operations difficult and costly, and in the end it was the Spitfires that enabled the British and French to evacuate across the water.

Merely the sight of a Spitfire soon became enough to make Me 109 pilots jumpy and cry out over the radio telephone (R/T) 'Achtung, Spitfeur!' In the haze of the morning of 1 June, Otto Hinze's *Schwarme* (four aircraft) spotted 'Spitfeurs' descending towards them. Even before contact Hinze's 109 was forced to pancake on the beach. He had been shot down by a nervous member of his own *Schwarme*, quite possibly his own wingman.

It was to many fighter boys' relief that at Dunkirk the 'Hun' was considerably less daring than legend – and Goebbel's propaganda department – suggested. Pilot Officer Johnny Allen declared at the time: 'Personally, I don't think that most of the

Hun pilots are very good. I have come across a few who seem to enjoy fighting, but the bulk of them don't.'

Doubtless, Allen's sentiment was pumped up for public propaganda but many of his comrades shared its gist. Squadron Leader Teddy Donaldson, who fought Me 109s over France, told trainee pilots at an Advanced Training Unit that the Germans were mediocre and ineffectual once they had lost their formation leader. (In the audience was Wilfrid Duncan Smith, a future Spitfire ace who was then making what felt like slow progress through the necessary training establishments before posting to a front-line squadron.) Allen's fellow squadron member, Pilot Officer Al Deere, took away another, equally positive impression from Dunkirk. Just before the evacuation Allen and Deere had escorted an air rescue mission to pick up the downed commanding officer of 74 Squadron from Calais. Above the town, Deere and Allen were attacked by a pack of Me 109s. It was the first meeting between the Spitfire and the Me 109, the premier fighter of the Luftwaffe. Deere later recalled:

While breakfasting with 'Wonky' I was called to the telephone to speak to 'Prof' Leathart, the flight commander.

'Al,' he said, 'will you collect Johnny Allen and get down here right away for immediate take-off? The Station Commander has suggested to Group that we fly the Master (a two-seater training type aircraft) over to Calais/Marck to pick up the C.O. of 74 Squadron. The A.O.C. has agreed and we have been given the job; I'll fly the Master and you and Johnny can act as escort in a couple of Spitfires. I understand that there is a lot of enemy activity over there now and I think we stand more chance of getting away with it if just the three of us go. We can nip across at sea level and should avoid being spotted by Hun fighters as the airfield is right on the coast.'

The trip to dispersal in my old barouche was made in record time. The plan was for the Master to land at Calais/Marck, pick up the squadron commander, if he was still on the airfield, and take-off again immediately without stopping the engine. Johnny and I were to remain orbiting the airfield to protect the Master whilst landing and taking off. It sounded a piece of cake. The trip out was uneventful and the Master landed without incident. There was broken cloud over the area which meant there was a likelihood of being surprised from above. I decided therefore to send Johnny above cloud, at about 8,000 feet, while I remained below circling the airfield. I watched the Master taxi towards a small hangar, and was wondering if his passenger was about, when an excited yell from the usually placid Johnny pierced my ear-drums.

'Al, they're here. Huns! About a dozen just below me and making towards the airfield. I'm going in to have a go at them.'

'OK Johnny, for God's sake keep me informed. I must remain in sight of the airfield to try and warn 'Prof' and stop him taking off.'

To warn the Master was not going to be easy. It carried no R/T and at best I could dive down towards where it stood on the airfield and waggle my wings hoping that 'Prof' would interpret this as a danger signal. With these thoughts in mind I wheeled my Spitfire around only to see the Master taxiing out for take-off. At the very moment I turned, a Messerschmitt 109 came hurtling through the clouds straight for the defenceless Master which by now was just becoming airborne. By the grace of God the hun flew right across my line of flight and I was able to give him a quick burst of fire which I knew had little hope of hitting him but which, I hoped, would divert his attention from the Master. It did, but not before a stream of tracer spouted from his guns and disappeared, it seemed, into the fuselage of the trainer. By this time my throttle was fully open and with the stick hard back to turn inside the Me 109 I was in range to fire. Just as I did so I heard Johnny screaming on the R/T.

'Red One – I'm surrounded, can you help me?'

'Try and hang on, Johnny, till I kill this bastard in front of me, and I'll be right up.'

In a last desperate attempt to avoid my fire, the Hun pilot straightened from his turn and pulled vertically upwards, thus writing his own death warrant; he presented me with a perfect no–deflection shot from dead below and I made no mistake. Smoke began to pour from his engine as the aircraft, now at the top of its climb, heeled slowly over in an uncontrolled stall and plunged vertically into the water's edge from about 3,000 feet. Immediately I broke back towards the airfield thankful to observe the Master parked safely by the perimeter fence apparently unharmed. Now to help Johnny.

'Hello, Red Two, how goes it?' I called over the R/T. 'I'm coming up now.'

Zooming up through the cloud I found myself crossing the path of two Me 109s which were diving inland. They must have seen me at the same moment because immediately the leader went into a steep turn. Again I found no difficulty in keeping inside the turn and was soon in range to fire. A long burst at the number two caused bits to fly off his aircraft which rolled on to its back and careered earthwards. Whether or not he was *hors de combat* I couldn't be sure but the leader was still there and must be dealt with. Reversing his turn very skilfully, he too dived towards the ground. Momentarily I lost distance, but I had got in range again before he flattened out above the tree tops and headed homewards. A quick burst caused him to whip into another turn and from this point onwards he did everything possible to shake me off. After a second burst I ran out of ammunition but determined to stay behind him for as long as possible, if for no other reason than the fact that I didn't know quite how to break off the engagement. I had the feeling that he must know I was out of ammunition and was just waiting for me to turn for home. Fortunately for me his next manoeuvre was to straighten out and determinedly head eastwards at which I pulled hard back on the stick and looped through the broken cloud before rolling out and diving full throttle towards the coast.

I now called Johnny on the R/T and was relieved to hear his cheerful but somewhat breathless voice answer.

'I'm just crossing out North of Calais but am rather worried about my aircraft. I can't see any holes but felt hits and she doesn't seem to be flying quite right. I'll make for the North Foreland at my present height of 8,000 feet. See if you can join up.'

We managed to join up in mid-Channel and sure enough his aircraft had been holed. However, it didn't seem too bad and on my advice he decided to continue back to Hornchurch rather than land forward at Mauston. He accomplished a safe landing to the accompaniment of a victory roll from me.

Excited pilots and ground crew clustered around us on the ground and our stories had to be recounted in detail. Johnny's only comment was that he hoped next time he encountered the Hun there would be fewer of them and he would not be alone; after all odds of 20-1 and 12-1 in consecutive engagements were too much for one's nerves.

Shortly afterwards 'Prof' arrived in the Master with his passenger, both none the worse for wear. From the safety of a ditch, into which he had dived on scrambling out of his aircraft, he had observed the air battle and was able to give his account of the affray. His story is best related by quoting verbatim from the official intelligence report he later made:

'. . . The moment I left the ground I saw from the activities of Red One that something was amiss. Almost at once a Me 109 appeared ahead of me and commenced firing. I pulled around in a tight turn, observing as I did so, the Messerschmitt shoot past me. I literally banged the aircraft on to the ground and evacuated the cockpit with all possible speed, diving into the safety of a ditch which ran along the airfield perimeter. Just as I did so I saw a Me 109 come hurtling out of the clouds, to crash with a tremendous explosion a few hundred yards away. Almost simultaneously, another Me 109 exploded as it hit the sea to my left.

From the comparative safety of the ditch my passenger and I caught momentary glimpses of the dogfight as first Me 109 and then Spitfire came hurtling through the cloud banks, only to scream upwards again. It was all over in a matter of about ten minutes but not before we observed a third enemy aircraft crash in flames. We waited about ten minutes after the fight ended and when it seemed safe, made a hasty take-off and a rather frightened trip back to England and safety.'

As a result of my prolonged fight with the last Me 109, it was possible to assess the relative performance of the two aircraft. In the early engagements between the British Hurricanes in France and the logs, the speed and climb of the latter had become legendary and were claimed by many to be far superior to that of the Spitfire. I was able to refute this contention and indeed was confident that, except in a dive, the Spitfire was superior in most other fields and, like the Hurricane, vastly more manoeuvrable. The superior rate of climb was, however, due mostly to the type of Spitfire with which my squadron was equipped. Aircraft of 54 Squadron were fitted with the Rotol constant speed airscrew on which we had been doing trials when the fighting started. Other Spitfires were, at that stage, using a two speed airscrew (i.e. either fully fine pitch or fully coarse) which meant that they lost performance in a sustained climb. There was a great deal of scepticism about my claim that the Spitfire was superior to the Messerschmitt log; there were those who frankly disbelieved me, saying that it was contrary to published performance figures. Later events, however, proved me to be right.

Deere subsequently received the Distinguished Flying Cross (DFC). Not all Spitfire pilots were as cold-nerved as the New Zealander Deere. Flight Lieutenant D.E. Gillam of 616 Squadron:

We had several casualties and as a very green squadron fatigue and losses were not understood. I remember one particular pilot, as he went to his aircraft, breaking down. Our medical officer went across and gave him a terrific punch and [a] few well chosen words and we had no further trouble.

Another 616 Squadron member, Pilot Officer Hugh 'Cocky' Dundas, admitted to something approaching panic in his debut dogfight on 28 May, when his flight encountered Me 109s on a sortie to Dunkirk:

With sudden, sickening stupid fear, I realized that I was being fired on and I pulled my Spitfire round hard, so that the blood was forced down from my head. The thick curtain of blackout blinded me for a moment and I felt the aircraft juddering on the brink of a stall. Straightening out, the curtain lifted and I saw a confusion of planes, diving and twisting. My eyes focused on two more Messerschmitts, flying in quite close formation, curving down towards me. Again I saw a ripple of smoke and the wink of lights; again I went into a blackout turn and again the bullets streaked harmlessly by.

At some stage in the next few seconds the silhouette of a Messerschmitt passed across my windscreen and I fired my guns in battle for the first time – a full deflection shot which, I believe, was quite ineffectual.

I was close to panic in the bewilderment and hot fear of that first dogfight. Fortunately instinct drove me to keep turning and turning, twisting my neck all the time to look for the enemy behind. Certainly the consideration which was uppermost in my mind was a sincere desire to stay alive.

As Spitfire pilots were discovering to their joy and to their salvation, the Me 109 could not hold on to a Spitfire in the turn. When Dundas felt it safe enough to straighten out, he realized that he had lost the pursuing Me 109 but he had also lost himself. Not recognizing any landmarks, panic set in for the second time that day and he blindly set out in what he prayed was the right direction for home. After several minutes, seeing nothing but the empty wastes of the North Sea before him, Dundas turned back towards Dunkirk 'cravenly thinking that I could at the worst crash-land somewhere off Dunkirk and get home in a boat'. Eventually he composed himself and forced himself to work out the simple navigational problem of locating England. On landing safely at Rochford, Essex, the squadron's base, jubilation replaced cravenness. 'I was transformed,' he recalled, 'Walter Mitty-like: now a debonair young fighter pilot, rising twenty, proud and delighted that he had fired his guns in a real dogfight, even though he had not hit anything.'

But not everybody returned from the engagement. For the first time Dundas heard the phrase that would become grimly familiar: 'One of our pilots is missing'. In the small tight-knit world of the fighter squadrons the losses were hard to bear, emotionally as well as numerically. Squadron leader J.E. McComb of 611 Squadron later recalled:

> On the day those close friends were killed we had laid on a drinks party for wives, in the Mess before lunch. We were ordered to Dunkirk and one of my chaps said, 'Shall we cancel the party?' I told him that if he could keep a Spit in the air for those hours he was a smart pilot and anyway we could not have Hitler interfering with our drinking habits.

As we were about to take off, Donald Little leapt on to my wing and said, 'Feed my dog tonight.' I bawled at him to get back into his cockpit and only after we were airborne did it occur to me that he could feed his dog himself but there was radio silence so said nothing. Little and Crompton, with their ninteen-year-old brides, shared one half of a cottage in Wellingore near Digby whilst my wife together with Barrie Heath (now Sir Barrie) and his wife shared the other half. That morning we ran into a cloud of Messerschmitts and got into all sorts of trouble and lost these two young pilots. We arrived back in ones and twos over a period of time, some having to land and refuel. Meanwhile the party had started, broken with a cheer as someone else turned up. Came the time when Lel Crompton realised, with June Little, that no more were coming back. Without a tear or word they quietly slipped out of the anteroom and went back to the cottage.

Fighter Command edged a victory at Dunkirk over a potent fighter plane, the Me 109, and veteran German pilots, some of them having been in combat since the Spanish Civil War. Yet it had been tight and vicious: some thirty Spitfire boys lost their lives protecting the evacuation. For Spitfire squadron after Spitfire squadron, Dunkirk was their blooding. 611 Squadron was no exception. Twenty-one-year-old Pilot Officer Peter Brown, an RAF regular, recorded the Squadron's debut in his combat report of 2 June:

When patrolling at 15,000 feet with A Flight, at 08.05 a.m., Me 109s suddenly appeared in our formation. I attacked a Me 109 using deflection, but saw no apparent hits. I then realized that a Me 109 was on my tail and firing. I dived to evade the enemy aircraft fire, but was followed down by the enemy fighter. My engine began missing and I went down towards the beach, where it picked up again. I went over Dunkirk at about 100 feet, still followed by the enemy aircraft. When I opened the boost full out, I felt no more shots from the enemy and found I had evaded him. Climbing up to 10,000 feet I saw two squadrons of Ju87Bs, about twenty-four aircraft, in the distance, but did not approach. I circled around for ten minutes, but could not see any sign of other aircraft. I then returned to England, arriving at Burnham-on-Crouch. I then followed the coast and landed at Southend aerodrome. My aircraft was hit by machine gun fire on the port mainplane, rudder, fin, fuselage, port tyre and possibly the engine.

Brown was lucky. Two of his fellow pilots were killed instantly in the 'bounce' by the Me 109s, confirming the adage that a fighter pilot's first fight was the most dangerous flight.

That Brown's Spitfire got him home safely was not luck. The Spitfire, beneath its slender beauty, was a tough old bird. Many Spitfire pilots, over the years of the Second World War, had occasion to thank the resilience of the Spit, none more so than Al Deere. Not only did he survive two crash landings during the Dunkirk operation, he also managed to nurse his Spitfire back across the Channel despite it having a gaping shell hole in the wing.

The evacuation from Dunkirk was finished on 4 June. At dawn on that day, Squadron Leader Douglas Bader led 'A' Flight 222 Squadron over Dunkirk. Smoke palled over the shattered town and beaches, which were littered with debris and abandoned equipment. (Navigation to Dunkirk was easy; the smoke from the burning oil refinery could be seen more than sixty miles away.) But not a person was to be seen. Bader's eye caught the white sail of a lone yacht heading towards England. It was the last ship to leave Dunkirk.

To use Churchill's phrase, Dunkirk had been 'a miracle of deliverance', since 338,000 soldiers had been brought home safe. There was even 'a victory inside the deliverance', for the RAF had triumphed over the Luftwaffe. Air Chief Marshal Sir Hugh Dowding felt moved to write to his men:

> My dear fighter boys. I don't send out many letters and signals but I feel I must take this occasion with the intensive fighting in northern France, for the time being over, to tell you how proud I am of you and the way you have fought since the Blitzkrieg started. I wish I could have spent my time visiting you and hear your accounts of the fighting, but I have occupied myself in working for you in other ways. I want you to know my thoughts are always with you and it is you and your fighting spirit that will crack the brow of the German Air Force and preserve our country through the trials which yet lie ahead. Good luck to you.

Over the period of the evacuation, Fighter Command had mounted 3,561 sorties, accounting for 156 enemy aircraft destroyed (according to the Luftwaffe's own records captured later in the war) for the loss of 106 RAF aircraft and 61 pilots and air gunners. Despite Churchill's commendation, and despite the statistics, Army accusations against the RAF for 'not doing their bit' festered on; the fighter pilots in their turn resented the charge that they had deserted the Tommies. Pilot Officer

Anthony 'Tony' Bartley of 92 Squadron wrote to his father in India:

Dear Pop,

I'm afraid that the fighter boys are in very bad odour at the moment over the Dunkirk evacuation operations. The BEF [British Expeditionary Force] have started stories that they never saw a single fighter the whole time they were being bombed. The feeling ran very high at one time, and some fighter pilots got roughed up by the army in pub brawls. Well, whatever you may have heard in India, this is the true story as I saw it over Dunkirk and Calais. Fighter Command were at first disinclined to send the Spitfires out of England at all. We are primarily home defence. Anyhow, we went, and at first just as single squadrons (12 Spitfires). You have had my accounts of how we used to run into fifty and sixty German machines every time we went over there, and fought them until our ammunition ran out. While this battle was going on up at 10,000 feet, the dive bombers, which did the chief damage, were playing havoc below us. The fact was that they had layers of bombers and fighters, with which twelve Spitfires had to cope. When eventually Fighter Command decided to send over more than one Squadron at a time, they forbade us to fly below 15,000 feet.

We were over Dunkirk on the second last day of the evacuation with more than our squadron. We went over in layers between 15,000 and 25,000 feet. Our squadron led the armada. We disobeyed orders and came down to 9,000 feet where we ran into thirty He 111s, which we drove back, destroying about eighteen of them. However, below us the dive bombers were operating the whole time.

No wonder the soldiers did not see us up at 10,000 feet but little do they realize that we saved them from the 'real bombs'; 500 pounders carried by the Heinkels. What reasons Fighter Command gave for forbidding us to below 15,000, I don't know.

Richard Hillary of 603 Squadron was one of those RAF pilots who were given a hard time in a pub by the Army:

After days on the beaches without sight of British planes, these men were bitter, and not unnaturally. They could not be expected to know that, had we not for once managed to gain air superiority behind them over Flanders, they would never have left Dunkirk alive. For us the evacuation was still a newspaper story, until Noel, Howes, and I got the day off, motored to Brighton, and saw for ourselves.

The beaches, streets, and pubs were a crawling mass of soldiers, British, French, and Belgian. They had no money but were being royally welcomed by the locals. They were ragged and weary. When Howes suddenly met a blonde and vanished with her and the car for the rest of the day, Noel and I soon found ourselves in various billets, acting as interpreters for the French. They were very tired and very patient. It had been so long. What could a few more hours matter? The most frequent request was for somewhere to bathe their feet. When it became obvious that there had been a mix-up, that some billets looked like being hopelessly overcrowded and others empty, we gave up. Collecting two French soldiers and a Belgian dispatch rider, we took them off for a drink. The bar we chose was a seething mass of sweating, turbulent khaki. Before we could even get a drink we were involved in half a dozen arguments over the whereabouts of our aircraft over Dunkirk. Knowing personally several pilots who had been killed, and with some knowledge of the true facts, we found it hard to keep our tempers.

Geoffrey Wellum was another who saw the cost of Dunkirk at first hand. The day after he arrived at Hornchurch, 92 Squadron went to war; the squadron lost four pilots for sixteen claimed kills:

Never shall I forget the sight of those pilots as they came into the Mess that first evening at Hornchurch after two days of hard fighting, The CO, my big blond Flight Commander Paddy Green and Pat Learmond were not among them. Pat Learmond was seen to go down in flames and Paddy badly wounded. Nothing has been heard of the others as yet. It gave me my first intimation of what war is all about. These pilots were no longer young men with little care in the world, they were older, mature men. On that day alone, most of them had been over Dunkirk three times and it was a day of the very fiercest fighting. No quarter asked and certainly none given. They now know fear. They also know what it takes to conquer fear because they have done it, not once but three times.

One commonplace method of conquering fear was that adopted by Old Etonian Tim Vigors of 222 Squadron, who simply convinced himself that 'it would be the other guy who "bought it"' and he would survive. (He did, just, despite being shot down in the Battle of Britain and then shot in his parachute later in the war when serving in the Far East.) At Dunkirk, Vigors found he could deal out death with equanimity, as well as face it. Flying home from his first kill (a Me 109) Vigors mused on the experience:

> I was more than happy to have made my first 'kill' and was experiencing that same satisfaction that I had known in Ireland when out pigeon shooting on a summer's evening.
>
> I was aware that I had killed a fellow human being and was surprised not to feel remorse. Of course, Hitler's atrocities had been well publicised and we had got into the way of identifying all Germans with their leader.

Squadron Leader Brian Lane (a.k.a. the author B.J. Ellan) concurred. Flying over the 'dreadful scene' of Dunkirk, he was overcome by 'a surge of hatred for the Hun and all his filthy doings . . . and I felt no mercy must be shown to a people who are a disgrace to humanity'. So, it was with no compunction at all that he shortly afterwards shot down a Stuka dive-bomber. 'I had wondered,' he said, 'what it would be like to shoot down an aircraft and bring it down. Now I knew and it was exhilarating.' Pilot Officer Tony Bartley of 92 Squadron, meanwhile, 'felt sick' after downing his first German plane, a Me 110 with a shark's jaw painted on the nose, which turned over and went straight down into the ground.

But even the most venomous of Spitfire boys conceded an admiration for the Luftwaffe's tactics. Luftwaffe fighter planes flew in a 'finger-four' formation of two close coupled pairs of aircraft about 200 yards apart. The RAF used a 'vic' formation, in which three planes flew in a V-shape, with the leader in the centre. The problem with the 'vic' was put succinctly by George Unwin of 19 Squadron: 'If you're flying in threes and you want to turn quickly, you can't without running into the other fellow.' Meanwhile, in the line astern formation favoured by the rule book's 'Number One Attack' the 'Tail End Charlie' tended to be easy, lonely pickings for predatory enemy fighters because he was so busy following the weavings of his fellows that he could not perform his intended role of looking out behind. Dunkirk planted in the mind of the Spitfire boys the embryo notion of adopting their own 'finger-four' formation.

There were other lessons learned at Dunkirk. Officially the Spitfire's eight machine guns were harmonized to hit a target at 400 yards, which pilots likened to taking a long range pot on the grouse moor. Better was harmonization for 250 yards, which encouraged the pilot to close in fast until the enemy filled the gun-sight, squirt and dart away – an altogether surer method of dealing aerial destruction.

As to the Spitfire itself, it had come through its first battle with flying colours. It was resilient and had killing power; above all, it was nimble. The tightness of its turn had enabled Al Deere to destroy a Me 109 and, by the same token, enabled Hugh Dundas to escape being destroyed by one. Experience suggested some improvements (73lbs of armour plating behind the cockpit, 2 inch thick protective glass on the front windscreen, a rear-view mirror, an alloy cover over the main fuel tank and, crucially, a constant-speed, variable-pitch airscrew, which were all subsequently fitted to the Mark I), but any lingering doubts in the corners of the Air Ministry about the Spitfire's suitability were banished by the blazing heat of its success. Dunkirk established the plane as the RAF's first choice fighter, beyond doubt, and production was increased.

Fighter Command badly needed more machines. The campaign in France and the evacuation from Dunkirk had reduced home defence to 331 Spitfires and Hurricanes. If Hitler invaded Britain immediately after the fall of France, Fighter Command was, in all likelihood, unable to prevent the occupation of the isles. But Hitler tarried, partly because his own armed forces had taken severe losses in recent months (the Battle of France alone cost the Luftwaffe 1,667 aircraft damaged or destroyed), and partly because he hoped that the British, now his last opponent standing, might come to terms. However, Hitler had misjudged the mood of Britain and its bulldog prime minister. On 18 June 1940, Churchill made a major speech to the Commons, the Shakespearean finale of which has echoed down the years and gave summer 1940 its title in the pages of history:

What General Weygand called the Battle of France is over. I expect the Battle of Britain is about to begin. Upon this battle depends the survival of Christian civilization. Upon it depends our British life and the long continuity of our institutions and our Empire. The whole fury and might of the enemy must very soon be turned on us. Hitler knows that he will have to break us in this island or lose the war. If we can stand up to him, all Europe may be free and the life of the world may move forward into broad, sunlit uplands. But if we fail, then the whole world, including the United States, including all that we have known and cared for, will sink into the abyss of a new Dark Age, made more sinister, and perhaps more protracted, by the lights of perverted science. Let us therefore brace ourselves to our duties, and so bear ourselves that, if the British Empire and its Commonwealth last for a thousand years, men will still say, 'This was their finest hour.'

The bulldog had barked and on 3 July it bit. On that day the Royal Navy appeared off French Morocco and ordered the French fleet anchored there to scuttle itself or follow into British captivity. Refusal, the British commander explained, obliged him 'to use whatever force may be necessary to prevent your ships from falling into German or Italian hands'. The French refused and at 5.53 p.m. the Royal Navy opened fire and crippled the French fleet, killing more than 1,200 French sailors. Understanding finally that Britain, under Churchill, would not come to a peace deal, Hitler issued War Directive No. 16, the order for the invasion of the isles. The War Directive included the clause:

2. The following preparations must be undertaken to make a landing in England possible:
(a) The English Air Force must be eliminated to such an extent that it will be incapable of putting up any substantial opposition to the invading troops.

An eerie quiet settled on the Channel and North Sea, as both sides made their preparations for the coming battle. The work of the Spitfire pilot settled into a round of patrols and interceptions of occasional Luftwaffe raiders. Some of the more badly mauled squadrons were reorganized and sent to recuperate, among them Pilot Officer Tony Bartley's 92 Squadron:

Our team was getting very weak and the only person who was enjoying himself was [Bob Stanford] Tuck, who took over the command of the squadron. And then it was over, as suddenly as it had begun. The evacuation of Dunkirk had been completed. A decimated, bloody but unbowed squadron was pulled out of the front line to lick its wounds and reform its ranks.

Other Spitfire boys, whose veins still coursed with the adrenaline of Dunkirk, even complained of boredom. Tim Vigors, to fill the time, spent days choreographing a Spitfire fly-past (at near ground level) which he photographed from the top of a control tower.

In those waiting days of June going on July 1940, as the sun shone on England, there were other ways of helping the war effort. At the Spitfire factories in Southampton, employees were working shifts of up to 72.5 hours a week. Driving them on was a potent mix of professional pride, patriotism and a demanding Minister of Aircraft Production, Lord Beaverbrook. Used to running his newspapers in a manner that bordered on the despotic and the piratical, 'The Beaver' looked to run the nation's aircraft production in much the same way. Many squeaked, but Beaverbrook got the job done; between February and June he tripled aircraft production from 141 fighters to 446. Churchill, sensibly, stood by him.

The activities of Beaverbrook extended beyond the factory gates. He determined that the whole of the British public should get involved in the war effort. Concerned that Germany controlled much of the world's supply of bauxite, one of the raw materials necessary for the production of aluminium, Beaverbrook made an imaginative 'Appeal for Aluminium' to the women of Britain:

Give us your aluminium. We want it, and we want it now. New and old, of every type and description, and all of it.

We will turn your pots and pans into Spitfires and Hurricanes, Blenheims and Wellingtons. I ask, therefore, that every one who has pots and pans, kettles, vacuum cleaners, hat pegs, coat hangers, shoe trees, bathroom fittings and household ornaments, cigarette boxes, or any other articles made wholly or in part of aluminium, should hand them over at once to the local headquarters of the Women's Voluntary Services.

There are branches of this organization in every town and village of the country. But if you are in any doubt, if you have any difficulty in finding the office of the WVS, please inquire at the nearest police station or town hall, where you will be supplied with the necessary information.

The need is instant. The call is urgent. Our expectations are high.

The response was overwhelming. Across the land, families cleared out their kitchens. A Staffordshire housewife, Elsie Cawser, penned a poem with a sentiment common to all donators. 'The Salvage Song (Or: The Housewife's Dream)' went:

> My saucepans have all been surrendered,
> The teapot is gone from the hob,
> The colander's leaving the cabbage
> For a very much different job.
> So now, when I hear on the wireless
> Of Hurricanes showing their mettle,
> I see, in a vision before me,
> A Dornier being chased by my kettle.

Not to be outdone, *Punch* magazine published several pieces of comic verse inspired by the 'Aluminium for Spitfires' campaign, including 'More About Aerial Scrap':

> Welcome! my departed Hoover, I admire your last
>   manoeuvre;
> Up above the world so high,
> Sweeping heinkels from the sky!

Beaverbrook asked the citizens of Britain for more than aluminium. He asked them for hard cash to buy Spitfires. 'Please give us anything you can spare – however small – so that we can increase the number of this most potent fighter plane,' he urged. To help publicize the fund, the Air Ministry published a price list of the major components of a Spitfire. The list is in old imperial currency, of pounds, shillings and pence.

	£	s	d
Engine	2,000	0	0
Fuselage	2,500	0	0
Wings	1,800	0	0
Undercarriage	800	0	0
Guns	800	0	0
Tail	500	0	0
Propeller	350	0	0
Petrol Tank (top)	40	0	0
Petrol Tank (Bottom)	25	0	0
Oil Tank	25	0	0
Compass	5	0	0
Clock	2	10	0
Thermometer	1	1	1
Sparking Plug		8	0

Additional items, such as paint, gauges and cables, added another £1,000 to the bill. The response to the Spitfire Fund was staggering; school boys and girls gave their pocket money, companies gave a slice of their income and foreign countries a dash of their GDP. In consequence, a good many Spitfires roared into the sky bearing the names of their sponsors – such as 'The Kalahari' (Bechuanaland), 'The Flying Scotsmen' (Railway workers) and 'The Canadian Policeman'. Members of the Kennel Club sponsored the aptly monickered 'The Dog Fighter.' *The Times,* meanwhile, reported on the 'Dorothy Spitfire':

> The Dorothys of Great Britain have made a promising start in raising funds to buy a fighter for the RAF to be called the 'Dorothy Spitfire'. The manager of the Sheffield branch of Lloyds bank has consented to act as trustee for the fund, and all amounts of £1 or less should be sent to him. Amounts of more than £1 should be paid into any branch of Lloyds Bank.

One of the Dorothys of Great Britain, the detective writer Dorothy L. Sayers, wrote to the *Daily Telegraph* explaining the 'good human, sentimental reasons' why the Spitfire Fund had so lit the public's imagination:

> First, a fighter plane is, comparatively speaking, a very small machine and there is something irresistibly endearing about a very small things that fights like hell . . .
>   Second, a fighter plane is less expensive [than a bomber]; the task before our town or name-groups seems a little less formidable, and our humble contribution just a little less adequate.

Third, when a ferocious giant has been coming at one with a club, this impulse to send the hat round for Jack the Giant-Killer is too strong to be restrained . . .

Possibly the most poignant donation to the Spitfire Fund came from South Wales, and was reported in *The Times* under the heading 'Spitfire in Memory of Airman Son':

Among the gifts received over the weekend was a cheque for 5,000 from the village of Michaelston-le-Pit, South Wales, received through Mr. H.H. Merrett, of Cwrt-yr-Ala, near Cardiff. 'On Sunday last,' Mr Merrett says in his letter to Lord Beaverbrook, 'we received the tragic news that my son, Flying Officer Norman Merrett, had lost his life somewhere in Britain while serving with the RAF. I cannot provide you with another gallant son. The one who has gone was my only son. But I want you to accept the enclosed cheque to purchase a Spitfire so that one of the ever growing number of lads from Britain and the Dominions, so anxious to defend us in the air, may be equipped with an instrument which, combined with that indomitable spirit, courage and fearlessness, will enable him, as his colleagues are now doing, to take severe toll of these inferior beings attempting, with increasing failure, to demolish the morale of our people. It is not a personal gift, but something to commemorate the passing of my son.'

By the time Beaverbrook's Spitfire Fund closed in early 1941, it has raised over £13 million and put thousands of Spitfires in the sky. The fund did something else too; it publicized the fighter and placed it into a treasured corner of the British public's heart.

It was *their* fighter. Previously the Spitfire had been a state-of-the-art plane. Thanks to Beaverbrook's Spitfire Fund, the aircraft was fast becoming a national icon. All the Spitfire needed for immortality was a defining role in history.

Hermann Göring, Commander-in-Chief of the Luftwaffe, was only too keen to provide the opportunity.

PART II

Finest Hours – The Battle of Britain, July–October 1940

On 3 July 1940, the Luftwaffe suddenly cranked up its activity over the Channel. This was not yet the invasion of Britain, 'Operation Sea Lion', but its overture, with Luftwaffe tasked with closing the Channel to British shipping and clearing the sky above it of RAF fighters. Without air superiority over the Channel and southern England, a German amphibious invasion would be easy prey for the RAF and Royal Navy. German intelligence considered that a month, at most, would be needed to destroy RAF's Fighter Command. Certainly, the Luftwaffe had the superior number of aircraft in this '*Kanalkampf*', or Channel War: Luftflotte 2, commanded by General 'Smiling' Albert Kesselring in Belgium, and Luftflotte 3, commanded by General Hugo Sperrle in France, could muster between them 2,009 serviceable aircraft, including 824 fighters.

At the beginning of July, Dowding's Order of Battle showed 52 fighter squadrons, of which 19 were equipped with Spitfires and 25 with Hurricanes (the remainder had Blenheims or Defiants, both of which were only suitable for night fighting).

Put bluntly, Dowding had 504 airworthy Spitfires and Hurricanes to protect Britain. He was also desperately short of pilots, commanding a mere 1,069.

The shield Dowding wielded may have been thin, but it had quality, in men, machines and organization. In charge of Fighter Command since 1936, Dowding had arranged Britain's air defence into four quadrants or 'Groups': No. 10 Group covered southwest England from Portsmouth onwards, No. 12 Group the Midlands, No. 13 northern England and No. 11 covered London and the southeast. The Group Commander of 11 Group was Air Vice Marshal Keith Park, a New Zealander who had been Dowding's right-hand man at Fighter Command's HQ at Bentley Priory. It was understood by all that 11 Group would have the bulldog's share of the fight. Each group was subdivided into sectors centred on a main fighter aerodrome.

Dowding and Fighter Command enjoyed one technical advantage over the Germans. Although late in adopting radar, Britain had, by summer 1940, constructed a chain of coastal radar stations that covered the southern and eastern approaches, and could detect approaching enemy aircraft up to a hundred miles away. The electronic information from the radar stations was sent to Bentley Priory's filter room, where it was matched with reports from the ears and eyes of the Observer Corps; volunteers who craned with binoculars from sandbagged posts. The sifted and sorted information was then passed on to the relevant group operations room where it was decided which sector should be 'scrambled' to intercept enemy aircraft. In the air, the scrambled fighters would be 'vectored' by the sector controller. Britain's air defence system was the most advanced, and the most efficient, in the world.

Which was just as well, for the Luftwaffe was sallying over the *Kanal* in ever increasing numbers. On the evening of 7 July, forty-five Dornier 17s, protected by sixty Me 109s, attacked a convoy near Dover. Six of the intercepting Spitfires from 65 Squadron were shot down, but among the victors that evening was 616 Squadron's Hugh Dundas, relieved to have finally hit a black-crossed aircraft:

On 7 July came the big moment when I at last scored hits on an enemy plane. Green section was scrambled and sent off at full speed out to sea, crossing the coast north of Spurn Point. George Moberley was leading; Sergeant Burnard and I followed him. There was a layer of broken cloud at about five thousand feet and we were ordered to keep below it. We thundered along at full throttle, bumping violently in the turbulent air just below the cloud. George gave the tally-ho and altered course sharply. Then I saw it – the pencil shape of a Dornier 17 twin-engined bomber just below the cloud, stalking a convoy.

As George went into the attack the Dornier pulled up into cloud. I climbed hard and in a few seconds burst through into the bright blue above. Almost immediately the Dornier also popped through close by and I was able to get in a short attack before it again disappeared into cloud. There followed an exciting chase as the German pilot tried frantically to elude us. But nowhere was the cloud solid, he was bound to come out into gaps and by good fortune we maintained contact with him, worrying at his heels like spaniels hunting in cover. He fought back gallantly – desperately would perhaps be a more appropriate word – and for a time his rear gunner returned our fire, though it was an unequal exchange, which must have been utterly terrifying for him. His tracer bullets streamed past and I received a hit on the outer part of my port wing. But the advantage was all in our favour. The rear gunner was silenced and the dying Dornier descended in its shroud of black smoke, to crash into the sea a few miles east of the convoy.

A second Dornier was sighted, scurrying away among the clouds. Sergeant Burnard and I managed to get in one attack each before our ammunition was all gone, but though we damaged it we did not see it crash.

Back at Leconfield I experienced for the first time the exhilaration of landing and taxiing in after a successful engagement with the enemy. Those who waited on the ground could always tell when a Spitfire's machine guns had been fired. Normally the eight gun ports on the leading edge of the wing were covered by little patches of canvas. But when the guns were fired these patches were, of course, shot away, leaving the ports open, and the plane made a distinctive whistling noise on the glide. This clear signal that you had been in action could be made more pronounced by a bit of side slipping, which, though sternly discouraged by the authorities, was hard to resist on such occasions. And so, when they recognized this signal of action, the ground crews, who identified themselves enthusiastically with the pilots whose planes they serviced, would run out in high excitement to hear the news. They regarded a victory for their plane as a victory for themselves – and justly so, for our reliance on their skills was absolute.

I felt twelve feet tall after that combat, which in retrospect certainly does not seem anything to be particularly proud of. At last I had broken my duck. I could only claim one-third of one enemy aircraft destroyed and one-half of another damaged – but that was better than nothing at all.

For the first time I was consumed by an insidious feeling which crept in on me many, many times in the months and years to follow. I heard the tempting tone of an inner voice which I was to hear again so often the next five years. It said, 'There, now, you have been in action several times and you have done some damage to the enemy. You are still alive and kicking. Even if you pulled out now, no one would ever be able to say you had not done your bit.'

It was the voice which expressed a sincere desire to stay alive, opposing a sincere desire to engage the enemy. It was muted and easy enough to muffle at that stage. But I was to learn how insistent it could become.

About 3,000 yards directly ahead of me, and at the same level, a Hun was just completing a turn preparatory to re-entering the fray. He saw me almost immediately and rolled out of his turn towards me so that a head-on attack became inevitable. Using both hands on the control column to steady the aircraft and thus keep my aim steady, I peered through the reflector sight at the rapidly closing enemy aircraft. We opened fire together, and immediately a hail of lead thudded into my Spitfire. One moment the Messerschmitt was a clearly defined shape, its wingspan nicely enclosed within the circle of my reflector sight, and the next it was on top of me, a terrifying blur which blotted out the sky ahead. Then we hit.

The force of the impact pitched me violently forward onto my cockpit harness, the straps of which bit viciously into my shoulders. At the same moment, the control column was snatched abruptly from my gripping fingers by a momentary, but powerful, reversal of elevator load. In a flash it was over; there was clear sky ahead of me, and I was still alive. But smoke and flame were pouring from the engine which began to vibrate, slowly at first but with increasing momentum, causing the now regained control column to jump back and forwards in my hand. Hastily I closed the throttle and reached forward to flick off the ignition switches, but before I could do so the engine seized and the airscrew stopped abruptly. I saw with amazement that the blades had been bent almost double with the impact of the collision; the Messerschmitt must have been just that fraction above me as we hit.

With smoke now pouring into the cockpit I reached blindly forward for the hood release toggle and tugged at it violently. There was no welcoming and expected rush of air to denote that the hood had been jettisoned. Again and again I pulled at the toggle but there was no response. In desperation I turned to the normal release catch and exerting my full strength endeavoured to slide back the hood. It refused to budge; I was trapped. There was only one thing to do; try to keep the aircraft under control and head for the nearby coast. The speed had by now dropped off considerably, and with full backward pressure on the stick I was just able to keep a reasonable gliding altitude. If only I could be lucky enough to hit in open country where there was a small chance that I might get away with it.

Frantically I peered through the smoke and flame enveloping the engine, seeking with streaming eyes for what lay ahead. There could be no question of turning; I had no idea what damage had been done to the fuselage and tail of my aircraft, although the mainplanes appeared to be undamaged, and I daren't risk even a small turn at low level, even if I could have seen to turn.

Through a miasmatic cloud of flame and smoke the ground suddenly appeared ahead of me. The next moment a post flashed by my wingtip and then the aircraft struck the ground and ricocheted into the air again, finally returning to earth with a jarring impact, and once again I was jerked forward on to my harness. Fortunately the straps held fast and continued to do so as the aircraft ploughed its way through a succession of splintering posts before finally coming to a halt on the edge of a corn field. Half blinded by smoke and frantic with fear I tore at my harness release pin. And then with my bare hands wielding the strength of desperation, I battered at the Perspex hood which entombed me. With a splintering crash it finally cracked open, thus enabling me to scramble from the cockpit to the safety of the surrounding field.

Convoy protection was a gruelling but necessary task throughout July, as the Luftwaffe tried to strangle Britain's supply lines and probe at the nation's air defences. 'We all disliked this work,' recalled Pilot Officer David Crook of 609 Squadron, 'the weather was brilliant and the Huns invariably used to attack out of the sun . . . Also we were always outnumbered, sometimes by ridiculous odds.' Patrolling off Weymouth in the dismal early evening of 9 July, Crook's 'Green section' of 609 Squadron, consisting of just three Spitfires, sighted a formation of Ju 87 dive bombers in the clouds out to sea and went to intercept. Despite being bounced by some Me 110s above them, David Crook managed, in this his first combat, to make a 'kill', downing a Ju 87:

The flames enveloped the whole machine and he went straight down for about 5,000 feet, till he was just a shapeless mass of wreckage. Absolutely fascinated, I saw him hit the sea with a great burst of white foam. Afterwards I was rather surprised to reflect that my only feeling had been one of considerable elation . . . A moment later I saw another Spitfire flying home on a very erratic course, obviously keeping a very good look out behind. I joined up with it and recognized Michael, and together we bolted for the English coast like a couple of startled rabbits. I made a perfectly bloody landing . . . I got out to talk to Michael and found my hand was quite shaky, and even my voice was unsteady.

Green section's Peter Drummond-Hay did not return from this action. It is thought that he left his radio set on 'Transmit' and failed to hear Crook's warning 'Look out behind!' when the Me 110s, known as Destroyers, pounced. Crook had shared a room with Drummond-Hay, and when he went up to it later:

Everything was just the same as Peter and had left it . . . his towel was still in the window, where he had thrown it during our hurried dressing. But he was dead now. I simply could not get used to such sudden and unexpected death, and there flashed across my mind the arrangements we had made to go up to London together the following day . . . I felt that I could not sleep in that room again, and so I took my things and went into Gordon's bed next door and slept there.

But I could not get out of my head the thought of Peter, with whom we had been talking and laughing that day, now lying in the cockpit of his wrecked Spitfire at the bottom of the English Channel.

Then, in the early, rainy afternoon of 10 July, now officially recognised as the first day of the Battle of Britain, sixty Ju 87 Stukas and seventy-five Dornier 17s stalked into the Channel with an escort of 200 Me 109 fighters. As the German airfleet approached a convoy, thirty Spits from 64 and 74 Squadrons came speeding in. 'Suddenly the Sky was full of British fighters,' remarked Hauptman Hannes Trautloft, a Me 109 pilot. But at Dowding's insistence the British fighter pilots avoided a free-for-all scrap with the German fighter escort and instead targeted instead the Luftwaffe bombers and dive-bombers. The Stukas were mauled to pieces; henceforth the Luftwaffe referred to them grimly as 'the Flying Coffins'.

No one would ever accuse Hugh Dowding of being an inspirational leader of men; in person, he was as inhibited as his nickname 'Stuffy' suggested. He was a poor communicator and some of his commanders and many of his pilots did not understand his strategy: to prioritize the destruction of the bomber over the fighter and to bleed the Luftwaffe to death by pinpricks. As strategies went, it wasn't glamorous and it failed to convince the pugnacious element in Fighter Command, headed by Squadron Leader Douglas Bader, who yearned for mass formations of fighters ('Big Wings') to take the aerial war to the enemy, but it worked. Like General Mikhail Kutuzov faced with the might of Napoleon in 1812, Dowding only had to keep his force together and active until the weather put an end to the possibility of invasion. Kutuzov's ally was 'General Winter'; Dowding needed to hang on until the arrival of 'General Autumn', when an amphibious invasion of Britain would become impossible. Later, on Dowding's death, a com-memorative bronze plaque was attached to the wall of Bentley Priory with the legend: 'To him the people of Britain and of the

Free World owe largely the way of life and the liberties that they enjoy today.'

Like Dowding, Hermann Göring had been a fighter pilot in the First World War. But there the similarities ended. Unlike the single-minded Dowding, Göring was as much a politician and a bon viveur as he was an airman. Burgeoning with overconfidence after the Luftwaffe's victories in Poland, the Low Countries and France, he failed to take proper control of the offensive against Britain. Consequently, the *Kanalkampf* was ad hoc, improvised, with some sorties nothing but opportunistic 'free hunts'. Inevitably, the Channel at Dover, being both the closest place to France and 'bottleneck' through which British shipping had to pass, became the Luftwaffe's favourite hunting ground; the British sailor and airman, on the receiving end, dubbed it 'Hellfire Corner'.

Charles Gardner, a BBC correspondent, witnessed a dogfight above the chalk cliffs of Dover on Sunday 14 July. Gardner's famous running radio commentary, spoken from his car, to the roof of which he had tied a bed mattress for protection, purveyed the drama of aerial fighting to millions, and gave the Spitfire yet another supercharged boost of publicity:

Ah! Here's one coming down now! There's one coming down in flames! There somebody's hit a German, and he's coming down. There's a long streak and he's coming down completely out of control – a long streak of smoke. Aah! – the man's baled out by parachute – the pilot's baled out by parachute! He's a Junkers 87 and he's going slap into the sea, and there he goes – SMASH! – a terrific column of water! and there was a Junkers 87. There's only one man got out by parachute, so presumably there was only a crew of one in it.

Now then – oh, there's a terrific mix-up now over the Channel. It's impossible to tell which are our machines, and which are the Germans. There's one definitely down in this battle, and there's a fight going on – you can hear the little rattles of machine gun bullets.

[CROOMPH] That was a bomb, as you may imagine. Here comes – there's one Spitfire, there are the little bursts – there's another bomb dropping. The sky is absolutely patterned now with bursts of anti-aircraft fire, and the sea is covered with smoke where the bombs have burst, but as far as I can see there's not one single ship hit, and there is definitely one German machine down, and looking across the sea now I can see the little white dot of parachute as the German pilot is floating down towards the spot where his machine crashed with such a big fountain of water about two minutes ago.

Well, now, everything is peaceful again for the moment. The Germans, who came over in about twenty dive bombers, delivered their attack on the convoy, and I think they've made off as quickly as they came. Oh, yes, I can see one, two, three, four, five, six, seven, eight, nine, ten Germans haring backwards France now for all they can go, and here are our Spitfires coming after them. There's going to be a big fight, I think, out there. You can hear the anti-aircraft batteries still going.

Well, that really was a hot little engagement while it lasted – and no damage done except to the Germans, who lost one machine, and the German pilot is still on the end of his parachute, though appreciably nearer the sea than he was. I can see no boat going out to pick him up, so he'll probably have a long swim ashore.

There are about four fighters up there, and I don't know what they're doing – one, two, three, four, five fighters fighting right over our head now. There's one coming right down on the tail of what I think is a Messerschmitt, and I think a Spitfire behind him. There's a dogfight going up there; there are four, five, six machines wheeling and turning round now. Hark at the machine guns going! – one, two, three, four, five, six – now there's something coming right down on the tail of another.

[Another voice interjects: 'Here they go! They're goin' back home!']

Yes, they're being chased home, and how they're being chased home! There are three Spitfires chasing three Messerschmitts now. Oh boy! Look at them going! And look how the Messersch – eh! that is really grand! And there's a Spitfire just behind the first two – he'll get them! Ah, yes! Oh, boy! I've never seen anything so good as this! The RAF fighters have really got these boys taped!

The RAF fighters might have had the Luftwaffe boys 'taped', but the size of the enemy formations was daunting. On 21 July Pilot Officer John Bisdee's 609 Squadron was scrambled from Warmwell in No. 10 Group to intercept an attack on Portland.

This was the first time I'd ever seen a really large German formation. The controller on the RT said, 'One hundred-plus bandits' and then told us the direction. Moments later he said, 'Very many bandits!' I happened to be flying L1082, which was our oldest Spitfire and slowest. I had some difficulty keeping up, however I did more or less. I remember the incredible sight of this great swarm of rotating

German aircraft, each following their own tail. The feeling
I had, and a lot of us had, was; what are these buggers doing
here? How dare they? It was really quite a shock to see this
vast number of black crosses and swastikas in the sky over
our country. Then we all plunged in.

Then we all plunged in. Despite the overwhelming numbers of
enemy aircraft, squadrons – even single flights – of Fighter
Command attacked and harried the enemy. On the morning of
24 July, 54 Squadron was vectored on to two heavily escorted
Luftwaffe bomber formations that were heading for the Thames
Estuary. A communications misunderstanding left Flying Officer
Al Deere and his flight of eight aircraft alone in the sky with the
largest enemy formation he had seen to that date, consisting 'of
about eighteen Dorniers protected by a considerable number of
escort fighters weaving and criss-crossing above and behind the
bombers'. Deere found 'an attack against such numbers was a
frightening prospect' but thought 'We must break them up'. All
Deere could do was take advantage of his height above the
bombers to work up a high overtaking speed, thus making it
difficult for the enemy fighters to intervene when his flight
stooped:

We turned into the attack. A momentary buffeting as I hit
the enemy bombers' slipstream, a determined juggling with
the control column and rudder, a brief wait for the range to
close, and the right hand bomber received the full impact of
my eight Brownings. In a matter of seconds, in which only
a short burst was possible, I was forced to break off the
attack for fear of collision. It was perhaps just as well as
the 109s were now all round us. In the next few minutes,

a frenzy of twisting and turning, I managed quick bursts at three enemy fighters, as singly they passed fleetingly through my line of fire, but without conclusive results. Suddenly, the sky was clear and I was alone; one moment the air was a seething cauldron of Hun fighters, and the next it was empty.

The 'empty sky phenomenon' never ceased to amaze fighter pilots throughout the long years of the Second World War. Such was the speed of combat, sometimes in excess of 400mph, that a move lasting mere seconds could take man and machine miles from the aerial battleground.

Deere's desperate plunge worked. Small numbers of Spitfires with aggressively minded pilots in the cockpits could work near miracles in breaking up enemy formations. When Deere re-found the battle he could see 'the enemy bombers making for France and safety'. The convoy that had been their target was unharmed and sailing serenely on.

Flight Lieutenant Brian Kingcombe of 92 Squadron favoured the 'head-on' tactics in this war of the 'Davids versus the Goliaths.' Later he recalled an engagement with one especially fearsome enemy formation:

They looked like a bloody great swarm of bees . . . in those days if you were diving down from a couple of thousand feet above them, which is what you probably tried to do, you were probably doing round about four hundred [mph] in your Spitfire. And they were probably doing somewhere about a hundred and eighty. So you were approaching not far short of six hundred miles an hour. So the gap closed very quickly. And so very soon the swarm of bees became a lot of bloody great aeroplanes. And then the tracer would come out. It's a little bit unnerving when they're firing at you because every third or fourth round – whatever their mixture was – was tracer. And tracer comes out at you apparently very slowly to begin with. You see these lazy, long smoke trails coming at you. They get faster as they reach you, then suddenly whip past your ear at the most amazing speed. Luckily most of them miss.

Of course you didn't always have the time to plan because sometimes you were sent off late. Maybe you hand only landed a short time ago from another sortie and hadn't had the time to rearm and refuel. It was when you were sent off in time you could do what I really preferred to do; climb to your height ahead of the enemy bombers, turn around and tackle head-on. A head-on attack did far more to destroy the morale of the approaching bombers than anything else . . . it upset the driver so much, the poor old pilot. He was the chap who then turned tail. When he was sitting and couldn't see the attack and was protected by a nice sheet of metal behind him and he had the gunners . . . he was in a much more relaxed frame of mind than when you were coming straight at him. And one would then go straight through the formation, turn round when you got through. And try and have another go from the rear then. But usually by that stage their fighters would come down . . . After that it was very much a free for all.

Of course, the cost to the 'Davids' of Fighter Command was high. On the day Deere so successfully broke up the intended enemy attack on the convoy, diffident, Bible-reading Johnny Allen, the hero of Dunkirk, was killed. A few days later 'Wonky'

Way was shot down. Deere heard the event over the RT, while he was patrolling nearby.

> At this juncture I recognized George's excited voice, 'Watch out, Blue One, 109s coming in from above – hundreds of them.' I immediately called control for permission to reinforce 'B' Flight but was refused, and ordered to stay over the convoy. Again I heard George, this time in urgency, 'Break, "Wonky", BREAK.' From the long silence that followed I had a premonition that the warning was too late. Again George's voice crackled in my earphones, this time in half-sobbing anger: 'Damn and blast this bloody war, they've got "Wonky".' So died another gallant airman; as with Johnny [Allen], not outfought but outnumbered.

Hearing the death of a fellow pilot, as it was relayed over the R/T, was always especially hard to bear. By now 54 Squadron had lost six pilots in three days. Of the seventeen pilots who had been in the squadron at the opening of the Dunkirk battle, only five remained. The morale of these five remained high but they were on the edge of exhaustion. The decision was made to send the squadron off to Catterick for a necessary rest and refit. As Deere noted, the decision showed just how closely Dowding, Commander-in-Chief of Fighter Command, controlled the battle 'with his finger on the pulse of operations'.

The withdrawal of 54 Squadron from the frontline coincided with the end of the *Kanalkampf* phase of the Battle of Britain. Round 1 had gone to Fighter Command; the Luftwaffe had lost about 180 aircraft, for the loss of 70 British fighters in this Channel war. But the strain on Fighter Command – as shown by 54 Squadron's record – had been heavy, for on most days 600 or more sorties had been flown. 'Over and over again,' notes the official history of the RAF about the campaign in July 1940, 'a mere handful of Spitfires and Hurricanes found themselves fighting desperately with formations of a hundred or more German aircraft'.

But the worst of the Battle was still to come.

On the morning of 1 August Göring gathered his subordinates together in the garden at the Luftwaffe HQ in The Hague. Resplendent in his white suit, Göring explained to the air commanders sitting in the sun that the Fuhrer's Directive No. 17 tasked them with overpowering the English air force 'in the shortest possible time'. Their objectives were to be 'flying units . . . ground installations . . . supply organizations, but also . . . the aircraft industry'. The elimination of Fighter Command and the achievement of absolute air superiority over England would take thirteen days. Then 'Operation Sea Lion', the invasion of Britain itself, could commence.

Not all Göring's commanders were convinced that the defeat of the RAF would be so short and so easy. The veteran Luftwaffe pilot 'Uncle' Theo Osterkamp of the Luftwaffe fighter wing JG 51 (Jagdgeschwader 51), who had flown in the First World War as well as at Dunkirk and over the *Kanal*, looked askance. Göring asked him what was wrong. Osterkamp expressed his reservations:

I explained to him that during the time when I was alone in combat over England with my Wing, I counted . . . about 500 to 700 British fighters . . . concentrated in the area around London. Their numbers had increased considerably [since] the beginning of the battle. All new units were equipped with Spitfires, which I considered of a quality equal to own our fighters.

Göring cut him off angrily: 'The Messerschmitt is much better than the Spitfire because the British are too cowardly to engage your fighters.'

Certainly, the Spitfire was not without competitors in the skies of summer 1940. The Hawker Hurricane, Britain's first monoplane fighter and Fighter Command's numerical mainstay in the coming battle, scored notable successes with its armament of eight .303-inch machine guns against the Luftwaffe's bombers: The Junkers 87 (the gull-winged Stuka), the Junkers 88, the Heinkel 111 and the veteran Dornier 17 'Flying Pencil' bomber. The top speed, however, of a Dornier 215, a Do-17 upgraded with more powerful Daimler-Benz engines, taxed the Hurricane to the utmost, reaching 311mph to the Hurricane's 328mph.

On the German predator side there were the Messerschmitt Bf110 and the Messerschmitt Bf109E fighters. A manoeuvrable lump of a machine, which would eventually need a fighter escort of its own, the twin-engined 110 still packed the gun-punch its nickname 'Destroyer' suggested. That escort was the wondrous Messerschmitt 109. When it ascended to the skies in September 1935, six months before the Spitfire, the tiny, quivering Messerschmitt 109 was a revolution in aviation; the first aeroplane to feature an all metal monocoque construction, closed canopy and retractable landing gear. Over 29,000 Me 109s were manufactured during the Second World War. No fighter before or since has been produced in such numbers.

The Me 109E or 'Emil' version encountered by the Spitfire in the Battle of Britain was powered by a 1,100hp Daimler-Benz 601A engine and was equipped with two 20mm cannon and two

7.92mm machine guns. The Emil was able to outdive the Spitfire.

Where the 109E lost the battle honours was in manoeuvrability. The Spitfire was more agile, with a tighter turn. The Spit's top speed of 361mph was 4mph faster than the 109. Another vital superiority was its firepower; while the wing-mounted Brownings were out ranged by German cannon, the Spitfire held a decisive concentration of fire. Pilots of the Emil also complained about the smallness of the cockpit – so legendarily small that Göring, the Luftwaffe chief, could not force his bulk into it – and that the narrow track of the undercarriage caused the plane to slew on landing. Their most bitter complaint was reserved for the smallness of the fuel tank, which handicapped the 109E's range. The Me109 could manage a bare ten minutes over the skies of southeast England, which was destined to be the main battle area.

The sky over England was not as unguarded as Göring had hoped. Thanks to the Herculean efforts of Beaverbrook and the nation's aircraft workers, 488 Hurricanes and Spitfires had been handed over to the RAF between 29 June and 2 August 1940. The strength of Fighter Command in the first week of August was 704 serviceable fighters. Even so, the task Fighter Command faced was daunting. It had to defend Britain not only against Kesselring's Luftflotte 2 in Belgium and Sperrle's Luftflotte 3 in France, but also Hans-Jürgen Stumpff's Luftflotte 5 in Denmark and Norway, which menaced the northeast of England and Scotland – a total force of 1,100 fighters and 1,900 bombers. In this bleak picture, the capabilities of R.J. Mitchell's Supermarine Spitfire was a small scintilla of hope.

Operation Eagle, the Luftwaffe's attack on Fighter Command, was fixed to begin on 5 August. The day broke damp and hazy and the *Adlertag* (Eagle Day) had to be postponed. It was a poor omen for such a grandiosely named campaign. The bad weather continued. There was a ferocious Luftwaffe attack on a convoy off the Isle of Wight on 8 August, followed by sporadic raids on airfields and radar stations over the next four days. Not until 13 August did the Eagle Day occur, with the Luftwaffe delivering the first of Göring's promised 'hard blows'; flying 1,485 sorties against targets across the south coast and Midlands (including a night attack on the Spitfire works at Castle Bromwich). David Crook of 609 Squadron was on patrol at above Weymouth when his commanding officer spotted a large German formation of Ju 87s escorted by Me 109s and 110s:

At about 4 p.m. we were ordered to patrol Weymouth at 15,000 feet. We took off, thirteen machines in all, with the C.O. leading, and climbed up over Weymouth. After a few minutes I began to hear a German voice talking on the R.T., faintly at first and then growing in volume. By a curious chance this German raid had a wavelength almost identical with our own and the voice we heard was that of the German Commander talking to his formation as they approached us across the Channel. About a quarter of an hour later we saw a large German formation approaching below us. There were a number of Junkers 87 dive-bombers escorted by Me 109s above, and also some Me 110s about two miles behind, some sixty machines in all.

A Hurricane squadron attacked the Me 110s as soon as they crossed the coast and they never got through to where we were.

Meanwhile the bombers, with their fighter escort still circling above them, passed beneath us. We were up at almost 20,000 feet in the sun and I don't think they ever saw us till the very last moment. The C.O. gave a terrific 'Tally ho' and led us round in a big semicircle so that we were now behind them, and we prepared to attack.

Mac, Novi (one of the Poles), and I were flying slightly behind and above the rest of the squadron, guarding their tails, and at this moment I saw about five Me 109s pass just underneath us.

I immediately broke away from the formation, dived on to the last Me 109, and gave him a terrific burst of fire at very close range. He burst into flames and spun down for many thousands of feet into the clouds below, leaving behind him a long trail of black smoke.

I followed him down for some way and could not pull out of my dive in time to avoid going below the clouds myself. I found that I was about five miles north of Weymouth, and then I saw a great column of smoke rising from the ground a short distance away. I knew perfectly well what it was and went over to have a look. My Me 109 lay in a field, a tangled heap of wreckage burning fiercely, but with the black crosses on the wings still visible. I found out later that the pilot was still in the machine. He had made no attempt to get out while the aircraft was diving and he had obviously been killed by my first burst of fire. He crashed just outside a small village and I could see everybody streaming out of their houses and rushing to the spot.

I climbed up through the clouds again to rejoin the fight but there was nothing to be seen, so I returned to the aerodrome, where all the ground crews were in a great state of excitement, as they could hear a terrific fight going on above the clouds but saw nothing except several German machines falling in flames.

Yes – they were all covered with black streaks from the smoke of the guns – everybody had fired.

There was the usual anxious counting – only ten back – where are the others – they should be back by now – I hope to God everybody's OK – good enough, here they come! Thank God, everybody's OK!

We all stood round in small groups talking excitedly, and exchanging experiences. It is very amusing to observe the exhilaration and excitement which everybody betrays after a successful action like this!

It soon became obvious that this had been our best effort yet. Thirteen enemy machines had been destroyed in about four minutes glorious fighting. Six more were probably destroyed or damaged, while our only damage sustained was one bullet through somebody's wing. I think this was the record bag for one squadron in one fight during the whole of the Battle of Britain.

Just after I broke away to attack my Messerschmitt, the whole squadron had dived right into the centre of the German formation and the massacre started. One pilot looked round in the middle of the action and in one small patch of sky, he saw five German dive-bombers going down in flames, still more or less in formation.

We all heard the German commander saying desperately, time after time, 'Achtung, achtung, Spit and Hurri' – meaning presumably, 'Look out, look out, Spitfires and Hurricanes.'

Novi got two Me 109s in his first fight and came back more pleased with himself and more excited than I have ever seen anybody before.

And so ended this very successful day, the thirteenth day of the month, and thirteen of our pilots went into action, and thirteen of the enemy were shot down. I shall never again distrust the number thirteen.

One member of the squadron remarked afterwards that he rather missed the 'glorious twelfth' this year – 'but the glorious thirteenth was the best day's shooting I ever had'.

Their [the ground crew's] loyalty to the squadron and their keenness and energy knew no bounds, and as a result we always had the very comforting feeling that our Spitfires were maintained as perfectly as was humanly possible.

I don't think my engine ever missed a beat throughout the whole summer, and this means a lot to you when you are continually going into action and any mechanical failure will have the most unpleasant consequences. Frequently in those hectic days they would work all through the night, in order to have a machine ready for dawn.

609 was an Auxiliary Squadron, formed before the war for 'weekend flyers'. The pilots of the Royal Auxiliary Air Force Squadrons, which drew their volunteer members from a defined locality (the West Riding of Yorkshire in the case of 609), tended to be 'Society' or at least rich. Hugh 'Cocky' Dundas of 616 Squadron might stand as the very model of the public school educated Auxiliary pilot, as remembered by Johnnie Johnson.

'Cocky' Dundas was a lanky, freckle-faced youth of nineteen who, after leaving Stowe, began to serve his articles to a Yorkshire solicitor. We were to fight together for a long time and became the best of friends; later Cocky was best man at my wedding and godfather to my younger son. Even at this early stage of his life he had developed an astonishing aptitude for expensive living. Once or twice each week he insisted on dining out of mess, when a bottle of wine with the meal, together with an assortment of drinks before and after, was the order of the day. Once, stranded at Brighton, he chartered a taxi all the way to Tangmere, because he disliked buses. His hair-oil came from an exclusive address in Bond Street. His uniforms were tailored in Hanover Square and lined with red silk, a custom followed by the Auxiliary pilots. To show his status as a member of the Auxiliary Air Force he should have worn two small brass 'A's, one on each lapel of his tunic. These symbols were present on Cocky's everyday uniform, but the left 'A' was much larger than its opposite number. This gave him a curiously lopsided appearance and was apt to irritate some of the more serious minded senior officers. He was a devout champion of what he called the 'Auxiliary attitude'.

Underneath their slight raffishness, the Auxiliary boys were as deadly earnest as any other RAF fighter pilot. Dundas' brother John, a pilot with 60 Squadron, was one of the Battle of Britain's top aces.

'Family' was a word often used about the Auxiliary Squadrons. They tended to be very tight knit, not just 'horizontally' but from top to bottom too, as evidenced in this exchange of letters on 15 August 1940 in 609 Squadron.

From: N.C.O.s and Men of No. 609 Squadron.

In view of the recent successes achieved by the R.A.F. and No. 609 Squadron in particular, we wish to offer all

Pilots our sincerest congratulations, and 'good Hunting' for the future.

We feel honoured to have such excellent Pilots in the Aircraft we service.

For and on behalf of N.C.O.s and Men of 'A' and 'B' Flights,

Flight-Sergeant Cloves, C.W. Flight-Sergeant Roberts, H.J.

The reply:

From: Officer Commanding, No. 609 Squadron.
To: All N.C.O.s and Airmen in Flights and Sections.
Date: 15th August 1940

On behalf of the Pilots of this Squadron, I thank you for your appreciation of our efforts.

Our results can only be achieved by confidence in our aircraft, and it is due to your hard work and skill that the engines have kept going, that the bullets have found their mark, and that the air is filled with Sorbo war whoops.

Keep going hard, with all your skill and might, for I shall have to ask you to keep up and increase this pace before this show is over.

(Sgd.) H.S. Darley
Squadron-Leader, Commanding
No. 609 Squadron, Warmwell

Darley was right. 609 Squadron's fitters and mechanics did have to up the pace. On that very day, in azures skies, all three Luftflotten went into action, with Luftflotte 5 targeting the north-east of England and Scotland. The fighting on 15 August was the most extensive in the whole Battle of Britain, with the Luftwaffe flying 520 bomber and 1,270 fighter sorties, with the attacks stretching from Northumberland to Dorset. Everywhere the Luftwaffe was opposed. Especially significant was the fighting in the north-east, where Fighter Command's 13 Group – involved in the battle for the first time – shot down eight He 111s and seven Me 110s for no loss. The Luftwaffe had hoped that Dowding had left the north undefended; he had not. So dismayed was the Luftwaffe by the interceptions of 13 Group that it never again launched daylight attacks across the North Sea.

But across the Channel, the Luftwaffe did not stop coming, flying 1,700 sorties on 16 August. On the 18th it struck in full force, chiefly against airfields in Kent, Surrey and Sussex, losing seventy-one aircraft to the RAF's twenty-seven in a day of violent, swirling fighting.

Each day, and often several times a day, the RAF's fighter boys rose to intercept the invaders. The fighting squadrons waiting to go into action were held on the ground at what was known as 'Readiness 5 Minutes'. Spitfires and Hurricanes sat on the airfield, sometimes protected by earth and brick revetments around the perimeter, and from time to time the ground crews would run the engines to warm them. Ronald Adams, a former actor, was an RAF Controller with 11 Group and later vividly recalled the scene at Hornchurch at the height of the Battle:

When we came out of that strange bungalow building so near the main hangars of the aerodrome, we would stroll around in the sunlight to the pilots' dispersal huts on the other side and see them stretched out on beds, or in wicker chairs fast asleep, with the Mae Wests slung loosely upon them, and their clumsy flying boots on their feet. Every time the telephone bell rang in the dispersal hut, or every time a voice was heard booming on the loudspeaker, all the sleeping figures would wake up and listen, and if it was not an urgent call for them, they would fall back and be asleep in an instant. Generally, the radio was on at full blast. That did not disturb them. The roar of aircraft taking off and the clatter of vehicles passing by – those did not disturb them either. But a telephone bell had them alert and grabbing for their flying helmets before it had stopped ringing. Often, they were pretty nearly out on their feet. For instance, after a long day's flying, one of our boys landed and the Spitfire trundled along the ground and came to rest – and nobody got out of it. The ground-crew rushed out and tried to help their pilot, but he was slumped in his cockpit. He was not wounded; he was just fast asleep. The ground crews themselves, stripped to the waist, worked day and night re-arming and refuelling and repairing; because the stock of replacements kept going down and the margin was getting narrower and narrower as the days went by. Occasionally, some lone ferry pilot would arrive with a replacement – a new or patched up Spitfire – but that was only on rare occasions. In those days and at the beginning of September, 1940, although I did not know it at the time, we were actually down to a few days' replacements, and that was all that stood between us and many grim possibilities.

Geoffrey 'Boy' Wellum, of 92 Squadron, was one of those fresh-faced pilots sat in the dispersal area, waiting, waiting, waiting:

Arrival at dispersal is for me always a moment. The drive round the perimeter track, masked headlights, the glow of somebody's cigarette and the squeal of brakes as the transport stops at the hut. No turning back now; committed; Here we go again.

I enter the hut and make for the flight board to check the 'Order of Battle'. Good, No. 2 to Brian. That makes me Red 2, suits me fine. I go to my locker and get my flying kit. It only seems ten minutes ago that we packed up for the day.

I remove my tie and open the collar of my shirt (far less sore on the back of the neck when you keep looking round). Now, where's my silk scarf? Don't say it's been lost. I take my parachute from the locker and, of course, my scarf is where I last threw it. I tie it round my neck, pick up my helmet and, slinging the chute over my shoulder, head for the door and the damp fresh early morning air. Walk steadily towards my Spitfire, which is dispersed about fifty yards away. The sky is clear. In the slowly strengthening light the ghostly figures of the ground crews work methodically on the aircraft, removing covers and plugging in the starter trolleys. I cut a corner, walk off the perimeter track and over the grass. Moisture collects on my flying boots from last night's heavy dew. It's going to be a lovely day . . .

Dispersal pen and my Spitfire. I pause and look at her. A long shapely nose, not exactly arrogant but, nevertheless, daring anyone to take a swing at it. Lines beautifully proportioned, the aircraft sitting there, engine turning easily and smoothly with subdued power. The slipstream blows the moisture over the top of the wings in thin streamlets. Flashes of blue flame from the exhausts are easily seen in the halfflight, an occasional backfire and the whole aeroplane trembling like a thoroughbred at the start of the Derby.

The engine note increases as my fitter opens up the Merlin to zero boost, whilst the rigger stands with his hand on the wingtip, watching expectantly. I think to myself, 'Don't open her up any more you twit, or the tail will lift and the whole shooting match will end up on its nose.' The engine note changes fractionally as the magnetos are tested. The fitter, intent on his instruments, red cockpit, lights reflecting on his face. Sounds OK, no problem there at all. Throttle back, mag check again at 1,500 revs by the sound of it and then throttle right closed, engine idling, smoke from the exhausts, cutout pulled and the engine splutters to a stop. Peace again.

Bevington, the fitter, looks from the cockpit and gives me the thumbs up. He levers himself out on to the wing and jumps to the ground. I walk forward and hang my parachute on the port wing for a quick getaway; you can easily put it on whilst the engine is being started, saves a lot of time.

Now to the cockpit. Up on to the wing and step in. Hang my helmet on the stick and plug in the R/T lead and oxygen tube. At the same time I check the bottle contents; full. Fuel? Press the fuel gauge button, reads full also. Now brake pressure. OK, that's fine. Trim? Let's adjust it now and then it's done with. Full rudder bias to help with the swing on take-off, elevators one degree nose heavy, that's good. Airscrew, full fine pitch. That's about it, then, ready to scramble when the time comes. Bound to come some-time. It'll be a miracle if we get through to midday without one.

I climb out of the cockpit and my fitter and rigger are waiting, as always. What stalwarts they are, both utterly loyal to 'their' pilot, dedicated and uncomplaining. They are both smiling and friendly.

'Twenty-five drop on both mags, sir. We found that oil leak last night. Nothing to worry about and in any case we reckon we've cured it.'

'Splendid; so we're at readiness, are we?'

'On the top line, sir.'

'Good men, see you both later, no doubt.'

'We'll be here.'

No need to tell them what is expected when the balloon goes up. It occurs to me and not for the first time, as I walk back to the dispersal hut, that the respect and feeling that these ground crews have for their pilots borders on affection. No standing to attention and shouted orders; we all get on together keeping Spitfires flying. To my mind, the atmosphere in a front-line fighter squadron is something approaching unique and certainly gives an inner feeling that will remain with me as long as I survive. I will never forget. I pause at the hut door and look at the ever brightening sky. Clear as a bell and I go inside.

As I put on my Mae West [an inflatable life jacket, so called in reference to the then popular busty American actress of that name] the telephone orderly at his blanket-covered table lifts the receiver.

I lie down on one of the camp beds and try to relax. Now all we have to do is wait. If I'm lucky I may be able to get a little sleep.

The light outside is getting stronger. Any time from now on things can start to happen and I wonder if the day will be opened by the normal Hun 'weather recce'. A section will be scrambled but won't get near it, of course. It'll be too high, have too much of a start and he won't come in very far anyway, not with the weather this clear. I suppose we are duty bound to have a crack at it, and that of course will only leave us with ten aircraft for the main interception. The weather is sure to be all right for him to give the OK for his chums to do their lousy bloody work. In the meantime, we must just wait and sweat it out, never an easy thing to do, even though we do get a lot of practice.

Waiting. Thoughts race through the mind. Some read. Some sleep, such as Butch Bryson. He's out to the wide; or is he? Could well be after the amount of Scotch he put away last night. I must say I enjoyed that little party a lot. You get a good pint in the White Hart. Pleasant crowd in there as well. Had a letter from a girl called Grace yesterday, sister of a school friend. She seemed interested; shall have to give a bit of thought to her sometime.

I must have nodded off into an uneasy doze. How long, I wonder. I find myself sitting bolt upright. The phone must have rung. Yes, that's it, the bloody phone again. I swear, that if ever I own a house I shall never install a telephone, so help me. All heads and eyes are turned towards the telephone orderly, AC2 Webber. He seems to be listening for an agonizingly long time. He turns his head.

'There will be no NAAFI van until later this morning, sir. It's got a flat battery. OK if I tell Chiefy, sir?'

What's the time? 06.15. That recce kite should have shown up by now if it's coming. Been here for two hours odd. This time yesterday, no, the day before it must have been, we were landing from our first sortie; at least, nine of us did. Not poor old John and Bill, though. Must all be a bit strung up with this waiting. Once you are on your way, well, things aren't too bad. However, as we aren't we'll just have to continue waiting and that's all there is to it. Relax; try to relax. I suppose that's the answer. Don't know the meaning of the word. Nevertheless, let's make a real effort. Hard work, relaxing.

Tommy gets up and walks to the door. He opens it quietly, thoughtfully surveys the scene for a moment and goes outside. I get up and go to the window. I see old Tom walking up and down very slowly. Every now and then he kicks at a stone or a piece of paper; sometimes, he stops and looks at the sky.

The phone rings again. The orderly picks it up and listens intently. Tommy has appeared in the doorway. Nobody speaks, everybody watches. The orderly turns to Brian.

'Squadron Leader Igoe would like a word with you, sir.'

He hands the phone to Brian, who listens to the Ops Controller, his face devoid of expression.

'OK, Bill. Right away. Yes, I expect so. No, I don't. Of course. OK, old boy. Cheers.' He puts the phone down and turns to us.

'Ops say that a pilot has appeared over Gris Nez and it looks like our recce chum. Two aircraft at standby. Tony, take Tommy as your No. 2 and call yourself Black Section. Off you go!'

They go at once and hurry away to their Spitfires. Intent, they do not look back.

'Two at standby, Chiefy.'

'Yes, OK, sir. Everything's under control.'

It would seem that the programme for today is starting to

move at last. I stand watching Butch and Wimpey playing a game of chess. How they can do that at this time of the day defeats me. Five minutes and the phone rings again.

'OK, sir, Black Section scramble.'

In Fighter Command 'scramble' was code for 'get airborne as rapidly as possible'. On receiving the order to scramble pilots ran to their planes, because every second of delay on the ground was ten metres less altitude in the air at the moment they encountered the enemy. A fighter pilot's first scramble always stuck in the mind, for suddenly the training was over and the real war – with all its attendant questions of morality and self-doubt – had arrived. Pilot Officer Richard Hillary of 603 Squadron experienced his first scramble from Hornchurch, where a colleague had warned him, 'You don't have to look for them [the enemy]. You have to look for a way out':

The voice of the controller came unhurried over the loud-speaker, telling us to take off, and in a few seconds we were running for our machines. I climbed into the cockpit of my plane and felt an empty sensation of suspense in the pit of my stomach. For one second, time seemed to stand still and I stared blankly in front of me. I knew that that morning I was to kill for the first time. That I might be killed or in any way injured did not occur to me. Later, when we were losing pilots regularly, I did consider it in an abstract way when on the ground; but once in the air, never. I knew it could not happen to me. I suppose every pilot knows that, knows it cannot happen to him; even when he is taking off for the last time, when he will not return, he knows that he cannot be killed. I wondered idly what he was like, this man

I would kill. Was he young, was he fat, would he die with the Fuehrer's name on his lips, or would he die alone, in that last moment conscious of himself as a man? I would never know. Then I was being strapped in, my mind automatically checking the controls, and we were off.

Roger Hall was a pilot officer with 152 Squadron, based at Warmwell near Weymouth, in 10 Group. The squadron, in addition to protecting the southwest coast, was also asked by Keith Park's 11 Group on occasion to defend the London area. As Hall records, an efficient 'scramble' meant that the squadron was aloft in about three minutes:

It was shortly before 7 o'clock when the telephone rang. The Orderly lifted the receiver and almost at once shouted 'Red Section scramble. Base angels ten.' I was up like a shot and out of the door before the others. I had a comparatively long way to go to my machine and I ran hard all the way. My mechanic was already at the starter battery when I got there. I leant on to the trailing edge of the port wing and slid open the cockpit hood, opened the small door underneath and got in. My mechanic was on the wing now and helping me to get into my parachute harness. I fumbled with it, my fingers shaking all the time. The parachute was fixed and the mechanic was holding the two upper straps of the Sutton harness above my shoulders waiting for me to fix the right lower one. Eventually all was set and I grabbed my helmet and put it on. My mechanic had taken up position again at the starter battery and was anxiously awaiting my signal to press the button. I switched the petrol and two magneto switches on and gave the priming pump three injections. I put my thumb up and received acknowledgment from the mechanic, who then pressed the button. At the same time I pressed both mine and the propeller started to turn. It fired after a few turns and blue exhaust swept past the open cockpit. The mechanic leant forward and uncoupled the lead from the starter battery, pulling the wheel chocks away at the same time. Finally he gave the all-clear signal and I opened the throttle to taxi towards the take-off point, at the same time making a cursory last minute cockpit check as I went.

Cocky and the sergeant pilot who, with me, made up Red Section, were just getting into position as I got there. I turned my machine to the left, using full left rudder and at the same time applying hand brake pressure from the lever on the stick. The machine slewed round nicely and I took up my position on the left side of Cocky. After a thumbs up signal to him to let him know that all was in order, Cocky opened his throttle and we started to move. Keeping an unrelaxing gaze towards his machine the three of us gathered speed rapidly. I saw Cocky's wheels leave the ground and at once felt my own free themselves. I eased out a bit to the left as Cocky, flying as Red one, retracted his undercarriage and in doing so rocked his machine about a bit. This was almost inevitable, for you had to change hands; the left hand from the throttle to the stick and the right hand from the stick to the wheel retracting lever. The small lock lever had to be moved fore and aft with a pumping action until the wheels finally locked themselves with a click into the wing recesses. The red light then appeared on the dashboard which meant 'wheels up'. This operation, although tedious to describe, took really very little time in practice but it always involved rather a lot of rocking about in the air. By the time we had finally taken off, not much more than three minutes had elapsed since the telephone had rung in the hut.

Other squadrons could manage an even faster scramble. Pilot Officer Tim Vigors flew with the formidable tin-legged Flight Lieutenant Douglas Bader in 222 Squadron:

Pilots on night readiness always slept down at dispersal. There was a lot of rivalry between different sections concerning who could get all three aircraft off the ground in the shortest space of time from the sounding of the alarm bell. Characteristically, Douglas was determined to prove that his section was the fastest. This led to many hours of rehearsal.

Our three camp beds were placed close to the door of the dispersal hut. Douglas's Spitfire was positioned slap bang outside the door with Hilary's and mine near by. In order to sleep better Douglas liked to remove his false legs before retiring. Lowering himself on to his bed he would hand his right leg to me and I would place it at the foot of my bed. Hilary's responsibility was the left leg. Wherever we were, Snipe liked to sleep on my bed and somehow or another he managed to squeeze himself beside me on the narrow mattress.

On the sound of the alarm bell my first responsibility was to seize Douglas's leg and place it on to the stump of his thigh which he would be sticking over the end of the bed. Hilary would be helping him with his left leg. At the same time his fitter and rigger, the two mechanics who were responsible for the maintenance of the engine and airframe of his aircraft, would have rushed through the door. Seizing him under the arms they would carry him bodily out of the door and down the steps on to the grass. Lifted by them on to the rear edge of the wing he would grab the sides of the cockpit and lever himself into his seat. Hilary and I would run to our Spitfires and hit the starting buttons as our bottoms touched the parachutes, already positioned on the metal seats. The three engines would splutter and roar into life and, with Douglas taxiing fast in front, we would head for the big floodlight which marked the end of the take-off area. Opening the throttles, we would roar off the ground in loose formation about twenty yards apart.

Spurred on by Douglas's unswerving determination, we managed to reduce the interval between the sound of the alarm bell and all three Spitfires being off the ground to two minutes and fifty seconds, at least thirty seconds better than the time achieved by any other section.

It was typical of Bader that he had rehearsed his section over and over again. The most famous RAF fighter of the war was a ruthless perfectionist. 'Egocentric' was a word often attached to him; 'bully' was another. However, Bader was an inspirational leader in wartime, a man to have on your side rather than the other. 'He was always, always looking for a fight,' noted Hugh Dundas. 'Here was a man made in the mould of Francis Drake – a man to be followed, a man who would win.' Johnnie Johnson, then a humble untested pilot officer but later to be Britain's greatest fighter ace, penned a memorable portrait of Bader, the warrior chief:

At Coltishall we found that Alert No. 1, 'invasion imminent and probable within twelve hours', had been declared by the responsible authorities and the defences were to be brought to the highest state of readiness. The scene in the mess could only be described as one of some confusion. Elderly officers, mobilized for the duration, darted about in various directions. Our own C.O. was not to be seen, and we tried to get a coherent explanation of the situation. We soon heard half a dozen different versions, the most popular of which was that the invasion was under way and some enemy landings were expected on the east coast. Perhaps the C.O. and the flight commanders were already at our dispersal, and I left the anteroom to make a telephone call from the hall. As I hastened along the corridor I almost collided with a squadron leader who stumped towards me with an awkward gait. His vital eyes gave me a swift scrutiny, at my pilot's brevet and the one thin ring of a pilot officer.

'I say, old boy, what's all the flap about?' he exclaimed, legs apart and putting a match to his pipe.

'I don't really know, sir,' I replied. 'But there are reports of enemy landings.'

The squadron leader pushed open the swing doors and stalked into the noisy, confused atmosphere of the anteroom. Fascinated, I followed in close line astern because I thought I knew who this was. He took in the scene and then demanded in a loud voice, and in choice, fruity language, what all the panic was about. Half a dozen voices started to explain, and eventually he had some idea of the form. As he listened, his eyes swept round the room, lingered for a moment on us pilots and established a private bond of fellowship between us.

There was a moment's silence whilst he digested the news.

'So the bastards are coming. Bloody good show! Think of all those juicy targets on those nice flat beaches. What shooting!' And he made a rude sound with his lips which was meant to resemble a ripple of machine gun fire.

The effect was immediate and extraordinary. Officers went about their various tasks and the complicated machinery of the airfield began to function smoothly again. Later we were told that the reports of the enemy landings were false and that we could revert to our normal readiness states. But the incident left me with a profound impression of the qualities of leadership displayed in a moment of tension by the assertive squadron leader. It was my first encounter with the already legendary Douglas Bader.

Few of the leading fighter aces had easy-going personalities. Bob Stanford Tuck, behind the hail-fellow-well-met exterior, was as dogmatic as Bader. And like Bader, he constantly wanted to engage the enemy. The Battle of Britain was won by the 'average' pilots who managed to make one-and-a-half or two kills before being shot down themselves, but a disproportionate amount of victories went to the small circle of men – led by Bader, Stanford Tuck, Eric Lock, John Dundas, Al Deere, Paddy Finucane and David Crook – who did not shy from combat. On the contrary, they tended to welcome it. On 18 August Stanford Tuck took to the air without orders, intent on finding the enemy, while visiting another airfield. In his subsequent combat report he confused Ju 88s with Me 110s, Göring's formidable 'Destroyers'. The self-same report might also serve as an advert for the resilience of the Spitfire:

I was on a visit to Northolt from Pembry (92 Squadron) and on hearing the Attack Action I took off at about 13.20 hrs and made for the South Coast. Whilst patrolling over Beachy Head at about 15,000 feet two JU 88s came straight towards me flying SSE. One immediately jettisoned its bombs into the sea, and both dived straight down to sea level on seeing me. I went down shallower and came down to sea level in front of the e/a [enemy aircraft]. I turned and made a head on attack at one of the JU88s. The e/a opened fire from its front gun at about 200 yards, but I held my fire until within range, and one short burst was sufficient to dispose of the enemy. It immediately slid sideways into the sea at a very fast speed. I turned and chased after the second, and getting in front of it proceeded to repeat the attack, but when about 800 yds from the e/a, the e/a opened fire and something very heavy hit the underside of my engine, which caused me to bump badly. A short burst was given at range, and the e/a was last seen crabbing along on its port engine only, leaving a trace of oil on the water. The e/a was almost at sea level and was then about 35 miles from the English Coast. My Glycol and all systems were very badly damaged, and after crossing the coast at 4,000 ft with the engine vibrating badly (the airscrew was badly damaged) I was unable to see for fumes, and baled out at about 800 ft. My parachute was still swinging when it reached the ground, and I sustained strains to my knee and ankle of my left leg. My aircraft landed near Tunbridge and is a complete write-off.

(Signed) R.R. Stanford Tuck

★

Fighter Command was more than holding its own. In addition to Stanford Tuck's Me 110 on the afternoon of 18 August, the fighter boys had destroyed 362 enemy aircraft in the previous ten days. Fighter Command's own losses were 211 Spitfires and Hurricanes. On the same afternoon as Stanford Tuck was on his unofficial lone hunt for the 'Hun', Churchill drove out to the RAF's Uxbridge headquarters with his Chief of Staff, General Hastings Ismay, to see for himself how the fighter boys were coping. When they left afterwards for Chequers, Churchill said to Ismay, 'Don't speak to me; I have never been so moved.' After a few minutes of silence, Churchill murmured, 'Never in the field of human conflict has so much been owed by so many to so few . . .'

So few – that was the problem. As Dowding was acutely aware, Fighter Command, despite its superior kill ratio, was running out of machines and men. The production lines of the aircraft factories were only making up 75 per cent of his losses; worse still, the training schools were only training 50 per cent of his lost fighter pilots, and the replacements were necessarily novices. The thin blue line was, however, joined by one consummate professional; Jeffrey Quill took a break from testing Spitfires and flew for nineteen days with 65 Squadron. He knew the Spitfire better than anybody, but as he had no combat experience to speak of, he wisely asked fellow officers in the mess at Hornchurch for advice. One of those officers was the steely South African 'Sailor' Malan of 74 Squadron, whose ideas on aerial combat soon became famous and were pinned to the walls of dispersal huts around the country. Malan liked to send German bombers back with a sole survivor, as a warning to the rest:

Ten of My Rules for Air Fighting
 1. Wait until you see the whites of his eyes. Fire short bursts of 1 to 2 seconds and only when your sights are definitely 'ON'.
 2. Whilst shooting think of nothing else; brace the whole of the body; have both hands on the stick, concentrate on your ring sight.
 3. Always keep a sharp lookout. 'Keep your finger out!'
 4. Height gives <u>You</u> the initiative.
 5. Always turn and face the attack.
 6. Make your decisions promptly. It is better to act quickly even though your tactics are not the best.
 7. Never fly straight and level for more than 30 seconds in the combat area.
 8. When diving to attack always leave a proportion of your formation above to act as top guard.
 9. INITIATIVE, AGGRESSION, AIR DISCIPLINE, and TEAM WORK are words that MEAN something in Air Fighting.
 10. Go in quickly – Punch hard – Get out!

With such 'nuggets of sound advice' under his helmet, Jeffrey Quill entered the aerial arena. He survived being dive-bombed and strafed as he took off from Manston ('those seconds when I was cold meat for any swooping Messerschmitt were interminable') to shoot down two Me 109s. His combat experience also led him to recommend some alterations to the Spitfire:

Nearly all our many engagements with Me 109s took place at around 20,000–25,000 ft. We had the edge over them in speed and climb and particularly in turning circle, but there were one or two glaring defects with the Spitfire which needed urgent action. I used to talk with Joe Smith on the telephone or write short notes with promises of a full report later. One point was the immense tactical advantage accruing to the side which saw an enemy formation first and in good time, and conversely the rapidity with which one was in trouble if one failed to see them first. One of the most remarkable pilots in 65 Squadron was Sergeant Franklin. He had eyes like a hawk and it was noticeable that he was often the first to see and identify distant specks in the sky and draw the leader's attention to them. I found my own ability to do this improved rapidly with practice, but I never achieved anything like the skill that Franklin and some others possessed. The Spitfire was fitted with a thick, armoured glass panel in the centre of its windscreen but the side panels were of curved perspex and the optical distortion from these made long distance visual scanning extremely difficult. I was determined to have the design altered and indeed I succeeded in getting optically true glass into the side panels by 1941.

When milling around in an engagement at around 25,000 ft or more at full power and usually at very low airspeeds, it was not long before the ethylene glycol, which comprised the coolant for the engine, began to boil at around 130°C, when it would eject a jet of steam from a small overflow pipe on the starboard side of the cowling and this would freeze all over the windscreen. Also if one had been flying at high altitude for some while and then suddenly dived down into the low, warm and moist air, the inside of the screen and canopy promptly became covered with an opaque layer of frozen condensation. This blinded one for several seconds or even minutes. However, this had already been reported during test flying and steps were in hand to cure it.

One engagement with several Me 109s at about 25,000 ft over the Channel sticks in my memory. It all happened very suddenly, in fact we were mildly 'bounced' and soon found myself behind two 109s in a steep left hand turn. I was able to turn inside the second one and fired at him from close range. He went on pulling round as sharply as he could and I followed him without any difficulty and went on firing bursts at him and saw puffs of black smoke and then a trail of white vapour streaming from him. By this time I could no longer see the first 109 and then realised he was on my tail. As I was by now just shuddering on the g stall, I quickly turned inwards and dived. I pulled up again when I was sure I had shaken him off and, as usual on these occasions, found myself apparently completely alone in the sky and thoroughly disoriented with wildly spinning compass and gyro instruments. Eventually I found one or two other aircraft and joined up with them to return to base. I was pleased with that little episode, partly because I was damn sure that the first 109 was not going to get home, and secondly, because I was now absolutely sure the Spitfire Mk I could readily out turn the 109, certainly in the 20,000 ft area, and probably at all heights.

On Monday 19 August 1940 the weather took a turn for the worse. Or the best, if one was a Spitfire pilot. 'Mainly cloudy, occasional showers in the East', the RAF meteorologists reported. In such weather, the Luftwaffe would not fly in force; the Spitfire squadrons needed the rest, a break from battle that the weather brought. The weather had a habit of being kind to Britain when she was under attack; another armada, 350 years previously, had been broken by Drake's guns and a gale. 'God breathed, and they were scattered' as the words stamped on the Armada medallion declared.

To the annoyance of Reichsmarschall Göring, the poor weather continued and his Luftwaffe could mount only sporadic attacks in the gloom. Nevertheless these raids too took their toll on the RAF, as Ulrich Steinhilper, a Me 109 pilot, recalled:

> Initially we had been positioned to fly cover for returning bombers. But soon after take-off we were ordered on to a ground attack on Mansion [Manston]. At first my heart was hammering in my chest, but when we pushed the noses of our aircraft down for the attack I calmed down. My mates who followed me in confirmed that I was doing well. I aimed at a fuel tanker which was filling a Spitfire, then at two other Spitfires, one after the other. The tanker exploded and everything began to burn around it. My other two Spitfires began to burn on their own.
>
> Only now do I realise what power is given to a pilot with those four guns.

Not until 24 August did the weather clear sufficiently for Göring to properly launch the third stage of the Battle of Britain; an all out offensive by the Luftwaffe against Fighter Command's airfields, especially those of 11 Group which ringed London. The resultant damage, believed Göring, would both impede Fighter Command's operations and force its fighters into the air, where they could be scythed down by his yellow-nosed Me 109s. For once, the vainglorious, obstinate Göring had learned a lesson from a setback henceforth the bombers were to go '*auf England*' in smaller numbers but with bigger fighter escorts.

For the Spitfire boys, the hardest fighting of the battle was now upon them. From six in the morning until midnight on the 24th, the Luftwaffe sent over more than 1,000 sorties over southern England, putting many forward airfields out of action and bombing Manston so badly that the demoralized ground staff refused to emerge from their air-raid shelters. Some 22 RAF fighters were either shot down or destroyed. (The RAF's losses that day included Spitfire L1082, which had been 609 Squadron's first Spitfire and had survived a year of active service; in the word's of L1082's mechanic, 'Our old crock was game to the last, being nursed back to base, where the tail end collapsed on landing.') In scenes of almost Armageddon-like destruction and confusion, the Spitfire once again gave hope. Thirty-eight Luftwaffe aircraft were destroyed over the course of the day, with a record 'bag' of five going to one pilot, Sergeant R.F. Hamlyn of 610 Squadron:

> Saturday was certainly a grand day. It started with the dawn. We were up at a quarter-past-four. We were in the air just after five o'clock. Shortly before half-past-eight we were in the air again looking for enemy raiders approaching the south coast from France. We saw three or four waves of Junkers 88s, protected by a bunch of Messerschmitt 109s above. We were at 15,000 feet, between the bombers and the fighters. The fighters did not have much chance to interfere with us before we attacked the bombers.
>
> I attacked one of the waves of bombers from behind and above. I selected the end bomber of the formation, which numbered between fifteen and eighteen. A burst of fire

lasting only two seconds was enough. It broke away from the formation, dived down, and I saw it crash into the sea.

I then throttled back so that I would not overtake the whole formation. I was getting quite a lot of crossfire from the other bombers as it was, though none of it hit me. If I had broken away after shooting down the first bomber I should have exposed myself to the full force of the enemy formation's crossfire. I didn't have time to select another bomber as target, for almost immediately a Messerschmitt 109 came diving after me. As I had throttled back he overshot me, and presented me with a beautiful target. He pulled up about 150 yards in front of me. I pressed the gun-button for two seconds. He immediately began to smoke, and dived away. I followed him and saw him go straight into the sea. When the sky was clear of German planes we went home for breakfast.

I didn't get any breakfast. I only had time for a hot drink before we were ordered to stand by again, and by half past eleven that morning we were patrolling the south-east coast. We were attacked by half a dozen Messerschmitt 109s, and of course, we broke up to deal with them individually. I had a dogfight with one, both of us trying to get into position to deliver an attack on the other, but I outmanoeuvred him. I got on his tail, and he made off for the French coast as hard as he could go.

The fight started at 10,000 feet. We raced across the Channel like mad. As we were going like that I saw one of our fellows shoot down another Messerschmitt, so I said to myself, 'I must keep the squadron's average up and get this one.' I didn't fire at him until we were actually over the French coast. Then I let him have it – three nice bursts of fire lasting three seconds each, which, as you may imagine, is an awfully long time!

I started the final burst at 8,000 feet, and then he began to go down, and I followed until I saw him crash into a field in France. Then I went back home without seeing any enemy at all. I carefully examined my Spitfire after I landed, certain that I must have been hit somewhere. But, no, not a mark. It was very satisfactory.

Our third show began just before four o'clock in the afternoon. We were flying towards the Thames Estuary at 5,000 feet when we saw anti-aircraft shells bursting in the sky to the north-east. We changed course and began to climb for the place where we thought we should meet the enemy. We did. They were flying at 12,000 feet. Twenty Junkers 88s in tight formation accompanied by about twenty Messerschmitt 109s above them. They were flying towards the London area. We could see the balloons shining in the sun. We pulled up towards the fighters. I got under one Messerschmitt and gave him two bursts.

Smoke started to pour out of him, and he went down out of control. Suddenly, tracer bullets started whizzing past my machine. I turned sharply, and saw a Messerschmitt attacking one of our pilots. I turned on the attacker and gave him a quick burst. Immediately he began to slow down and the aircraft began to smoke. I pressed the gun button a second time, and the Messerschmitt caught fire.

I fired a third time, and the whole machine became enveloped in flames and pieces began to fly off. Finally, as it went down, more pieces came off, all burning. As it tumbled down towards the Thames Estuary it was really a bunch of blazing fragments instead of a whole aircraft. It was an amazing sight. That was my fifth for the day and the squadron's ninety-ninth. The squadron brought the score over the century the next day.

There is a lot of luck about air fighting. I mean it's a matter of luck whether you get into a good scrap or not. I was right through the Dunkirk show and didn't get a thing. But recently I seem to have been lucky. Fights are over so quickly that unless you are right there at the beginning you are liable not to see anything at all. None of the fights today lasted more than five minutes each.

The understatement in Hamlyn's account of his exploit was typical of the RAF's fighter boys. 'Shooting a line', exaggeration or boasting, was a cardinal sin.

As David Crook of 609 Squadron noted, whereas in a normal English summer 'it is quite impossible to get fine weather for one's holidays . . . in wartime, when every fine day simple plays into the hands of German bombers, we had week after week of cloudless blue skies'. Between 24 August and 6 September 1940 the clear blue skies allowed the Luftwaffe to send, on average, 1,000 German aircraft over southern England each and every day, of which as many as 750 were Me 109 fighters – the special acknowledged preserve of the Spitfire squadrons, because the 'Hurris' could barely touch them. In the same period, the Luftwaffe made thirty-three major raids, of which two-thirds stormed the airfields of Fighter Command. Flying Officer Richard Hillary was at Hornchurch on 31 August when the bombs dropped:

At that moment I heard the emotionless voice of the controller.

'Large enemy bombing formation approaching Horn-church. All personnel not engaged in active duty take cover immediately.'

I looked up. They were still not visible. At the Dispersal Point I saw Bubble and Pip Cardell make a dash for the shelter. Three Spitfires just landed, turned about and came past me with a roar to take off downwind. Our lorry was still trundling along the road, maybe halfway round, and seemed suddenly an awfully long way from the Dispersal Point.

I looked up again, and this time I saw them – about a dozen slugs, shining in the bright sun and coming straight on. At the rising scream of the first bomb I instinctively shrugged up my shoulders and ducked my head. Out of the corner of my eye I saw the three Spitfires. One moment they were about twenty feet up in close formation; the next catapulted apart as though on elastic. The leader went over on his back and ploughed along the runway with a rending crash of tearing fabric. No. 2 put a wing in and spun round on his airscrew, while the plane on the left was blasted wingless into the next field. I remember thinking stupidly, 'That's the shortest flight he's ever taken,' and then my feet were nearly knocked from under me, my mouth was full of dirt, and Bubble, gesticulating like a madman from the shelter entrance, was yelling, 'Run, you bloody fool, run!' I ran. Suddenly awakened to the lunacy of my behaviour, I covered the distance to that shelter as if impelled by a rocket and shot through the entrance while once again the ground rose up and hit me, and my head smashed hard against one of the pillars. I subsided on a heap of rubble and massaged it.

'Who's here?' I asked, peering through the gloom.

'Cardell and I and three of our ground crew,' said Bubble, 'and, by the Grace of God, you!'

I could see by his mouth that he was still talking, but a sudden concentration of the scream and crump of falling bombs made it impossible to hear him.

The air was thick with dust and the shelter shook and heaved at each explosion, yet somehow held firm. For about three minutes the bedlam continued, and then suddenly ceased. In the utter silence which followed nobody moved. None of us wished to be the first to look on the devastation which we felt must be outside. Then Bubble spoke. 'Praise God!' he said, 'I'm not a civilian. Of all the bloody frightening things I've ever done, sitting in that shelter was the worst. Me for the air from now on!'

It broke the tension and we scrambled out of the entrance. The runways were certainly in something of a mess. Gaping holes and great gobbets of earth were everywhere. Right in front of us a bomb had landed by my Spitfire, covering it with a shower of grit and rubble.

The attacks on Hornchurch saw Al Deere in yet another improbable, death defying escapade:

I was not quite airborne when a bomb burst on the airfield, ahead of me and to my left. 'Good, I've made it,' I thought. To this day I am not clear exactly what happened next; all I can remember is that a tremendous blast of air, carrying showers of earth, struck me in the face, and the next moment thinking vaguely that I was upside down. What I do remember is the impact with the ground and a terrifying period of ploughing along the airfield upside down, still firmly strapped in the cockpit. Stones and dirt were thrown into my face and my helmet was torn by the stony ground against which my head was firmly pressed.

Finally the aircraft stopped its mad upside down dash leaving me trapped in the cockpit, in almost total darkness, and breathing petrol fumes, the smell of which was overpowering. Bombs were still exploding outside, but this was not as frightening as the thought of fire from the petrol now seeping into the ground around my head. One spark and I would be engulfed in flames.

'Al, Al, are you alive?' urgently, and to me miraculously, the voice of Pilot Officer Eric Edsall, who had been my number three in the section, penetrated to my dazed senses.

'Yes, but barely. For God's sake get me out of here quickly,' I answered breathlessly, desperately afraid of fire.

'Can you reach the release wire on the door, Al? If you can free the catches I might be able to lever it open; I can just get my hand underneath it.'

It was no mean feat to move my right hand across, locate the spring loaded release wire, and exert sufficient pressure to free the locks. But somehow I managed it, and after a tremendous struggle Eric managed to force the door outwards. The next problem was to free myself from the parachute harness, as the small aperture created by the now opened cockpit door was barely large enough to wriggle through, without the extra impediment of a parachute pack. This too I eventually managed, and after a frantic struggle squeezed my way out into the blessed fresh air.

Few had Al Deere's luck. On most days the RAF suffered near thirty pilots killed or wounded, out of a fighting strength of around a thousand. As a result pilots were rushed through the training units to fill the gaps in men, but some had only a few hours flying time on Spits in their log books when they arrived at a squadron. Flight Lieutenant Al Deere of 54 Squadron remembered the arrival at Hornchurch of Mick Shand, a fellow New Zealander:

Pilot Officer Mick Shand, who came to my flight, certainly looked promising until I learned the grim details of his flying experience. Mick was a rugged, aggressive looking New Zealander typical of the type one would expect to find in the second row of an 'All Black' pack. He had a most cheerful and easy going disposition and was a great favourite among his fellow officers, as I was to learn sometime later when we again served together. On this occasion there was to be little time in which to assess his value.

'Hello,' I said greeting him at dispersal that afternoon. 'I hear you're a fellow countryman of mine.'

'Too right, and glad to be here,' was the cheerful rejoinder.

'What flying experience have you got?'

'I've got a total of 140 hours approximately, mostly on Wapitis (an outmoded bi-plane). I only managed to get twenty hours on Spitfires at O.C.U. and it was hardly enough to get the feel of flying again after a two months' layoff. As a matter of fact I know damned all about fighters, I was trained as a light bomber pilot.'

'Have you fired the guns on the Spitfire yet?'

'No, I haven't; apart from a very little free gunnery from a rear cockpit, I've no idea of air firing.'

'What about the reflector sight, do you understand it?'

'Good grief,' I thought. 'It does seem a shame to throw him into battle so soon.' There was no alternative, and certainly no time or aircraft to fit in any further training.

'Get yourself kitted out, and when you are ready come and find me and I'll run over things with you. You will be required to fly later on today, if things warm up a bit.' I said this as cheerfully as possible in order not to give him any hint of my thoughts.

This was typical of the replacement pilots arriving in the squadrons (although the circumstances were a little different for New Zealanders trained in their own country, because of the time taken to get to England); all desperately keen to get cracking but all lacking in basic flying experience.

I took Mick Shand as my number two on his first trip, having first briefed him to stick close to my tail and not to attempt to get mixed up with the 109s until he had had an opportunity to see a little of what was going on. 'There will be time enough,' I urged.

At the end of the following day neither Mick nor his compatriot was with us. Both were in hospital somewhere on the south coast, having fallen foul of 109s over the famous 'Hell's Corner'.

Shand was far from alone in knowing next to nothing about dogfighting. Then proceeding through No. 7 Operation Training Unit at Hawarden, his last stop before joining a squadron, Wilfrid Duncan Smith found much of his combat instruction very down to earth:

Our main ground activity concerned practice interceptions,

pedalling round the parade ground on tricycles equipped with battery operated radio sets and compasses while 'controllers' vectored us on to an 'enemy' in the shape of another tricycle. The proceedings usually finished in a boisterous free-for-all with the 'enemy' being rammed from all angles.

About a fifth of the new pilots sent to the squadrons were born outside Britain. As Flying Officer John Dundas wrote in 609's official diary at the end of August:

> It will be seen that the Squadron was becoming cosmopolitan. One might think that this heterogeneity would interfere with teamwork or morale, but this was not so. Under Squadron Leader Darley's quietly firm and competent leadership, the Squadron steadily gained in skill and confidence, and remained a veritable 'Band of Brothers'.

The 'Band of Brothers' at the moment that Dundas entered his note in the diary consisted of four Auxiliaries, six Regulars, five Volunteer Reservists, one Dominion, three U.S. and two Polish pilots. There were: S/Ldr H.S. Darley, F/Lt F.J. Howell, F/Lt H.G. MacArthur, F/O J.C. Dundas, P/O D.M. Crook, P/O M.J. Appleby, P/O G.M. Gaunt, P/O C.N. Overton, P/O J.D. Bisdee, P/O J. Churchin, P/O R.G. Miller, P/O N. le. C. Agazarian, P/O M.E. Staples, F/O T. Nowierski, F/O P. Ostaszewski, F/O J.C. Newbery, P/O E.G. Tobin, P/O A. Mamedoff, P/O V.G. Keough, P/O A.K. Ogilvie and Sgt Feary.

David Crook thought the Americans in 609 Squadron 'grand fellows' and added: 'I think it was a very fine gesture on their part to come over here and help us to fight our battles, and they came at a time when trained pilots were worth a great deal in Fighter Command.'

Whether they had come for the adventure or because of a deep political desire to resist Nazi tyranny, these American volunteers knew, eyes wide open, what they had let themselves in for. Pointing to his newly acquired wings on his tunic, one American told Crook with a knowing grin, 'I reckon these are a one way ticket, pal.' Like the Americans, the Polish pilots were rated highly – despite their tendency to impenetrable chatter on the R/T that caused flight commanders nervous breakdowns – and with just cause: Poles made up 5 per cent of the Few, but were responsible for 15 per cent of the Luftwaffe's losses. Flight Lieutenant Brian Kingcombe of 92 Squadron noted:

> I can also tell you that some of our own chaps even shot the odd pilot in a parachute after they had shot down his plane. If you hit them with a shell you could knock them right round the parachute. I know of more than one Pole who did that – but you could understand it in their case. Some of those Poles had seen their families slaughtered, and they had the most desperate hatred of the Germans.

Generally, however, the fighter boys played by the rules of war and baled out enemy aircrew were left alone. Enemy aircraft, unless they surrendered by putting down their wheels, were fair game, whatever their condition. David Crook confessed to a reluctance to 'finish off' a smoking Me 109 which was hightailing it for home. 'But if I let him go,' concluded Crook, 'he would come back to England another day and possibly shoot down some of our pilots.' It was a judgement with which most fighter boys would have agreed. Crook fired his remaining ammunition into the Me 109 and watched it crash into the sea.

Just one-third of the 609 'Band' would survive the war; those who did not included John Dundas himself, shot down over the Isle of Wight on 28 November 1940. His last words, heard over the R/T were 'Whoppee! I've got a 109.' The Me 109 Dundas destroyed belonged to the Luftwaffe ace Helmut Wick, Kommodore of JG 2 (Richthofen) Geschwader. It was the thirteenth victory of Flight Lieutenant John Dundas, DFC and Bar, and 609's greatest warrior. John Bisdee said of him, 'He got everything he could out of a Spitfire.' Languid, amusing, gregarious, principled, honourable, Dundas was the last of the squadron's Auxiliary officers.

609 Squadron was far from unique in its blood loss. Other squadrons were also haemorrhaging. On 31 August Tim Vigors joined the dwindling band of those shot down who lived to tell the tale:

On the last day of August I came close to getting killed myself. We were diving from 25,000 feet on to a big formation of bombers. There was a lot of cloud and we suddenly found ourselves in the middle of them. I blazed away at a Dornier and then, like a fool, pulled up into a sharp left-hand turn without checking what was behind me. Suddenly there was a crash as a cannon shell, fired by a 109, tore broadside into my engine. The next one struck just behind the cockpit and exploded with a bang, sending most of its particles whistling round the armour plating at my back. My instrument panel disintegrated in front of my eyes. The control column was nearly torn from my hands as a third shell hit the tail unit. Smoke and glycol poured from the engine and for a moment I was sure that I was on fire. I was just reaching for the harness release when I found myself in thick cloud. There were no flames so, protected from the enemy for the moment by the enshrouding cloud, I decided to stay put until I could better assess the damage. My blind flying instruments had all shattered so I had no way of telling whether I was flying upwards or downwards, or if I was the right way up or on my back. A moment later I slithered into clear air once more to find that I was diving straight at the centre of London.

I started to pull out of the dive. The controls felt funny, which was not surprising as more than half of the control surfaces on my tail unit had been shot away, and most of my port aileron was missing. But the aircraft was still controllable and although there was a lot of smoke, there was no flame. I decided to sit tight and try and land the aircraft in one piece. I started to glide in an easterly direction and, whilst losing height, searched desperately for a suitable landing site. I had already turned off the petrol and, although there was still a lot of white smoke coming from the broken glycol leads, I assessed the danger of fire as reasonably remote. The controls, particularly the fore and aft reactions, felt very sloppy. Also, in order to see in front of me, I had to crab the aircraft to make the smoke fly off to one side. When I was down to about 2,000 feet I spotted a large field about 300 yards square, surrounded by small suburban houses. Other than vegetables and some bushes, the area seemed clear of obstructions although some high tension cables ran across the centre of the field.

Although the field was certainly not an easy place to

land a Spitfire under the very best of conditions, by now I had no alternative and was too low to bail out. But I was going to need a lot of luck to pull it off. As I glided down towards the field, I tried to judge my speed. Once before I had found myself landing a Spitfire without the aid of the airspeed indicator when, for some reason, the instrument had broken. On that occasion I had a 1,000 yard grass airfield in front of me and could get a good idea of the speed I was travelling at from the feel of the controls. But this time I only had, at the most, 300 yards of landing area, and because of the damage done to my elevators and port aileron, it was virtually impossible to get any guidance from the stick and rudder. If I allowed the speed to drop too low I would stall, dive into the ground, and almost certainly be killed. On the other hand, if I came in too fast, I would not be able to get the aircraft to stall when I levelled out, and would fly straight into the houses at the far end. The only way I had of making that vital assessment was visually, by watching the ground passing beneath me.

In my life, before and since, I have had hairy experiences in aircraft, when extreme skill and a lot of luck were needed to survive. None of those experiences compare with the circumstances of that particular landing.

Crabbing my way along to keep the smoke away from my forward line of sight, I glided down towards the houses which lined the near side of my landing area. Passing a few feet over their roofs, I flung the Spitfire into a steep sideslip to drop off height. In order to cut down my landing run, I had of course left the wheels retracted in the wings. Now, levelling off a few feet above the vegetables, I started to kick the rudder right and left so as to drop off speed again. About two-thirds of the way across the field I realised I was going too fast and wasn't going to make it. Emergency action was needed, otherwise I was going to end up in the drawing room of the red brick house which was rushing towards me. I muttered a quick prayer and took the only course open. Flinging over the stick to the left, I drove the port wing tip into the ground. There was a grinding noise as the wing dug into the soil and then I was cartwheeling. Landing on its belly, facing back the way we had come, the aircraft was now slithering backwards. The tail struck the hedge dividing the field from the small garden of the house. In a cloud of dirt and branches, we came to a juddering halt. There was a sudden and complete silence, one of the most welcome I have ever known.

As I heaved myself from the cockpit, a lady appeared through the gate from the garden. In her hand she bore a mug. 'Are you alright, dear?' she cried. 'I thought you might like a cup of tea to steady your nerves.'

'Thank you Madam,' I replied, taking the proffered mug. 'But do you suppose your husband would have a drop of whisky to put in it? That might help to make my nerves even steadier.'

'Of course he has,' she said. 'Come on into the house and I'll get it for you.' I followed the lady back into the house. She took a bottle of whisky from the cupboard and poured a generous measure into my tea. It tasted good.

Vigors' cordial reception on the ground ended at London's Fenchurch Street Station:

There were no trains to Hornchurch that morning, though the ticket clerk said there may be a bus. I left the station and, hoisting my parachute on to my shoulder once more, walked where the clerk had indicated. I asked two police-men for directions to the bus stop, adding that I was in a hurry to get back to join my squadron. 'We'll give you a hand, Sir,' one of them said, 'and take you to the bus queue.'

We walked through to the road and there, sure enough, was a queue of about 100 people lined up by the bus stop. As we approached, a number of people started looking at us curiously. Then a murmur arose and some people in the crowd surged towards us. The blue/grey colour of my RAF uniform was not dissimilar to that worn by pilots of the Luftwaffe. In those days my head was covered by a crop of light blond hair. My parachute, helmet and flying boots made me look like somebody who had just got out of an aircraft. With a policeman on each side of me they had taken me for a captured German.

It all started to look nasty. 'Quick Sir!' one of the policemen cried, realising what had happened, 'get against the wall.' We all three of us backed against the station wall but the leaders were on us. 'RAF RAF,' one of the policemen yelled. But some were beginning to claw at me. 'Can't you see,' said the other policeman, 'he's RAF, you bloody fools!' I was scared. These wretched people, who had seen their homes going up in flames, meant business. Thankfully, the policemen's words had had an effect and those people at the front of the crowd realised what they were doing. The ferocious hatred in their eyes turned to horror.

'He's RAF!' they yelled and started to try to push back the crowd behind them. But those at the back of the mob pressed on, determined to reek their share of revenge and it was getting unpleasantly crowded up against the wall by the time they realised their mistake.

Then the reaction set in. I was quickly hoisted on to the shoulders of a few of the front division and carried through the crowd with everybody cheering and trying to clap me on the back. If anything, this part of the whole incident was more uncomfortable, though less frightening, than the few moments when it appeared certain that I was going to be lynched.

Like Tim Vigors, Flight Lieutenant Brian Kingcombe of 92 Squadron had long sustained himself with the belief that being shot down 'can never happen to me'. Kingcombe was shot down, however – by his own side:

There had been an engagement, and I was gliding back to Biggin Hill after using up all my ammunition. I remember it was a beautiful day and I could see Biggin Hill in the distance.

I throttled back at about 25,000 feet. There was nothing in the sky except three Spitfires behind me.

Then, suddenly – bang! The aeroplane was full of holes. I was bloody indignant I can tell you.

All at once I realised, 'Christ! I've got to bail out!' I had a bullet through one leg and my controls had gone. I had to get out!

As I was parachuting down, I remembered that I was wearing a German Mae West! It was one that had been taken from a crashed plane – they were a sight more comfortable than ours. At that I began to get very worried.

There I was, dangling on my parachute going down outside Maidstone, and I could see a crowd gathering below. What if someone decided to take a shot at me, I thought!

I believe there were instructions then to the Home Guard on how to deal with parachutists – apparently some of the Germans were coming down disguised as nuns! So one instruction said, 'In order to ascertain sex of parachutist, put hand up skirt.' Those were certainly desperate times!

Anyhow, I landed safely, and the crowd soon realised from my language that I was English.

In fact, as I said, it was by no means uncommon to be shot down by your own planes. I could name you half a dozen who were; the commander of Biggin Hill for one. And another chap I know of was *deliberately* shot down and killed by his own squadron. They didn't like him, apparently.

While the loss of pilots, either by enemy action or 'friendly fire', affected the overall combat strength of Fighter Command, it also personally affected those left behind, even someone as psychologically robust as Tim Vigors, for the dead were sometimes their closest friends, veritable brothers in arms:

The next morning we attacked a large bunch of bombers just north off Dover. We had another squadron from the wing above us who had agreed to look after the escorting fighters. All guns blazing, we dived on the Dorniers as tracers started to tear through us from behind. A cloud of smoke engulfed a Spitfire on my right. 'My God,' I thought, 'that's Hillary!'

I had no time to look round to see if the pilot was able to get out. My hands were full, taking evasive action to shake off the 109 who was on my tail. But, back at Hornchurch, I waited in dread of what might be. No sign of Hillary. All the squadron's aircraft were home safe and I knew that the aircraft I had seen in flames must have been Hillary's. 'He must have got out. He must have got out,' I repeated to nobody in particular.

An hour passed and still no news. I had no appetite for lunch and waited by the telephone at dispersal. At about 2.00 p.m. the news came through from Group Head-quarters. The wreckage of a Spitfire bearing Hillary's markings had been found in a field near Sevenoaks. The pilot was dead.

A wave of misery swept over me. Up till now I had been able to shrug off the deaths of even my closest friends. But this was different. Hillary had been like a brother to me. For the past nine months we had pooled all our thoughts, hopes and fears and had somehow managed to support each other through the trauma of those times. Now he was gone. I just couldn't get my mind to accept it. I just could not believe that Hillary, who I had laughed with last night after my near miss with the bomb, who I had shared the draughty ride home with so few hours before, was never to be laughed with again. That he was dead.

Flying Officer Richard Hillary of 603 Squadron, an Oxford graduate, was one of those who paid a high price. The recurrent nightmare of the Spitfire pilot was to be trapped in the cockpit as their plane burned up; on 3 September the nightmare came true for Hillary:

September 3 dawned dark and overcast, with a slight breeze ruffling the waters of the Estuary. Hornchurch aerodrome, twelve miles east of London, wore its usual morning pallor of yellow fog, lending an added air of grimness to the dimly silhouetted Spitfires around the boundary. From time to time a balloon would poke its head grotesquely through the mist as though looking for possible victims, before falling back like some tired monster.

We came out on to the tarmac at about eight o'clock. During the night our machines had been moved from the Dispersal Point, over to the hangars. All the machine tools, oil, and general equipment had been left on the far side of the aerodrome. I was worried. We had been bombed a short time before, and my plane had been fitted out with a new cockpit hood. This hood unfortunately would not slide open along its groove; and with a depleted ground staff and no tools, I began to fear it never would. Unless it did open, I shouldn't be able to bale out in a hurry if I had to. Miraculously, 'Uncle George' Denholm, our Squadron Leader, produced three men with a heavy file and lubricating oil, and the corporal fitter and I set upon the hood in a fury of haste. We took it turn by turn, filing and oiling, oiling and filing, until at last the hood began to move. But agonizingly slowly: by ten o'clock, when the mist had cleared and the sun was blazing out of a clear sky, the hood was still sticking firmly halfway along the groove. At ten-fifteen, what I had feared for the last hour happened. Down the loudspeaker came the emotionless voice of the controller: '603 Squadron take off and patrol base; you will receive further orders in the air: 603 Squadron take off as quickly as you can, please.' As I pressed the starter and the engine roared into life, the corporal stepped back and crossed his fingers significantly. I felt the usual sick feeling in the pit of the stomach, as though I were about to row a race, and then I was too busy getting into position to feel anything.

Uncle George and the leading section took off in a cloud of dust; Brian Carbury looked across and put up his thumbs. I nodded and opened up, to take off for the last time from Hornchurch. I was flying No. 3 in Brian's section, with Stapme Stapleton on the right. The third section consisted of only two machines, so that our Squadron strength was eight. We headed south-east, climbing all out on a steady course. At about 12,000 feet we came up through the clouds. I looked down and saw them spread out below me like layers of whipped cream. The sun was brilliant and made it difficult to see even the next plane when turning. I was peering anxiously ahead, for the controller had given us warning of at least fifty enemy fighters approaching very high. When we did first sight them, nobody shouted, as I think we all saw them at the same moment. They must have been 500 to 1000 feet above us and coming straight on like a swarm of locusts. I remember cursing and going automatically into line astern. The next moment we were in among them and it was each man for himself. As soon as they saw us they spread out and dived, and the next ten minutes was a blur of twisting machines and tracer bullets. One Messerschmitt went down in a sheet of flame on my right, and a Spitfire hurtled past in a half roll. I was weaving and turning in a desperate attempt to gain height, with the machine practically hanging on the airscrew. Then, just below me and to my left, I saw what I had been praying for; a Messerschmitt climbing and away from the sun. I closed in to 200 yards, and from slightly to one side gave him a two second burst: fabric ripped off the wing and black smoke poured from the engine, but he did not go down. Like a fool I did not break away, but put in another three second burst. Red flames shot upwards and he spiralled out of sight. At that moment, I felt a terrific explosion which knocked the control stick from my hand, and the whole machine quivered like a stricken animal. In a second, the cockpit was a mass of flames. Instinctively, I reached up to open the hood. It would not move. I tore off my straps and managed to force it back; but this took time, and when I dropped back into the seat and reached for the stick in an effort to turn the plane on its back, the heat was so intense that I could feel myself going. I remember a second of sharp agony, remember thinking, 'So this is it!' and putting both hands to my eyes. Then I passed out.

When I regained consciousness I was free of the machine and falling rapidly. I pulled the ripcord of my parachute and checked my descent with a jerk. Looking down, I saw that my left trouser leg was burnt off, that I was going to fall into the sea, and that the English coast was deplorably far away. About twenty feet above the water, I attempted to undo my parachute, failed, and flopped into the sea with it billowing round me. I was told later that the machine went into a spin at about 25,000 feet and that at 10,000 feet I fell out – unconscious. This may well have been so, for I discovered later a large cut on the top of my head, presumably collected while bumping round inside.

The water was not unwarm and I was pleasantly surprised to find that my life jacket kept me afloat. I looked at my watch; it was not there. Then, for the first time, I noticed how burnt my hands were; down to the wrist, the skin was dead white and hung in shreds; I felt faintly sick from the smell of burnt flesh. By closing one eye I could see my lips, jutting out like motor tires. The side of my parachute harness was cutting into me particularly painfully, so that I guessed my right hip was burnt. I made a further attempt to undo the harness, but owing to the pain of my hands, soon desisted. Instead, I lay back and reviewed my position. I was a long way from land; my hands were burnt, and so, judging from the pain of the sun, was my face. It was unlikely that anyone on shore had seen me come down and even more unlikely that a ship would come by. I could float for possibly four hours in my Mae West. I began to feel that I had perhaps been premature in considering myself lucky to have escaped from the machine. After about half an hour my teeth started chattering, and to quiet them I kept up a regular tuneless chant, varying it from time to time with calls for help.

Hillary tried to commit suicide in the water by releasing the air from his Mae West life jacket but was so enmeshed in his parachute that he could not force his head underwater. Some hours later he was rescued by the Margate lifeboat, which was somehow appropriate, because Hillary's ancestor, Sir William Hillary, had founded the Lifeboat Service 110 years before. As Richard Hillary thawed out, waiting for the ambulance, 'the agony was such that I could have cried out'. Admitted to hospital he was given an anaesthetic and blacked out. He endured months of plastic surgery to his ravaged face and hands. But, typically of the fighter breed, he returned to action. He was killed later in the war in a night flying accident.

Flying Officer Eric Marrs should have gone up in petrol fuelled flames, but somehow did not, in what must have been one of the luckiest escapes of the battle:

I got in a burst of about three seconds when – crash! The whole world seemed to be tumbling in on me. I pushed the stick forward hard, went into a vertical dive and held it until I was below cloud. I had a look around.

The chief trouble was that petrol was gushing into the cockpit at the rate of gallons, all over my feet, and there was a sort of lake of petrol in the bottom of the cockpit. My knee and legs were tingling all over as if I had pushed them into a bed of nettles. There was a hole in the side of the cockpit where a bullet had come in and hit the dashboard, knocking away the starter button. Another bullet, I think an explosive one, had knocked away one of the petrol taps in front of the joystick, spattering my leg with little splinters and sending a chunk of something through the backside of my petrol tank near the bottom. I had obviously run into some pretty good crossfire from Heinkels.

I made for home at top speed to get there before all my petrol ran out. I was about fifteen miles from the aerodrome and it was a heart-rending business with all the petrol gushing over my legs and the constant danger of fire. About five miles from the drome, smoke began to come from under the dashboard. I thought the whole thing might blow at any minute, so I switched off my engine. The smoke stopped.

I glided towards the drome and tried putting my wheels down. One came down and the other remained stuck up. I tried to get the one that was down up again! It was stuck down! There was nothing for it to make a one wheel landing.

I switched on my engine again to make the aerodrome. It took me some way and began to smoke again, so I hastily switched it off. I was now near enough and made a normal landing, touching down lightly.

In circumstances where Fighter Command was losing thirty pilots a day, promotion could be rapid, as Tim Vigors himself discovered:

By the time the airfield at Coltishall came into view ahead of me, I had managed to talk myself out of my depression and face up once more to the job in hand. I ordered the squadron into line astern and joined the circuit for our landing. As I touched down I received directions to the dispersal area which had been allotted to us and led the way over to our new home. The station commander was there to greet us and I explained Johnny Hill's absence. He looked with some surprise at the pilot officer's stripes which still adorned my shoulders. 'Where are the two flight commanders?' he asked.

'I am one, Sir,' I replied, 'and the other flight commander is just pulling up over there. He's also a pilot officer,' I added. He eyed me with respect and looked at the ribbon of the Distinguished Flying Cross which was sewn on to my tunic below my wings. Obviously, he remained slightly bewildered that the squadron was being led by a pilot who still only held the lowest officer rank in the RAF.

'We don't have any flight lieutenants or flying officers left, Sir,' I explained. 'Actually, I was promoted to flying officer last week but I haven't had the time to get the new stripes.'

'Alright Vigors,' he said, 'get all your pilots together and I will arrange for some transport to take you over to the Officers' Mess.'

Johnny Hill flew in that evening and the next morning we held a council of war, or maybe more aptly described as 'a council of rest from war'.

'I see you haven't put up your flying officer's stripes yet,' was Johnny's opening remark. 'Well it's just as well as they told me at Group Headquarters yesterday that you are being promoted to acting flight lieutenant. Congratulations, you've deserved it!'

Tim Vigors was nineteen.

Fighter pilots of any sort became so scarce that Bomber Command, Coastal Command, the Navy and the Army were all canvassed for volunteers; those that came through underwent a futile six day conversion course. Normally a fighter squadron remained in the line for six weeks, but such was the intensity of the fighting and losses that some units had to be replaced after a week. To refresh and replenish his resources, Dowding swapped around the fighter squadrons. Hugh Dundas' 616 Squadron moved south to join 11 Group, in 'hilarious mood, eager to take off for . . . glory'. The optimism was soon dashed when they encounted Kenley aerodrome and the 615 pilots stationed there:

When we landed at our new airfield our spirits were quickly subdued. Kenley had been heavily and successfully blitzed the day before. Much of the station lay in ruins. Wreckage of aircraft and motor transport spattered the periphery of the field. Newly filled craters dotted the landing ground. The atmosphere in the officers' mess was taut and heavily overlaid with weariness.

Both the station operations staff and the pilots of 615 Squadron, led by Squadron Leader Walter Churchill, showed signs of strain in their faces and behaviour. The fierce rage of the station commander when a ferry pilot overshot the runway while landing a precious replacement Spitfire was frightening to behold.

Within a fortnight of landing at Kenley, 616 Squadron had lost half of its pilots and had to be withdrawn from the front-line. It had, however, given more than it had received; within that period 616 claimed sixteen enemy aircraft definitely destroyed, six probables and fifteen damaged. Pilot Officer Bobby Oxspring's 66 Squadron was also transferred to front-line Kenley. Arriving at the beginning of September 1940, after four days leave, Oxspring was sobered by what he found:

There I was met by a bunch of 66 pilots. They looked a sorry sight, a couple of them sporting bandages and all of them exceedingly scruffy. A flow of facetious remarks greeted me such as, 'What kept you?' and 'Wait till you get a basin of this lot!' . . . The squadron's casualties were alarming. We had lost eight aircraft and six pilots in two days fighting. Dunworth was promoted to take over 54 Squadron and Ken Gillies, who had flown with 66 for over four years, was now A Flight Commander . . . He gave me some sound tactical advice as how to react when I made my baptism in battle the following day. His concluding remark was, 'Whatever circus you get tangled up in, Bobby, for Christ's sake watch your tail!'

His words were prophetic, as Oxspring discovered:

Shortly after ten o'clock next morning, the squadron was scrambled and vectored to the Maidstone area. We climbed at full bore to around 15,000 feet and as we levelled off, a sighting was called by one of our pilots. '*Fibus Leader bandits eleven o'clock level.*' The rest of us eyeballed the indicated area. At least one other among us was impressed for a voice transmitted the highly useless comment, 'God, look at 'em, hundreds of the bastards.'

Up front the squadron leader, Rupert Leigh, did not have time to admonish the culprit, but merely gave the Tally Ho and ordered us into attack formation. The leading German bomber waves were now on our port side and slightly below. As the CO's six Spits peeled down on to them, we in B flight positioned to follow behind and I noticed a dog-fight in progress above and up sun. Four grey painted Messerschmitt 109s flew close over the top of us, climbing away. As we started to follow the CO, a 109 flashed vertically down in front of my nose. His belly was toward me so close I could distinguish rivets and oil streaks on his fuselage. Flames and black smoke were streaming from his engine as he disappeared beneath me; the vanquished victim of one of our hawk-eyed boys up top in the dogfight.

Still turning toward the bombers, I saw another 109 crossing ahead at my level. I throttled up to max power to reduce the distance and get my sights on. Just getting to firing range, I suddenly thought of Ken's 'watch your tail' warning. I looked back over my left shoulder and sure enough, another 109 was below my tail pulling a bead and about to let go. There was no point sticking around to see if he could shoot straight and my reactions were unbelievably fast. I parked everything in the left-hand corner. Cranking on full left aileron and rudder, at the same time I shoved the throttle through the gate for emergency power.

Hauling back on the stick, I reefed into a blacked out turn. As I was in the grey out stage, I noticed I'd got the nose above the horizon, which gave some assurance that, on recovery, I would have gained precious feet in altitude. The blood drained from my eyes as the G forces blacked me out. Sweat ran down my face greasing the chamois-lined oxygen mask which slid a couple of inches down my nose.

I held the turn for a number of seconds which from experience I judged had completed about 270 degrees.

Then with the pressure relaxed my eyesight returned, and I peered rearwards to seek my aggressor. He was nowhere in sight, but then nor was the rest of my flight. The bombers had moved on and were hardly visible. Some combats were still raging high above me and I tried to gain height to join them, but they faded away before I could.

On the other side of the Channel, the vital importance of the Spitfire was also being acknowledged. Infuriated by the losses to his bomber force, Göring ordered the fighter commanders to meet him at Kesselring's forward headquarters in the Pas-de-Calais. There, standing in a wind-blown field, Göring berated the senior fighter officers for failing to protect the bombers. Adolf Galland recalled the meeting:

We received many more harsh words. Finally, as his [Göring's] time ran short, he grew more amiable and asked what were the requirements for our squadrons. Molders asked for a series of Me 109s with more powerful engines. The request was granted. 'And you?' Göring turned to me. I did not hesitate long, 'I should like an outfit of Spitfires for my group.'

With that Göring, speechless with rage, stomped off to his Mercedes.

Göring's anger was misplaced. Despite the supremacy of the Spitfire over the Me 109 (narrow, but enough), despite the formidability of the Hurricane as a gun platform against bombers, despite Sir Hugh Dowding's strategic genius, despite Keith Park's brilliant operational control, despite radar, despite the selfless heroics of the pilots, despite the tireless hard work of the 'erks' (airmen), despite the efforts of the aircraft industry workers, the Battle of Britain was being won by the Luftwaffe. It was a simple matter of mathematics. The Luftwaffe had greater reserves; ipso facto, in a war of attrition, it could outlast Fighter Command, even with the RAF's superior kill ratio. Fighter Command needed help. It was given it, un-wittingly, by Göring himself.

With the gales of autumn just over the calendar page, Göring knew that if the invasion fleet was to get across the Channel in 1940, it had to sail within the next few weeks. To definitively break the tiresome resistance of Fighter Command, Göring decided once again to switch the focus of the Luftwaffe's attack – this time to London. As Luftwaffe ace Adolf Galland explained, only by attacking London would 'the

English fighters leave their dens and be forced to give us open battle'.

And so the Battle of Britain moved to its climax: the daylight assault upon what Galland called the 'seven-million-people city on the Thames . . . brain and nerve centre of the British High Command' by dense formations of Heinkel, Junkers and Dornier bombers, protected by phalanxes of Messerschmitt fighters. As Göring hoped, Fighter Command rose to the occasion. What the overconfident, dilettantish commander of the Luftwaffe did not appreciate was how skilful and determined would be Fighter Command's defence of the capital. Or how Fighter Command's lot was made easier by the simple fact that it could take-off and land unhampered at airfields now ignored by the Luftwaffe.

The first of the big raids on London came on 7 September 1940. At 4.30 p.m. 350 Luftwaffe bombers and 600 fighters appeared above the Thames heading towards London. Fighter Command, expecting the continued raiding of its airfields, was, for once, caught flat-footed and could only scramble four squadrons for the initial interception. 'There were so many enemy fighters layered up to 30,000 feet', recalled one Spitfire pilot, 'that it was just like looking up the escalator at Piccadilly Circus'. Even veteran pilots such as Sandy Johnstone of 602 Squadron were awed by the Luftwaffe formation as it droned through the sky:

> 602 was naturally first to break through the haze, although, when we did, I nearly jumped clean out of my cockpit. Ahead and above, a veritable armada of German aircraft was heading for London, Staffel upon Staffel for as far as the eye could see, with an untold number of escorting fighters in attendance. I have never seen so many aircraft in the air all

at one time. It was awe inspiring. They spotted us at once and before we had time to turn and face them, a batch of 109s swooped down and made us scatter, whereupon the sky exploded into a seething cauldron of aeroplanes; swerving, dodging, diving in and out of vapour trails and the smoke of battle. A Hurricane on fire pulled up in front of me and span out of control, whilst to the right, a 110 flashed across my line of sight, only to disappear before I could draw a bead on it. Earphones were filled with a cacophony of meaningless sounds. A mass of whirling impressions; a Do 17 spinning wildly with a large section of airplane missing, pulling sharply to one side to avoid hitting a portly German as he parachuted past me with his hands raised in an attitude of surrender. Streaks of tracer suddenly appearing ahead when I instinctively threw up an arm to protect my face.

Johnstone, running low on petrol, set out for his home aerodrome of Westhampnett in Sussex, but came under fire from a trio of Me 109s:

I let fly at the nearest, whose canopy shattered into a thousand pieces as he pulled away in an inverted dive, whereupon I banked steeply to meet the others head on, only to find I was out of ammunition when I pressed the button. I don't know whether they were aware of my predicament, but they were certainly incensed by my impertinence.

After a near vertical dive, 'foot on the throttle, weaving madly', Johnstone managed to elude his pursuers.

It was not only Sandy Johnstone who had never seen so many aircraft in the air before; no one had. The Luftwaffe raid of the afternoon of 7 September was the largest in history and wreaked havoc on London's docks and East End. Desmond Flower, a young Army lieutenant, recalled the view from the ground on this, the first day of the 'Blitz':

> Suddenly we were gaping upwards. The brilliant sky was criss-crossed from horizon to horizon by innumerable vapour trails. The sight was a completely novel one. We watched, fascinated, and all work stopped. The little silver stars sparkling at the heads of the vapour trails turned east. This display looked so insubstantial and harmless; even beautiful. Then with a dull roar which made the ground across London shake as one stood upon it, the first sticks of bombs hit the docks. Leisurely, enormous mushrooms of black and brown smoke shot with crimson, climbed into the sunlit sky. There they hung and slowly expanded, for there was no wind, and the great fires below fed more smoke into them . . .

Even as the bombs were dropping on London's docks and East End, Dowding was scrambling more squadrons – including a 'Big Wing' of three squadrons led off by Douglas Bader from Duxford – to attack the German formation as it turned and sped for France. By the end of the day, Fighter Command had downed thirty-nine Luftwaffe war planes, for the loss of thirty-one of its own.

Tim Vigor's 222 Squadron had been in the thick of the fighting, as the squadron's combat report for the afternoon recorded:

SECRET
FIGHTER COMMAND COMBAT REPORT
TO: H.Q. FIGHTER COMMAND
FROM: H.Q. NO. 11 GROUP.
INTELLIGENCE PATROL REPORT 222
SQUADRON. 16:50–18:50 hours. 7.9.40

Thirteen aircraft left Hornchurch to patrol base at 15,000 feet. On reaching height, the Squadron at once intercepted enemy bombers, escorted by Me 109s in large numbers and the combat took place over a wide area between Southend and Lympne. A large number of combats took place, but out of these at least eleven ended definitely in our favour, as detailed below, without any casualties in the Squadron. It was observed that some of the Me 109s had yellow wing tips and spinners. The bombers were escorted on the flanks as well as from above. The whole Squadron had landed by 1850 hours, with the exception of Sgt. Burgess, who arrived later after a forced landing.

ENEMY CASUALTIES

1 Me 109 destroyed – P/O Broad Hurst – e/a engine on fire – destroyed on land.

1 Me 109 destroyed – Sgt. Hutchinson – e/a engine on fire – destroyed in Estuary.

1 Me 109 destroyed – Sgt. Marland – e/a engine on fire – destroyed in sea.

1 Me 109 destroyed – Sgt. Burgess – volumes of white smoke – appeared to dive to ground.

1 Me 110 destroyed – Sgt. Scott – one engine o[n] fire and was observed to dive to ground.

1 Do 17 probable – P/O Vigors – one engine on fire – losing height – crew out of action.

1 Do 215 probable – P/O Whitbread – one engine on fire.
1 Me 109 probable – Sgt. Johnson.
1 Do 215 probable F/O van Meutz – bits of tail plane fell off.
1 Me.109 probable – F/O van Meutz – glycol or petrol pouring out.
1 Glenn Martin damaged – S/Ldr. Hill – Pieces observed flying off. N.B. This machine had French markings – twin engined and had green camouflage.
OUR CASUALTIES. Nil
1 aircraft category 2.

On the ground, however, a total of 448 civilian Londoners were killed by the Luftwaffe's bombing attacks, which continued well into the night. The excitable Göring rang his wife Emmy in Berlin to tell her 'London is in flames'. But even as Göring gloated, the fires were being put out by 600 engines and thousands of fire fighters, professional and voluntary. From being cowed by the Luftwaffe, the citizens of London seemed to take perverse pleasure in being on the front-line of the war. James Reston, the *New York Times*' man in London, having watched the events of the day, cabled his paper: 'One simply cannot convey the spirit of these people. Adversity only angers and strengthens them. That curious gentility among their men folk confuses us. We underestimate them . . . The British people can hold out to the end.'

So could Fighter Command now. Flying over London in his personal Hurricane on the following day, 11 Group's commander Keith Park recalled: 'It was burning all down the river. It was a horrid sight. But I looked down and said, "Thank God for that," because I realized that the methodical Germans had at last switched their attack from my vital aerodromes on to the cities.'

On the other side of the Channel, the veteran Theo Osterkamp cried 'tears of rage and dismay' over Göring's decision to bomb London instead of the RAF's fighter airfields 'at the very point of victory'.

London, in the parlance of the time, 'could take it'. Yet it still needed defending; its citizens could not be left as staked lambs in a trap for the beast. In days of blue heavens and brilliant sun remembered by all participants, the skies of southeastern England were filled by the sight and sound of German raiders proceeding towards London to be intercepted by British fighters rising to engage them. Piloting one of them was Roger Hall of 152 Squadron from 10 Group:

I was flying White two behind Ferdie as White one. The new Yellow Section in 'A' Flight was made up from a F/O just returned from leave and a new sergeant pilot who had arrived at the station from O.T.U. [Operational Training Unit] that very day. Black two was now P/O Watty, who had been standing down during the morning.

In the absence of the C.O., Bottle was leading the squadron as Red one and Maida Leader. We taxied out and formed up in Squadron formation for take-off. Bottle always seemed to prefer it this way when he was leading. White Section were on the port side of the 'V' and with a fore and aft movement of his hand Bottle started to move, the remainder of the squadron opening up their engines simultaneously.

It must have looked an impressive sight, I thought, to anyone watching from the ground. The noise must have seemed deafening as the twelve 'Merlin' engines reached their ultimate boost for take-off.

Off the ground, we quickly slid into position, the number twos behind their number ones and the whole of 'B' flight slightly behind 'A' flight. Turning to gently port, Bottle called up control to say that Maida squadron were now airborne. Control answering confirmed that we were to patrol base at angels ten. We continued to spiral round the aerodrome gaining altitude at the rate of approximately two thousand feet a minute. At ten thousand feet we levelled out and Bottle called up to say that we were now in position. Control acknowledged his call and said that for the present we were to stay put.

For about ten minutes we remained over the airfield, which, as we looked down on it, seemed a compact little affair difficult to reconcile with what from the ground appeared to be nothing more than a number of wooden huts of various sizes strung together in a haphazard fashion. I could see it now as the planners must have seen it on the drawing board. Looking to the east I could see a few miles away my old regimental depot with its tank tracks leading conspicuously away from the buildings over the heather to the driving and testing grounds.

'Hallo Maida Leader' called up control, 'Increase angels to two-five – increase your angels to two-five – Mandrake to Maida Leader – over.' 'Hallo Mandrake, Maida Leader answering – understand angels two-five – listening and out,' came the reply from Bottle.

Once again we started to climb, this time very steeply in an attitude which was generally known as 'hanging on the prop'. My airspeed was not much in advance of 140mph which was not at all comfortable as it precluded any sudden change of direction should it have become necessary. The aircraft was not far from its stalling speed.

'Hallo Maida Leader, Mandrake calling – Hallo Maida Leader – Victor 080 degrees – angels three-zero – over.' 'Hallo Mandrake – Maida Leader answering – your message received and understood – Vectoring 080 degrees, angels three-zero—listening out.'

We had reached thirteen thousand feet when this order came through and, still climbing, we started on our new course which was a little north of due east and would bring us into the region of South London.

'Hallo Maida Leader – Mandrake calling – What are your angels?' called control. 'Hallo Mandrake – Maida Leader answering – angels one-four – over' came Bottle's reply, rather curtly I thought, as if to give the impression to control that he was getting a bit fed up with him.

'Hallo Maida Leader' cut in Mandrake again; Mandrake was now excited and talking fast, running away with himself, 'Very many bandits approaching bomb-dump from the south – repeat – very many bandits approaching bomb-dump from the south – gain angels as fast as you can – Buster – Buster – over to you – over.' 'OK Mandrake – your message received – we're doing our best – listening out' replied Maida Leader. I looked at my code-card and identified 'Bomb-Dump' as being London. I thought how apt this was.

I switched on full oxygen and turned my trigger button on to 'Fire' at the same time adjusting my reflector sight. At twenty-five thousand feet we entered the base of stratus cloud and closed up our formation to penetrate it. At twenty-seven thousand feet we were out of it. Above it the sun was brilliant as ever.

'Buster – Buster – Maida Squadron' – Mandrake kept calling. 'Get off the bloody air Mandrake, you stupid clot – what the bloody hell do you think you're doing?' Someone, I don't think it was Bottle, replied. There was silence over the ether after that for the time being.

Beneath us, as we reached thirty thousand feet and levelled out, there was a flat carpet of cloud, pure white in the bright sunlight. Above us, apart from a few delicate and remote wisps of cirrus, the sky was an intense blue, the sort of blue you find on an artist's palette. Behind us and slightly to our starboard the sun was still high in the sky and was dazzling to look into. To the east the stratus cloud was beginning to disperse and we could see across the North Sea to the Dutch Islands. Visibility was limited only by the curvature of the Earth.

The entire firmament, the vault of the heavens, was revealed to us. It stretched from Lille and St. Omer in the rolling plains of the Pas-de-Calais to the south, eastwards down the sandy coastline of Northern France, past Dunkirk to the Belgian frontier, beyond that to the Dutch Islands and past them to the faint line of the German coast, and up as far north as the Norfolk coast of our own country. Such was a panorama that confronted us as we levelled out five miles above the earth and higher than the highest mountain.

'Hallo Mandrake,' Maida Leader called. 'Maida Squadron now at angels three-zero – Bandits in sight – Tally Ho.' 'Well done, Maida Leader – Good luck – Good luck – over to you,' Mandrake replied.

Yes, there they were all right. Very many bandits, too. The sky was full of black dots, which, from where we were at the moment, might have been anything; but we knew only too well what they were. They were coming from the south; squadron upon squadron, fleet upon fleet, an aerial Armada the size of which I don't suppose Jules Verne or even Wells had envisaged. The main body of them was below us by quite ten thousand feet, but above them as escort, winged the protective fighter screen proudly trailing their long white plumes of vapour.

Our position was somewhere over Surrey at that moment, and as we approached the enemy formations which were still some miles away, we saw our own fighters – the eleven group squadrons and some from twelve group in the Midlands – coming up from the north. There seemed to be quite a number of us. They too were black dots, climbing in groups of twelve or thirty-six in wing formation. Most of them were Hurricanes.

The enemy appeared to be disposed in three distinct and separate groups each comprising a hundred or more bombers. Above each group were about fifty fighters – Me 109s, and Me 110s. The bombers were Heinkels, Dorniers and Junkers 88s.

'Line astern formation – Maida squadron,' ordered Maida Leader. We took up our battle formations at once, with 'A' Flight in the order of Red, Yellow and White. There were two machines behind me and three in front. 'Come up into line abreast "B" Flight' came the next order from Red one. When we had completed this change the squadron was disposed in two lines of six machines flying abreast and at a distance of about fifty yards between each Flight.

145

We were ready to attack. We were now in the battle area and three-quarters of an hour had elapsed since we had taken off.

The two bomber formations furthest from us were already being attacked by a considerable number of our fighters. Spitfires and Hurricanes appeared to be in equal numbers at the time. Some of the German machines were already falling out of their hitherto ordered ranks and floundering towards the earth. There was a little ack-ack fire coming from up somewhere on the ground although its paucity seemed pathetic and its effect was little more than that of a defiant gesture.

We approached the westernmost bomber formation from the front port quarter, but we were some ten thousand feet higher than they were and we hadn't started to dive yet. Immediately above the bombers were some twin-engined fighters, Me 110s. Maida Leader let the formation get a little in front of us then he gave the order 'Going down now Maida aircraft,' turning his machine upside down as he gave it. The whole of 'A' Flight, one after the other, peeled off after him, upside down at first and then into a vertical dive.

When they had gone 'B' Flight followed suit. Ferdie and I turned over with a hard leftward pressure to the stick to bring the starboard wing up to right angles to the horizon, and some application to the port or bottom rudder pedal to keep the nose from rising. Keeping the controls like this, the starboard wing fell over until it was parallel to the horizon again, but upside down. Pulling the stick back from this position the nose of my machine fell towards the ground and followed White one in front, now going vertically down on to the bombers almost directly below us. Our speed started to build up immediately. It went from three hundred miles per hour to four and more. White one in front, his tail wheel some distance below me but visible through the upper part of my windscreen, was turning his machine in the vertical plane from one side to the other by the use of his ailerons. Red Section had reached the formation and had formed into a loosened echelon to starboard as they attacked. They were coming straight down on top of the bombers, having gone slap through the protective Me 110 fighter screen, ignoring them completely.

Now it was our turn. With one eye on our own machines I slipped out slightly to the right of Ferdie and placed the red dot of my sight firmly in front and in line with the starboard engine of a Dornier vertically below me and about three hundred yards off. I felt apprehensive lest I should collide with our own machines in the melee that was to ensue. I seemed to see one move ahead what the positions of our machines would be, and where I should be in relation to them if I wasn't careful. I pressed my trigger and through my inch thick windscreen I saw the tracers spiralling away hitting free air in front of the bomber's engine. I was allowing too much deflection. I must correct. I pushed the stick further forward. My machine was past the vertical and I was feeling the effect of the negative gravity trying to throw me out of the machine, forcing my body up into the perspex hood of the cockpit. My Sutton harness was biting into my shoulders and blood was forcing its way to my head, turning everything red. My tracers were hitting the bomber's engine and bits of metal were beginning to fly off it. I was getting too close to it, much too close. I knew I must pull away but I seemed hypnotised and went still closer, fascinated by what was happening. I was oblivious to everything else. I pulled away just in time to miss hitting the Dornier's starboard wing tip. I turned my machine to the right on ailerons and heaved back on the stick, inflicting a terrific amount of gravity on to the machine. I was pressed down into the cockpit again and a black veil came over my eyes and I could see nothing.

I eased the stick a little to regain my vision and to look for Ferdie. I saw a machine, a single Spitfire, climbing up after a dive about five hundred yards in front of me and flew after it for all I was worth. I was going faster than it was and I soon caught up with it – in fact I overshot it. It was Ferdie all right. I could see the 'C' Charlie alongside our squadron letters on his fuselage. I pulled out to one side and back again, hurling my machine at the air without any finesse, just to absorb some speed so that Ferdie could catch up with me. 'C' Charlie went past me and I thrust my throttle forward lest I should lose him. I got in behind him again and called him up to tell him so. He said, 'Keep an eye out behind and don't stop weaving.' I acknowledged his message and started to fall back a bit to get some room. Ferdie had turned out to the flank of the enemy formation and had taken a wide sweeping orbit to port, climbing fast as he did so. I threw my aircraft first on to its port wing tip to pull it round, then fully over to the other tip for another steep turn, and round again and again, blacking out on each turn. We were vulnerable on the climb, intensely so, for we were so slow.

I saw them coming quite suddenly on a left turn; red tracers coming towards us from the centre of a large black twin engined Me 110 which wasn't quite far enough in the sun from us to be totally obscured, though I had to squint to identify it. I shouted to Ferdie but he had already seen the tracers flash past him and had discontinued his port climbing turn and had started to turn over on his back and to dive. I followed, doing the same thing, but the Me 110 must have done so too for the tracers were still following us. We dived for about a thousand feet, I should think, and I kept wondering why my machine had not been hit.

Ferdie started to ease his dive a bit. I watched him turn his machine on to its side and stay there for a second, then its nose came up, still on its side, and the whole aircraft seemed to come round in a barrel roll as if clinging to the inside of some revolving drum. I tried to imitate this manoeuvre but I didn't know how to, so I just thrust open the throttle and aimed my machine in Ferdie's direction and eventually caught him up.

The Me 110 had gone off somewhere. I got up to Ferdie and slid once more under the doubtful protection of his tail and told him that I was there. I continued to weave like a pilot inspired, but my inspiration was the result of sheer terror and nothing more.

All the time we were moving towards the bombers; but we moved indirectly by turns, and that was the only way we could move with any degree of immunity now. Four Spitfires flashed past in front of us; they weren't ours though, for I noticed the markings. There was a lot of talking going on on the ether and we seemed to be on the same frequency as a lot of other squadrons. 'Hallo Firefly Yellow Section – 110 behind you' – 'Hallo Cushing Control – Knockout Red leader returning to base to refuel.'

'Close up Knockout "N" for Nellie and watch for those 109s on your left' – 'All right Landsdown Squadron – control answering – your message received – many more bandits coming from the east – over' – 'Talker White two where the bloody hell are you?' – 'Going down now Sheldrake Squadron – loosen up a bit' – 'You clumsy clot – Hurricane "Y" Yoke – what the flaming hades do you think you are doing?' – 'I don't know Blue one but there are some bastards up there on the left – nine o'clock above' – Even the Germans came in intermittently: 'Achtung, Achtung – drei Spitfeuer unter, unter Achtung, Spitfeuer, Spitfeuer.' 'Tally Ho – Tally Ho – Homer Red leader attacking now.' 'Get off the bastard air Homer leader' – 'Yes I can see Rimmer leader – Red two answering – Glycol leak I think – he's getting out – yes he's baled out he's OK'

And so it went on incessantly, disjointed bits of conversation coming from different units all revealing some private little episode in the great battle of which each story was a small part of the integral whole.

Two 109s were coming up behind the four Spitfires and instinctively I found myself thrusting forward my two-way radio switch to the transmitting position and calling out, 'Look out those four Spitfires – 109s behind you – look out.' I felt that my message could hardly be of less importance than some that I had heard, but no heed was taken of it. The two 109s had now settled themselves on the tail of the rear Spitfire and were pumping cannon shells into it. We were some way off but Ferdie saw them too and changed direction to starboard, opening up his throttle as we closed. The fourth Spitfire, or 'tail-end Charlie', had broken away, black smoke pouring from its engine, and the third in line came under fire now from the same 109. We approached the two 109s from above their starboard rear quarter, and taking a long deflection shot, from what must have been still out of range, Ferdie opened fire on the leader. The 109 didn't see us, for he still continued to fire at number three until it too started to trail Glycol from its radiator and turned over on its back, breaking away from the remaining two. 'Look out Black one – look out Black Section Apple Squadron – 109s – 109s' came the belated warning, possibly from number three as he went down. At last number one turned steeply to port, with the two 109s still hanging on to their tails now firing at number two. They were presenting a relatively stationary target to us now for we were directly behind them.

Ferdie's bullets were hitting the second 109 now and pieces of its tail unit were coming away and floating past underneath us. The 109 jinked to the starboard. The leading Spitfire followed by its number two, had now turned full circle in a very tight turn and as yet it didn't seem that either of them had been hit. The 109 leader was vainly trying to keep into the same turn but couldn't hold it tight enough, so I think his bullets were skidding past the starboard of the Spitfires. The rear 109's tail unit disintegrated under Ferdie's fire and a large chunk of it slithered across the top surface of my starboard wing, denting the panels but making no noise. I put my hand up to my face for a second.

The fuselage of the 109 fell away below us and we came into the leader. I hadn't fired at it yet but now I slipped out to port of Ferdie as the leader turned right steeply and over on to its back to show its duck egg blue belly to us. I came up almost to line abreast of Ferdie on his port side and fired at the under surface of the German machine, turning upside down with it. The earth was now above my perspex hood and I was trying to keep my sights on the 109 in this attitude, pushing my stick forward to do so. Pieces of refuse rose up from the floor of my machine and the engine spluttered and coughed as the carburettor became temporarily starved of fuel. My propeller idled helplessly for a second and my harness snaps bit into my shoulders again. Flames leapt from the engine of the 109 but at the same time there was a loud bang from somewhere behind me and I heard, 'Look out Roger' as a large hole appeared near my starboard wing tip throwing up the matt green metal into a ragged rent to show the naked aluminium beneath.

I broke from the 109 and turned steeply to starboard, throwing the stick over to the right and then pulling it back into me and blacking out at once. Easing out I saw three 110s go past my tail in formation but they made no attempt to follow me round. 'Hallo Roger – Are you OK?' I heard Ferdie calling.

'I think so – where are you?' I called back.

'I'm on your tail – keep turning' came Ferdie's reply. Thank God, I thought Ferdie and I seemed to be alone in the sky. It was often like this. At one moment the air seemed to be full of aircraft and the next there was nothing except you. Ferdie came up in on my port side telling me at the same time that he thought we had better try to find the rest of the squadron.

Landing back at Warmwell, Hall gave his combat report to 'Brains' [the Intelligence Officer]. It was now late evening and as there would be no further flying that day,

Hall and his colleagues relaxed in model fighter boy fashion with an epic drinking session.

There was no further flying that day and we were released at nine o'clock. We went up to the mess as usual and after some drinks we got into our cars and left the camp. We were to rendezvous at The Sunray.

We got to The Sunray after five minutes or so. It wasn't far from the aerodrome and was tucked away at the end of a lane leading from the main Weymouth-Wareham road.

The Sunray was blacked out and it was pitch dark outside when we switched off our lights. We groped our way to the door which Chumley seemed able to find in some instinctive manner. He opened the front door calling to me, 'Switch your radar on Roger' and pulled aside a blanket which had been rigged up to act as a further precaution, to prevent the light from escaping as the main door was opened. We got inside to find the others already drinking. Cocky seemed to be in the chair as Chumley and I came in and he called out, 'Lost again White Section — biggies coming up for both of you.'

The Sunray was an old pub and full of atmosphere. The ceilings were low and oak beams ran the entire length of them. In between the beams the ceiling itself was made of wood of the same colour. It seemed dark at first but there was a liberal amount of lamps, not on the ceiling itself but on the walls, and these gave a soft light that was distinctly cosy. There were tables of heavy oak around which were chairs made out of highly polished barrels, and each containing soft plushy cushions. Around the walls ran an almost continuous cushion covered bench and the windows, from what I could see of them, for they were heavily curtained, were made of bottle glass and were only translucent. The serving bar in the middle of the room was round and from it hung a varied assortment of brilliantly polished copper and brass ornaments. There were roses in copper vases standing on some of the tables and a bowl or two on the bar itself. There were sandwiches beneath glass cases and sausage rolls as well. The visible atmosphere in the room was cloudy with tobacco smoke which seemed to reach its optimum height a foot or so from the ceiling, where it appeared to flatten out and drift in horizontal layers, until someone passed through it and then it appeared to follow whoever did so for a moment. There was wireless somewhere in the room, for I could hear music coming from near where I was standing.

I was by the bar with the others and I had finished my third pint of bitter and was talking to Cocky. The night was quite early yet and Bottle was standing up at the bar with Dimmy, Chumley and Pete. They were all laughing at the top of their voices and a bit further along was Ferdie listening to what I think might have been a rather long-drawn-out story from one of the sergeant pilots, while two others seemed impatiently trying to get him to the point. Ferdie seemed to be quite amused at the process. There were two of our Polish pilots here too, both non-commissioned and their names were so difficult to pronounce that we simply called them 'Zig' and 'Zag'. They didn't seem to take any offence at this abbreviation. They were excellent pilots, both of them.

The wireless now started to play the theme of Tchaikovsky's *Swan Lake* ballet and when I'd got my sixth pint I mentally detached myself from the rest for a moment.

'Wotcher Roger, mine's a pint of black and tan – have one yourself.' I was jolted back to reality by this, accompanied by a hearty slap on the back from Ferdie, who had wormed his way across to me.

I had my seventh pint with Ferdie and we both edged up closer to the bar, where the main body of the squadron seemed to have congregated. It was Cocky who, high spirited and irrepressible as ever, said, 'Come on boys, we've had this – next stop The Crown.' We picked up our caps and made for the door.

'Mind the light,' someone shouted, as the protective blanket was thrust aside for a moment. The air outside was cold and it hit me like a cold shower for a brief second while I gathered my wits. Chumley piled into the passenger seat. I was feeling perhaps a little too self-confident after the drinks but I felt sure I would make it somehow.

We got on to the main road again and Chumley directed us to The Crown in Weymouth. The road was fairly free of traffic and I gave the little car full rein for a while. It was dark and just in front of me there seemed to be an even darker but obscure sort of shape, which I found difficulty in identifying for a moment. 'For Christ's sake, man' Chumley shouted. Cocky's large Humber had pulled up on the verge and its occupants were busy relieving themselves by the roadside, but one of them was standing in front of the rear light and obscuring it. We were travelling at not much less than 75mph when Chumley shouted at me and the Humber was only about thirty yards from us when I recognised it. My slow-wittedness only now became evident but I felt quite confident and in complete control of my faculties as I faced the emergency. I pulled the wheel over to the right, not abruptly but absolutely surely and with a calculated pressure to allow me only inches, inches enough to guide the left mudguard past the Humber's off rear bumper. At the time I was in full control and thinking how fine and assured were my reactions, how much finer they were now than they ever were when I had had no drink. The sense of complete infallibility and the consequent denial of any risk had overtaken me and the feeling, if anything, became accentuated when the little car had passed Cocky's large Humber, which it did by the barest fraction of an inch, to the accompanying shout of 'Look out, 109s behind' from those who were standing by the verge and otherwise engaged. 'No road sense, those boys' Chumley remarked.

The Crown was quite a different sort of place from The Sunray. From the outside it was distinctly unpretentious in appearance, just a flat sided building flanking the back street down by the harbour. It had four windows, two top and bottom and a door in the middle. We went in, and as I had rather expected, it was an ordinary working man's pub. There were no furnishings to speak of, the floor was just pain wooden boards and the few tables were round with marble tops and the conventional china ashtrays advertising some type of lager or whisky. The bar occupied the whole one side of the room and the barman greeted us warmly as we arrived. Chumley ordered two pints of bitter. Apparently the squadron were well known and held in high esteem.

The others arrived soon after we got there and the drinks were on me this time. There was a dartboard in the corner of the room and, not surprisingly, we threw badly. What did it matter how we played I thought, as long as we let off some steam.

When we left The Crown at closing time I was drunk, but we didn't return to the aerodrome. Bottle had some friends in Bournemouth and it was to Bournemouth that he'd decided to go. I was too drunk to drive and so was Chumley, who had left The Crown before closing time and taken up his position in the passenger seat of my car where he was now fast asleep. Dimmy and I lifted him out, still asleep, into the back of Cocky's Humber. Dimmy, who so he claimed, was more sober than I, said he would drive my car. I made no protest. I relapsed into the passenger seat and fell asleep as the car gathered speed towards Bournemouth. I woke up as soon as the car came to a standstill, feeling a lot more sober. It was about half-past eleven when we went through the door of this quite large private house. Bottle's and Cocky's car had already arrived and the occupants had apparently gone inside. The door opened and a girl greeted us. 'I'm Pam, come on in the others are here,' she said. Everyone was seated in or on some sort of chair or stool and all had a glass of some sort in, their hand. There were two other girls there besides Pam.

I was beginning to feel rather tired about this time and I would have been glad to get back to camp, especially as I had to be on dawn readiness again. The atmosphere here didn't seem conducive to any sort of rowdery like The Crown or The Compass and the girls didn't somehow seem to fit into the picture. They weren't on the same wavelength. It was about two-thirty in the morning when we finally left.

We arrived back at the mess just after four o'clock, having stopped at an all night cafe for eggs and bacon and coffee. I had to be on readiness at five-thirty and it seemed hardly worthwhile going to bed, so I decided to go straight down to dispersal, to find I was the only one there. I had just an hour and a half's sleep before I was due to take-off on dawn patrol.

Doubtless the petrol that powered Hall's pub crawl was aviation fuel. As Tim Vigors recalled, pilots considered 'borrowing' aviation fuel a perk of the job:

Petrol rationing had, by this time, really started to bite. It had not affected us pilots too badly as, quite illegally, we used to top up the tanks of our cars from the petrol bowsers used for refuelling aircraft. As long as this was done reasonably discreetly the authorities kindly turned a blind eye. What effect 100 octane fuel was having on the pistons and cylinders of my Ford 8 remained to be seen. So far EGO [his car] was going like a bomb. In fact the diet seemed to suit her.

Tim Vigors' cure for the 6 a.m. hangover that was endemic among Spitfire pilots, was to turn on the Spitfire's oxygen system to full. Hangover or no, the ferocity with which the RAF's fighter boys were engaging the Luftwaffe alarmed the German pilots. Flying over London on 8 September, Me 109 pilot Ulrich Steinhilper recalled:

Now we really came up against the full force of the RAF. If the calculations of our High Command had been correct there should have been minimal fighter opposition to us now. But whilst we saw numerous head-on and flank attacks on the bombers below, we were often too busy with our own defence to intervene. There were constant dogfights with aircraft wheeling and diving, pursuing each other, sometimes with success sometimes not. There were stark black lines diving down, showing the path of a stricken aircraft and parachutes floating in the thin, cold air. There was tragedy too, as I watched one parachute begin to burn, its helpless charge falling faster and faster. Hard to take too, were the accidents of identification. I sat helpless with the hard lump of frustration boiling in my chest as I saw below me a '109 latch on to the tail of another of our fighters and then to see them suddenly linked by four straight grey lines as the guns were fired. Quickly the yellow tail of the leading fighter ignited and it rolled out to dive towards the ground. In such tense and charged surroundings, such mistakes were inevitable.

Pilot Officer Eric Lock of 41 Squadron was one of Fighter Command's natural-born hunters. On a lone spotter patrol between Dungeness and Ramsgate on the morning of September 14, the diminutive 'Sawn-off Lockie' saw an enemy fighter formation coming over at around 28,000 feet. Lock's almost suicidal determination to close in combat with the enemy is evident from his combat report:

I was out on patrol to the south coast to give information. I was flying at 31,000–33,000 feet, when I saw a formation of twelve Me 109s, travelling east of the coast between Dover and Deal. I attacked the last section of the formation; they were flying in a diamond formation. I was just about to close in when I was attacked from above by some other Me 109s. They peeled off from about 3,000 feet above me and carried out a head-on attack on me. I waited until one of them was in range and gave him a long burst. He passed a few feet above me; I carried out a sharp turn to the right and saw him in flames. Just then I was attacked again from head-on. I waited till he was at point-blank range. I saw my bullets go into the enemy aircraft, and as he went past underneath me, I gave him a very long burst of fire. I saw some more enemy aircraft coming down on me, so I half rolled and dived through the clouds. I had just passed through the clouds when I saw someone who had baled out. I followed him down to the ground. I am pretty certain it was a Me 109 pilot, I saw the troops rush up to him and he appeared to be holding his arms up. I flew low over the field and he waved back. This was afterwards confirmed by the police.

Eric Lock would prove one of the most successful RAF fighter pilots in the Battle of Britain. Lock had the hunter's gifts of eyesight, the ability to spot weakness in his prey and the skill to get into the killing position, as well as the underestimated virtue of patience. All these attributes were to the fore in an earlier encounter with Me 109s, which Lock stalked with rare skill. His combat report for the occasion stated:

I was Yellow 1, patrolling with 41 Squadron on the Maidstone patrol line. We dived through cloud, when my section became split up. When we came through the clouds I found myself about 2,000 feet above and behind the squadron formation. My No. 2 and 3 were missing, so I remained in this position. The squadron then turned northeast. I then saw a large formation of Me 109s come between the squadron and myself, so I climbed back into the sun to gain more height. I then sighted several formations of Me 109s in line abreast, so I joined one of the last formations of 109s. I waited for quite a while and then had a short burst at one on the extreme left. He went into a dive with smoke and glycol coming from the engine. I then gave the next aircraft a short burst, and he started to sideslip. I gave him two more short bursts and he went into a vertical dive with flames coming from the engine and bits and pieces flying off. It crashed between West Malling and Ashford.

Lock's Spitfire was one of 269 serviceable Spitfires and 533 Hurricanes in front-line units on 14 September. The estimate of Fighter Command's strength by Beppo Schmidt, the Luftwaffe's chief of intelligence, was fifty planes in total. Thus it was with considerable surprise that, on the very next day, Sunday 15 September, the Luftwaffe found its all out effort against London spectacularly rebuffed.

At 10.30 in the morning Churchill, sensing that the crisp autumn weather was right for the enemy (and doubtless sensing too the arrival of an historic moment) dropped in on Air Vice-Marshal Park at 11 Group HQ, Uxbridge:

> We must take 15th September as the culminating date. On this day the Luftwaffe, after two heavy attacks on the 14th, made its greatest concentrated effort in a resumed daylight attack on London.
>
> It was one of the decisive battles of the war, and like the Battle of Waterloo, it was on a Sunday. I was at Chequers.

I had already on several occasions visited the headquarters of No. 11 Fighter Group in order to witness the conduct of an air battle, when not much had happened. However, the weather on this day seemed suitable to the enemy, and accordingly I drove over to Uxbridge and arrived at the Group Headquarters. No. 11 Group comprised no fewer than twenty-five squadrons covering the whole of Essex, Kent, Sussex, and Hampshire, and all the approaches across them to London. Air Vice-Marshal Park had for six months commanded this group, on which our fate largely depended. From the beginning of Dunkirk, all the daylight actions in the South of England had already been conducted by him, and all his arrangements and apparatus had been brought to the highest perfection. My wife and I were taken down to the bomb proof Operations Room, fifty feet below ground. All the ascendancy of the Hurricanes and Spitfires would have been fruitless but for this system of underground control centres and telephone cables, which had been devised and built before the war by the Air Ministry under Dowding's advice and impulse. Lasting credit is due to all concerned. In the South of England there were, at this time, No. 11 Group HQ and six subordinate Fighter Station Centres. All these were, as has been described, under heavy stress. The Supreme Command was exercised from the Fighter Headquarters at Stanmore, but the actual handling of the direction of the squadrons was wisely left to No. 11 Group, which controlled the units through its Fighter Stations located in each county.

The Group Operations Room was like a small theatre, about sixty feet across, and with two storeys. We took our seats in the Dress Circle. Below us was the large-scale map table, around which perhaps twenty highly trained young men and women, with their telephone assistants, were assembled. Opposite to us, covering the entire wall where the theatre curtain would be, was a gigantic blackboard divided into six columns, with electric bulbs for the six fighter stations, each of their squadrons having a sub-column of its own, and also divided by lateral lines. Thus the lowest row of bulbs showed as they were lighted the squadrons which were 'Standing By' at two minutes' notice, the next row those at 'Readiness', five minutes, then at 'Available', twenty minutes, then those which had taken off, the next row those which had reported having seen the enemy, the next – with red lights – those which were in action, and the top row those which were returning home. On the left hand side, in a kind of glass stage box, were the four or five officers whose duty it was to weigh and measure the information received from our Observer Corps, which at this time numbered upwards of fifty thousand men, women, and youths. Radar was still in its infancy, but it gave warning of raids approaching our coast, and the observers, with field glasses and portable telephones, were our main source of information about raiders flying overland. Thousands of messages were therefore received during an action. Several roomfuls of experienced people in other parts of the underground headquarters sifted them with great rapidity, and transmitted the results from minute to minute directly to the plotters seated around the table on the floor and to the officer supervising from the glass stage box.

On the right hand was another glass stage box containing Army officers who reported the action of our anti-aircraft batteries, of which at this time in the Command there were two hundred. At night it was of vital importance to stop these batteries firing over certain areas in which our fighters would be closing with the enemy. I was not unacquainted with the general outlines of this system, having had it explained to me a year before the war by Dowding when I visited him at Stanmore. It had been shaped and refined in constant action, and all was now fused together into a most elaborate instrument of war, the like of which existed nowhere in the world.

'I don't know,' said Park, as we went down, 'whether anything will happen today. At present all is quiet.' However, after a quarter of an hour the raid-plotters began to move about. An attack of '40 plus' was reported to be coming from the German stations in the Dieppe area. The bulbs along the bottom of the wall display panel began to glow as various squadrons came to 'Stand By'. Then in quick succession '20 plus', '40 plus' signals were received, and in another ten minutes it was evident that a serious battle impended. On both sides the air began to fill.

Park, the consummate tactician, began feeding his fighter squadrons into the air, so they could harry the 200 German aircraft which were now airborne all the way from the Channel to London. Despite slashing attacks by the RAF's fighter squadrons, detachments of German bombers began to unload their ordinance on the capital at around 12.05 p.m. However, if the pilots of these bombers thought they had escaped the British fighter boys, they were mistaken. Park had concentrated six fighter squadrons over London. These now turned to the attack. Pilot Officer Bobby Oxspring of 'B' Flight from 66 Squadron remembered:

B flight was the last to attack and we selected the nearest vic of bombers. Firing a long deflection burst on my target without any apparent result, I broke underneath and then up and away to the side. George Corbett stuck with me and whilst deciding the next move, we saw a solitary Spitfire ahead of us. It was Ken Gillies, and as we joined up with him he recognized my markings and called, 'Hang on, Bobby, we'll shake this lot up.' He then led us forward and then turned around into a head-on attack. Flying line abreast we fired all the way in to point-blank range on the leading vic of Heinkels.

As we broke down and away beneath out targets we saw the formation had separated. But the main stream still advanced on London and at that moment we witnessed the glorious sight of five squadrons from the Duxford wing, led by Douglas Bader, come sailing into the raid. The impact of a further sixty Hurricanes and Spitfires charging in on the already sorely harassed bomber fleet was too much. Bombs were jettisoned indiscriminately on south-east London, and the raiders fled for home.

In this noon action Bader's 'Big Wing' claimed twenty enemy bombers; it seemed a vindication of the airman's multi squadron tactic over the cautious commitment of single or double squadrons favoured by Park and Dowding. In truth, in the confusion of fighting, Bader's squadrons heavily overclaimed their 'kills'. The Big Wing controversy would grumble on, but in one respect it was resoundingly successful; its appearance in near-formation order over Brixton at 12.08 p.m. shot a hole in the morale of the Luftwaffe. From Kent onwards, the Luftwaffe had been slashed at by the 'last fifty Spitfires' – only to find another 'last fifty Spitfires' over London.

Pilot Officer 'Polly' Pollard of 611 Squadron was flying of those 'last fifty Spitfires' in Bader's Big Wing at high noon over London. His subsequent Combat Report stated:

Attacked thirty Do 215 [from] about 4,000 Ft above them – short burst in dive – so result seen. Chased one Do 215 from London towards Rochester with one other Spitfire and 1 Hurricane. Do 215 lost height rapidly between Rochester and Herne Bay – smoke from Port Engine – Crew of two bailed out and aircraft crashed on the edge of a wood approx 4–5 miles south of Herne Bay – Burst into flames on hitting ground. Four No. 1 attacks carried out.

In Fighter Command's Uxbridge HQ, the plotters shadowed the attacks of Pollard and his fellow pilots, and moved the markers representing German formations back across the Channel into France. A beaming Prime Minister offered his congratulations to the operations team. All over southern England, Spitfires and Hurricanes flew back to their bases in ones and twos to be refuelled and rearmed as soon as possible. Speed was of the essence because at 1.45 p.m., a new wave of 475 'hostile' aircraft appeared on British coastal radar. Fifteen minutes later, Park once again scrambled his fighter squadrons. Churchill resumed his 'Dress Circle' seat:

Presently the red bulbs showed that the majority of our squadrons were engaged. A subdued hum arose from the floor, where the busy plotters pushed their discs to and fro in accordance with the swiftly changing situation. Air Vice-Marshal Park gave general directions for the disposition of his fighter force, which were translated into detailed orders to each Fighter Station by a youngish officer in the centre of the Dress Circle, at whose side I sat. Some years after, I asked his name. He was Lord Willoughby de Broke. (I met him next in 1947, when the Jockey Club, of which he was a Steward, invited me to see the Derby. He was surprised that I remembered the occasion.) He now gave the orders for the individual squadrons to ascend and patrol as the result of the final information which appeared on the map table. The Air Marshal himself walked up and down behind watching every move in the game with vigilant eye, supervising his junior executive hand, and only occasionally intervening with some decisive order, usually to reinforce a threatened area. In a little while all our squadrons were fighting, and some had already begun to return for fuel. All were in the air. The lower line of bulbs were out. There was not one squadron left in reserve. At this moment Park spoke to Dowding at Stanmore, asking for three squadrons from No. 12 Group to be put at his disposal in case of another major attack while his squadrons were rearming and refuelling. This was done. They were specially needed to cover London and our fighter aerodromes, because No. 11 Group had already shot their bolt.

The young officer, to whom this seemed a matter of routine, continued to give his orders, in accordance with the general directions of his Group Commander, in a calm, low monotone, and the three reinforcing squadrons were soon absorbed. I became conscious of the anxiety of the Commander, who now stood still behind his subordinate's chair. Hitherto I had watched in silence. I now asked: 'What other reserves have we?'

'There are none,' said Air Vice-Marshal Park. In an

account which he wrote about it afterwards he said that at this I 'looked grave'. Well I might. What losses should we not suffer if our refuelling planes were caught on the ground by further raids of '40 plus' or '50 plus'! The odds were great; our margins small; the stakes infinite.

Another five minutes passed, and most of our squadrons had now descended to refuel. In many cases our resources could not give them overhead protection. Then it appeared that the enemy were going home. The shifting of the discs on the table below showed a continuous eastward movement of German bombers and fighters. No new attack appeared. In another ten minutes the action was ended. We climbed again the stairways which led to the surface, and almost as we emerged the 'All Clear' sounded.

Churchill, the former cavalryman, had understood what Göring, the former fighter pilot, had failed to appreciate – that Fighter Command's squadrons were at their most vulnerable when they were refuelling and rearming. If Göring had ordered his second wave of bombers to attack the RAF's forward airfields instead of London, 11 Group might have been caught on the ground and annihilated. (Later in the war, the Japanese would lose the sea battle of Midway to the US in five fatal minutes, precisely because their fighters were attacked whilst refuelling on the decks of their carriers.) Instead, when Göring's second wave of aircraft came over at 2 p.m., Fighter Command was in the air, ready and waiting. Eric Lock, scrambled on his second sortie of the day, relished the opportunity such numbers of 'hostiles' presented:

We delivered our attack and I broke away to starboard. I started to climb again and sighted a formation of three

Dornier 17s escorted by Me 109s, just above the clouds. I saw a Hurricane attack the Me 109s, so I joined him. He shot one down in flames as I was attacking. I attacked from behind and underneath, firing a rather long burst. He went into a vertical dive on fire. The Hurricane pilot then beckoned me to attack the three Dornier 17s, so we selected one each. We both delivered an astern attack, to stop the rear machine gunner, this seemed rather effective. We then carried out our attacks. When I delivered my second attack, the starboard engine burst into flames and the aircraft dived into the sea. By now the two other Dornier 17s had dived to sea level. We carried out a quarter beam attack on the remainder. After a while, the starboard engine caught fire and he also landed in the sea by a convoy.

Eric Lock was gazetted the Distinguished Flying Cross on 1 October. His citation read, 'This officer has destroyed nine enemy aircraft, eight of these within a period of one week. He has displayed great vigour and determination in pressing home his attacks.'

So much for Fighter Command being *kaput*. By the end of the day, Fighter Command had shot down fifty-six German aircraft for the loss of only twenty-six of its own. Rightly, 15 September 1940 has become officially immortalized as 'Battle of Britain Day', the moment when the battle turned against the Germans. The proof came two days later, when Hitler postponed the invasion of Britain until further notice.

The postponement of 'Operation Sea Lion', however, did not yet mean the end of Operation Eagle. Göring, clinging to the thin hope that a continued Luftwaffe offensive might yet force Britain to surrender, allowed the battle to straggle on. The hectic

skirmishes of October provided the Battle with one of its
immortal moments. Bobby Oxspring of 66 Squadron recalled:

One exhausting day involved us in prolonged scraps starting
around 30,000 feet and inevitably the combats worked
down to lower altitudes. Having lost height on one of these
inconclusive mills, I collected some of my flight together
and prepared to climb back to the action.

Bodie elected to weave above the rest of us as lookout,
and suddenly he called, 'Give me a hand, Bob, I've got a
problem.'

I'd lost sight of him for a moment and said, 'OK, where
are you?'

As he replied, the gravity of his predicament was
emphasized by the wheezing of heavy breathing in the
backtone of his mike, 'Hurwheez, six o'clock high.'

Then I spotted him a couple of thousand feet up in the
middle of half a dozen 109s desperately reefing around and
fighting for his life. We poured on the coals as I called,
'Hang on, Bogle, we've got to get some height.' In fully
fine pitch we practically stood on our tails, and just to
encourage him I transmitted, 'Be with you in a minute,
Bogle.'

Back came his comment, 'Hurwheez, don't panic, I've
got 'em surrounded!'

We staggered into the melee with practically no forward
speed, but our sudden appearance diverted the 109s'
attention from Bodie because they broke the engagement.

Our speed was too slow for us to give effective chase
except for Bodie, who fastened on to one. He gave it the
hammer and despatched his tormentor into a Kentish field.

Bodie was a natural fighter pilot; aggressive, tenacious and tough, he would take on any odds and usually did. Son of an Essex dentist, it was sad that his life was wasted when he died in an accident to his Spitfire the following year.

Belatedly, the Luftwaffe decided to cut off the Spitfire problem at the source, attacking the Spitfire factories at Southampton on 24 and 26 September, killing 130 Supermarine workers. At the end of the month, the new Spitfire plant at Yeovil was hit. The Castle Bromwich plant was out of range for almost all German bombers – and it was this plant that made the new Mark II Spitfire. Fitted with the Merlin XII engine and a two stage supercharger, the Mk II brought more dismay to battered Luftwaffe pilots. Ulrich Steinhilper wrote to his father:

> The British have . . . a new engine in their Spitfires and our Me 109s can hardly keep up with it. We have also made some improvements and have also some new engines, but there is no more talk of absolute superiority. The other day we tangled with these newer Spitfires and had three losses against one success. I got into deep trouble myself and my *Rottenhund* (Sigi Voss) was shot down. I ended up against two Spitfires with all weapons jammed. There was no alternative but to get the hell out of it. When I got back I found three hits, fortunately none of them in any vital spots.

Oberleutnant Ulrich Steinhilper was less lucky. On 27 October, he was shot down during a sortie over England and made a POW. By that time even Joseph Goebbels was forced to acknowledge that daylight raids on England were a lost cause. The Battle of Britain was over.

★

The Few deserved their plaudits. Some 2,500 pilots – some as young as eighteen, one as old as forty – had alone saved Britain from invasion. The Battle had been, like Waterloo, a damn close run thing; during the all important months of August and September 1940, when the battle was at its height, Fighter Command had lost 756 fighters and the Luftwaffe just 668. It was loss of 600 bombers that made the scorecard read so unfavourably to the attacker.

Fighter Command's defeat of the Luftwaffe had far-reaching consequences. It finished the myth of Nazi invincibility once and for all; in much the same way that Napoleon's repulse at Aspern-Essling in 1809 gave hope to a demoralized Europe that the Grand Army could be conquered. After the war, the German General Gerd von Rundstedt was asked by a delegation of Russian officers what he considered to be the turning point of the war. They expected him to name Stalingrad. He replied, 'The Battle of Britain'.

Few of the Few were aware that they had made history. According to Sergeant Pilot George Unwin, 'In fact, when Churchill said something about "Never in the field of human conflict has so much or something been owed to so few," my CO always reckoned he was referring to the unpaid mess bills.'

Then there was the Spitfire itself. Although the Hurricane had made an invaluable contribution to the Battle of Britain, a meeting of ministers in October agreed that, 'the Hurricane is found not a match for the Messerschmitt. The Spitfire retains its superiority.' Subsequent research by the historian John Alcorn has backed the opinion of the men from the Ministry. Alcorn, having analysed the statistics of Luftwaffe and Fighter Command combats losses, concluded 'The 19 Spitfire units gained 521 victories, an average of just over 27 per squadron. The 30 fully engaged Hurricane units gained 655 victories, an average of just under 22 per squadron. On those figures the Spitfire was 1.25 times more effective in action than the Hurricane.'

The attitude of the Spitfire boys themselves towards their aerial steed was summoned up by an American pilot from 609 Squadron, who gave an anonymous interview to the BBC in October 1940: 'I guess the Spitfire is the finest fighter aircraft in the world. It's rugged and has no vices. I'd certainly rather fight with one than against one.'

609 Squadron had certainly tested the limits of the Spit's ruggedness. Late in the Battle of Britain, 609 was sent to patrol the Dorset coast. 'It was always a grand sight to see twelve Spitfires sweeping along together in formation,' recalled David Crook. The squadron then sighted six Me 109s below them and swept down to attack:

The victim that I had selected for myself was about 500 yards ahead of me, and still diving hard at very high speed. God, what a dive that was! I came down on full throttle from 27,000 feet to 1,000 feet in a matter of a few seconds, and the speed rose with incredible swiftness – 400mph, 500, 550, 600mph. I never reached this speed before and probably never shall again. I have a sort of dim recollection of the sea coming up towards me an incredible speed and also feeling an awful pain in my ears . . . I pulled out of the dive as gently as I could, but the strain was terrific and there was a sort of black mist in front of my eyes, though I did not quite black out.

David Crook's Spitfire had reached the borderland of the speed of sound. Only days before, 609 Squadron's J.P. Newbery and P. Ostaszewski had pulled out of power dives with such violence that they had bent their Spit's wings. But the wings had held.

PART III

Tally-Ho! – The Spitfire Offensive 1941–5

Specification No. 7/30
1 October 1931
Single Seater Day and Night Fighter
1. General Requirements
(a) The aircraft is to fulfil the duties of 'Single Seater Fighter' for
day and night flying.

Over the years the Spitfire would be a day fighter, a dive-bomber, a photo reconnaissance spy plane, a floatplane and a mail plane, but no one ever accused it of being an adequate night fighter. Somehow, somewhere in the Spitfire's gestation, R.J. Mitchell, Supermarine and the Air Ministry forgot that the original specification was for a 'day and night fighter'. The chief problem with the Spitfire at night was its long nose, as Hugh Dundas, recalled:

The Spitfire was, from the pilot's point of view, far from ideal for night flying under wartime conditions. With the tail down in the landing or take-off position, the long, broad engine cowling in front of the cockpit reduced forward vision, so that you could only see out at an angle of about forty-five degrees on either side. The single line of 'glim-lamps', which was all we were allowed as a flare path, was masked in such a way that the lights could only be seen from a narrow angle on the line of approach.

When the Spitfire was actually airborne at night, the pilot found himself blinded by the glow from the exhaust manifolds. Sometimes blinkers were fitted over the exhausts to blank out the flames, but these restricted the already limited view from the plane's cockpit. Some of the terror of landing a Spitfire at night was recalled by Geoffrey Wellum, whose friend Laurie had been killed performing a night landing:

A black void, no horizon and so straight on to the instruments and a steady climb ahead up to 1,500 feet. Levelling off and turning to port, I am just able to pick out the glim lamps showing me where my friends are and the aerodrome is located. Yes it's dark all right, think I'd better have a quiet fly around for a little while. Still feel on edge about something. Probably just plain scared. I'm not finding things easy for some reason, so a few minutes of local flying may help to settle things down a bit. Throttle well back, reduce the revs and trim her out to assume a comfortable cruise. The glow from the exhausts, helped by blinkers, is acceptable at these engine settings.

After ten minutes or so things feel a little better. Except for the flare path there is nothing else I can see. A line of glims is not very bright in the best of circumstances and there is not the faintest suggestion of a horizon, no use worrying about it, there's nothing I or anybody else can do about it so perhaps I'd better try a landing.

My first effort is a wretched exhibition. On the final approach I completely lose sight of the line of flares. There is a moment of bewilderment. Those bloody lights were there a few moments ago, so better open up and go round again. Come on Geoff, look lively, don't waste any more time or you'll be into the deck. I open the throttle wide, wheels up, flaps up, not too much of a hurry and away up to 1,100 feet again.

Well, what on earth happened there? Surely they wouldn't switch those lights off? I suppose they might have done it if there was a Hun about, but even then, not with a chap on the last stages of his final approach. Impossible anyway, glim lamps have individual switches. They are not connected to any main switch as far as I'm aware. In any case, there are the lights off to port now so let's have another go and take it easily and quietly.

Exactly the same thing happens again and as I overshoot, and climb away for the second time I realize that I'm doing something radically wrong. That time on the overshoot I caught a quick glimpse of the flares and I seemed to be crossing them at a good 30 degrees to the line. No Eddy Lewis to assist this time. My night flying during training was good and it was OK last night, so why not tonight? For goodness sake, think.

For the life of me I can't work it out, can't seem to apply my mind to the problem. The urge to just sit here and make believe the whole thing is not really happening and to quietly run out of petrol and crash is overwhelming. When I force myself to snap out of it, I merely get the sensation of having my hands very full of aeroplane. It's a horrible feeling. A bloody fine pilot you are, I don't think.

Well, I can't stay up here all night so let's try again. Help me God, please don't let me do a Laurie. I'm a bit frightened and lonely up here in the dark. I start my third attempt to land. As I turn crosswind, keeping my eyes on the flare path, the blackness seems to close in around me. I know in my own mind that I haven't solved the problem. I'm not certain exactly what it is that I'm doing wrong. However, turning in on to finals I manage to line up nicely on the line of flares. This one looks altogether better, much better. A quick glance at the instruments to check my speed. I'm a shade too slow and perhaps a little short of height, nothing much but just a fraction. Correct, Geoff laddie, a touch of throttle and keep your line on those flares for Christ's sake.

Look out of the cockpit for the final effort and the friendly line of flares has vanished. Oh, God, no: please! This is bloody impossible.

There is absolutely nothing to see but a jet black void, and I mean black. Sod it! It just cannot be. Those bloody lights were there a couple of seconds ago. Think, Geoff, quickly for God's sake. I feel a sweat break out and experience fear; stark unblemished fear. I am incapable of movement or thought, things must take their course. A voice of reason in my mind; for God's sake, Geoff, for God's sake, there's going to be a crash. You are about to die. So this is what it's like. One is composed and reconciled. I picture what will happen when I hit the ground. A blinding flash and a noise of tearing and tortured metal. Glare, a white light, very bright and a mass of sparks from the exhaust. Never seen so many before. Perhaps I've throttled back or, more likely, I'm on fire and going to burn. Oh, Dad! What a waste of money on my education. Poor Mum, she will be heartbroken. What a fool of a son they've got. I just don't understand anything anymore, just don't know what is happening except that I'm in the process of crashing and dying. Come on then, God, get it over with or I'll go over to the other side, you see if I don't. Ask the Devil. What was it the man said, 'If you break one there will be merry hell to pay'?

Presumably instinctive reactions. Opposite rudder and stick back into my tummy. I sit waiting for it. No longer frightened strangely enough; just totally resigned. I'm amazed it hasn't happened yet. It's terribly dark, only a sort of rushing sound, almost soothing and I close my eyes. A heavy thud; something's touched. I wonder what? Come on, why delay it any longer?

Listen, God, you're not only difficult to find but you're also a hard task master. All is now so quiet. It's peaceful. Another fearful thump followed by a bump and a strange sensation of what appears to be the rumble of wheels over rough ground. I just do not understand it, or is it that I'm dead? That probably is the answer. Yes, that's it because we seem to be stationary and it's so quiet. We've stopped, I'm sure we have. Am I alive or is this death? I think I'm alive and that's all that matters, but it's very very still and quiet. Perhaps I've bought it after all; then again, perhaps not. It's all so confusing. The red cockpit lights still glow and the cockpit itself is almost cosy. Induces a drowsy feeling, but why is it so quiet? I don't think the engine is running, which is odd. Of course it's not odd, you stupid bastard, if you've crashed. But if we are sitting on the ground in a more or less normal attitude, then surely it should be running? It all happened so quickly, whatever is going on.

It would appear that the ignition switches are off. That would be the reason for the engine being stopped and the stillness. I must have switched the magneto switches off somewhere along the line but I don't remember doing it. Must have acted pretty quickly. I just sit strapped to my seat. It's quite comfortable and peaceful. I wonder what has happened. What really occurred?

Well, I suppose I'd better make a move and see if I can get out of this thing and then that would prove once and for all if I really any alive or not. I can't open the door. I must be dead. Someone is standing on the wing beside the cockpit. The red cockpit lights reflect on his face. He's ghostly; ah! that's it, the Holy Ghost or a ghost of some sort. Or is it Brian? The figure looks at me for a few seconds.

'What the bloody hell do you think you're up to? What are you doing? Come on. Don't just sit there.'

'I don't know and please don't rush me.'

'Look Geoffrey, come on. Get out of this aeroplane. Come on. Make a move, we can't stay out here all night. Here, I'll give you a hand.'

'OK.'

'What the blazes went wrong with you? You hit the Chance Light one hell of a crack.'

'Oh, is that what I did?'

'I'll say, and furthermore, you've not only written-off the Chance Light but at least a quarter of your port wing is stuck on what was the top of it. By God, Wellum, you were lucky. I've never seen a prang like it, how bloody lucky can you get? You should have been killed.'

'Yes. I must have been very lucky indeed.'

The end of the Battle of Britain in October 1940 and the resultant shift by the Luftwaffe to the night-time bombing of British cities brought the nocturnal inadequacy of the RAF's premier fighter into sharp relief. Although Hugh Dowding had no responsibility for the Spitfire's design, he seemed to have no answers either, to the need to bolster Britain's defences against the German nocturnal menace. In the weeks following the Battle, the Air Chief Marshal found other complaints about him mounting; he was too old, he was fatigued, and – most damningly of all – he failed to appreciate the Big Wing beloved of Douglas Bader. Dowding, the architect of Britain's aerial salvation, was sacked in November 1940 after behind-the-scenes political manoeuvring led by Lord Trenchard, 'The Father of the RAF', Archibald Sinclair, the Air Secretary, and the Tory MP Peter Macdonald, who also happened to be the adjutant of Bader's squadron at Duxford. With Dowding went Air Vice-Marshal Keith Park. Dowding's 'chicks' were dismayed on hearing the news of his departure. Wilfrid Duncan Smith wrote later:

The news came as a shock to most of us because he had schemed the victory, held Fighter Command together in the Battle of Britain through critical periods and proved himself an all-time great among air commanders. Though he was relatively unknown personally to many pilots, a great bond of affection and respect flowed between them in the knowledge that he was expert in making decisions of far reaching effect and would go to any lengths to support his subordinate commanders and squadrons.

Dowding's replacement as Commander-in-Chief Fighter Command was Sholto Douglas, the former Deputy Chief of the Air Staff. Trafford Leigh-Mallory, the former commander of 12 Group, took over Park's 11 Group. Both Douglas and Leigh-Mallory believed in the Big Wing as the means to stop the Luftwaffe, both were more offensively minded than Dowding and Park. 'We have stopped licking our wounds,' wrote Leigh-Mallory. 'We are going over to the offensive. Last year our fighting was desperate but now we are entitled to be cockier.' The era of the Rhubarb, Circus and Ramrod had arrived.

In the lingo of the Spitfire pilot, a Ramrod was a bombing mission with a definite target in Occupied France or the Low Countries. A Circus was a bomb raid with the objective of smoking out the Luftwaffe. For both Ramrods and Circuses, Spits acted as escorts. A Rhubarb was a low-level strafing attack by Spitfires, in pairs or fours. The jocular nouns belied the dangerousness of the missions. Even an 'average' sortie over Occupied France was guaranteed to be hair-raising. Sergeant Jo Van Schaik of 609 Squadron filed the following combat report following a typical Circus over Lille in summer 1941:

I was Blue 3, 609 Sqdn. Acting as Escort Cover Wing during Circus operation against Lille. Shortly after leaving the target area I was attacked by two Me 109Fs out of the sun, and felt my A/C struck in the tail. I broke away downwards and headed for home, rapidly losing height. I was down to 3,000ft. Over Calais and was planning an attack on a gun post on the beach when tracer appeared from astern and turning round I saw two Me 109Fs on my tail, these presumably being the same ones as before. All three of us went into a turning circle at 500ft over the housetops. I broke away, as my A/C was not perfectly functioning and headed across the Channel. Both E/A, however, attacked me again and I was hit in the starboard mainplane. Then I did a steep turn on to the tail of one E/A, fired with cannon and I saw his starboard wing tip drop off. This E/A then departed and the other attacked me head-on. We both fired together; I with M/G. I noticed no damage to this A/C then, but after a further turning circle at sea level, I hit him with cannon fire, and oil and glycol were emitted. He beat it homeward, still streaming. Previously I had called 'M'aidez' on button D, and now in answer to the Controller's enquiry, I said I thought I could make the coast, which I successfully did at Manston.

A procession of Spitfire pilots who survived the Battle of Britain would not survive the Ramrod, Rhubarbs and Circuses of 1941–2.

Fighter Command's new offensive spirit required both more Spitfires and a beefier Spitfire. Production was increased to a point where it exceeded losses, so that by September 1941, twenty-seven squadrons operated Spitfires, compared to nineteen at the height of the Battle of Britain. Fighter Command also got a new production Spitfire in 1941, the Mark V, to deal with the Luftwaffe's latest Me 109, the Me 109F. Intended as a stopgap, the Mark V became the most numerous mark ever; no less than 6,787 were built. The main production version of the Spitfire V carried an armament of two 20mm Hispano cannon and four 7.7mm (.303in) Browning machine guns. The Rolls-Royce

Merlin 45 engine developed 1,4070hp. Maximum speed was 371mph at 20,000 feet. The service ceiling was 38,000 feet. There was another improvement to the Spitfire.

Hitherto the Spitfire had suffered one crucial disadvantage compared to its Luftwaffe rival, the Me 109. The Merlin engine did not possess fuel injection, so would 'conk out' in a negative G-dive. Tests on a captured Me 109 had shown the Me 109's fuel injector pumps to be an 'outstanding characteristic'. Beatrice Shilling, a scientist at the Royal Aircraft Establishment in Farnborough, devised a temporary solution in 1941, which became known jokily among the thankful pilots as 'Miss Shilling's orifice'. The said 'orifice' was a hole punched through a metal diaphragm fitted across the Merlin's SU (Skinners Union) carburettors, and this prevented petrol swamping the top of the carburettors when the Spitfire went into the dive. A true fuel injection system for the Spitfire, the Bendix-Stromberg carburettor, had to wait until 1942.

'I loathed those Rhubarbs with a deep, dark hatred,' recalled Johnnie Johnson of 616 Squadron. He was not alone; aside from the stirred up, waspish Luftwaffe fighters to deal with, there was invariably a gauntlet of flak to run on a Rhubarb. Johnson's squadron leader, on the other hand, was only too delighted to carry the war to the enemy. The spring and summer of 1941 were the heyday of Douglas Bader's all guns blazing 'Tangmere Wing', recently joined by 616 Squadron and novice pilot officer Johnnie Johnson. Johnson may not have loved Rhubarbs, but he came to love Bader, the sky warrior. Johnson recalled his first mission with Bader:

Climbing and still holding a close formation, we curved across the Channel. I was in the number three position in

Bader's section and ahead of me were Cocky and the wing commander. Behind me, in the unenviable tail-end Charlie position, was an apprehensive Nip. Suddenly I sported three lean 109s only a few hundred feet higher than our formation and travelling in the same direction. Obviously they hadn't seen us and would make an ideal target for a section of 145 Squadron, who were still higher than the 109s. I should have calmly reported the number, type and position of the 109s to our leader, but I was excited and shouted, 'Look out, Dogsbody!' [The call sign of Bader was derived from his initials – D.B.]

But the other pilots of the wing weren't waiting for further advice from me. To them 'look out' was a warning of the utmost danger – of the dreaded bounce by a strong force of 109s. Now they took swift evasive action and half-rolled, dived, aileron-turned and swung out in all directions, like a wedge of fast moving teal avoiding a wild-fowler on the coast. In far less time than it takes to tell, a highly organized wing was reduced to a shambles and the scattered sections could never be re-formed in time to continue the planned flight. I was the last to land, for I had realized the error and knew the consequences would be unpleasant. They were all waiting in the dispersal hut.

'Close the door, Billy,' ordered Bader. And then:

'Now who's the clot who shouted "look out"?'

I admitted that I was the guilty party.

'Very well. Now tell us what we had to "look out" for?' demanded the angry wing commander.

'Well, sir, there were three 109s a few hundred feet above . . .'

'Three 109s!' interrupted Bader. 'We could have clobbered the lot. But your girlish scream made us think there were fifty of the brutes behind.'

This public rebuke hurt deeply, but it was well justified, for our first operation together had been a complete failure, thanks to my error. Bader went on to deliver an impromptu lecture on tactics. We were utterly dependent upon each other for cross cover and accurate reporting. In future the words 'look out' would not be used. In dire emergencies we would cry 'break port, blue section' or even 'break port, Ken', for Bader preferred the use of Christian names. The pilot who called the break would then be responsible for controlling the safety of the formation until it was out of danger. In all other instances enemy aircraft would be reported according to the clock code, with full details, thus: 'Dogsbody from red two. Six 109s at two o'clock, high. About 2,000 yards.'

Bader concluded his lecture, and since he was always quick to forgive, he gave me an encouraging grin when he stumped out of the dispersal hut. I never forgot this lesson.

One morning shortly afterwards we were released until noon after some night patrols. I had not flown during the night and Ken had left instructions that I was to check the Spitfires of our flight and carry out any air tests that were necessary. I was discussing the aircraft with our flight sergeant when the wing commander swaggered in. We sprang to attention.

'Sit down, old boy. Where's the chaps?'

'In bed, sir,' I answered. 'They were all up late on a fighter night and we don't come to readiness until one o'clock.'

'Any luck?' he enquired.

'No, sir. None of them had a squirt,' I replied.

Bader grunted. 'The Spitfire's not as good as the Hurricane at night. More room in the cockpit and a better view. And the Spit's much trickier to land at night on that little, narrow undercarriage.' He paused to light his pipe and continued, 'I'm having a Hurricane sent down which I'll fly at night. Sailor [Adolph Malan] got a couple of Heinkels one night last year, and there's no reason why we shouldn't hack clown a few more.' And after a further pause, 'What are you doing now?'

'Flight Lieutenant Holden sent me down to check our aircraft, sir. I've got a couple of air tests,' I answered.

'Good show,' grinned Bader. 'You and I will slide up through this bit of cloud, nip across the Channel and see if we can bag a couple of Huns before lunch. It will be a pleasant surprise for Flight Lieutenant Holden, eh?'

I said there would be little doubt on this score!

We took off together and climbed through several layers of cloud. When we finally broke out into the warm sunshine, Bader grinned and waved his hand before his face, the signal for me to take up a wide abreast position.

I could hardly believe that I was flying as wingman to the legendary pilot. But there he was only a few yards away with his initials and wing commander's pennant painted on the fuselage of his Spitfire. There would be no reporting mistakes this time.

The radio buzzed with static, and the Tangmere controller broke the silence.

'Dogsbody, from Beetle 1. You receiving?'

Bader was equally abrupt. 'Loud and clear, out.'

And soon afterwards the controller again: 'Dogsbody, what are your intentions?'

Silence from Dogsbody. Now Bader was curving our Spitfires to the south. Beachy Head should be below and in ten minutes we would be crossing the French coast.

'Dogsbody. I say again, what are your intentions? The station commander would like to know.' This, of course, was an order that could not be ignored.

'Tell him that Dogsbody section, two aircraft, are going on a little snoop over the Channel. Nothing exciting, just a little routine snoop. Out.'

The controller acknowledged this information, but he was on the air main within a few seconds.

'Dogsbody, you are not to proceed with your flight. You are to return immediately. I say again, return immediately. Is this understood?'

Bader said that it was fully understood and uttered a strong oath that stung the ears of the controller and startled the Waaf plotters in the ops. room, for all our conversations were broadcast by loudspeakers. But we turned about and dropped through the cloud to pick up the Sussex coastline.

'Line astern. Johnnie. And I'll show you how to get on the tail of a 109. A steep climb, a tight turn. Tighter yet. We can always turn inside the brutes and' – (a rude noise meant to imitate machine gun fire) – 'nothing to it. A piece of cake, isn't it? Once more.'

It was while with the Tangmere Wing that Bader and Hugh 'Cocky' Dundas evolved the 'finger formation', the British version of the Luftwaffe's standard fighter formation. As Flying Officer Dundas of 616 Squadron wrote later:

We sat up late in the mess one evening, several of us together, discussing battle formations. We were expressing dissatisfaction with the formations adopted in the past. In 1940 the squadrons of Fighter Command had all flown the same basic formation. The twelve aircraft of a squadron were divided into four sections of three aircraft each. Normally these sections flew in 'Vic' formation – that is to say, one plane on each side of the leader and a little behind him. When going into action this formation would be changed to line astern. The last man in the last section was responsible for 'weaving'; swerving from side to side in order to keep a good look out to the rear.

Having frequently flown in that tail-end position, I knew well the difficulties and hazards involved. It you weaved too much, you got left behind. If you did not weave enough, you got picked off. I said that I thought it was a lousy formation and that no variation of it would be any good. For instance, we had been experimenting with the idea of flying in three sections of four, aircraft line astern. The last man in each section was still excessively vulnerable. We needed to find something quite different, some way of flying which would cut out all that weaving around and enable everyone to cover everyone else's tail.

The half pints went down again and again, while we argued the toss. I was in favour of trying line-abreast formation, already extensively used by the Germans. I argued that four aircraft flying side by side, each one about fifty yards from his neighbour, could never be surprised from behind. The two on the left would cover the tails of the two on the right, and vice versa. No enemy plane could get within shooting distance without being seen. If attacked, you would break outwards, one pair to port, the other pair to starboard.

Next morning I was sitting at breakfast feeling just a little queasy and concentrating on black coffee, when Bader came and sat at the same table. He never drank beer, or anything else containing alcohol, and he appeared quite the reverse of queasy. Bright, breezy and aggressive are the words which came to mind in describing his demeanour. I did not pay too much attention when he referred to our discussion of the previous evening. I just went on concentrating on the coffee. When he said that he had been thinking about the idea of line-abreast formation and had decided to try it, I let the matter pass. His next remark, however, riveted my attention.

'We'll give it a try this morning – make a pass down the Pas de Calais. Probably find something there. You'd better come with me, Cocky. I'll fix it with Woodie (the Station Commander) and let you know what time.'

He told Paddy Woodhouse, the CU of 610 Squadron, who was sitting with us, to get himself a number two and to stand by to come along too. Then he stumped off to make the arrangements.

'Oh God,' I thought, 'you bloody fool, Dundas. That will teach you to keep your big mouth shut.' I pushed my coffee cup away and left the room feeling queasier than ever.

The Tangmere Wing's first try at finger four was a near disaster, resulting in Cocky Dundas being shot down, but thankfully not hurt. In the irony of ironies, the Luftwaffe pilot who downed Dundas on the afternoon of 8 May 1941 was likely Oberst

Werner Mölders – the very self-same Werner Mölders who had first devised the four plane fighter formation.

In a lyrical note, written in the high summer of 1941, Dundas caught for posterity the extraordinary atmosphere around the Tangmere Wing of Douglas Bader:

It was hot in the garden, lying face down on the lawn, a pot of iced shandy by my hand, Robin [my golden retriever] huffing and puffing and panting at the ants. Odd to be lying there peacefully, listening to the click of croquet balls, the blur of voices, the gramophone. The shandy sharp, cold, stimulating.

'Hullo, Cocky.'

'Hullo, Johnnie.'

'Get a squirt this morning, Cocky?'

'Yes, Johnnie, I got a squirt. Missed the bastard as usual, though.'

'Another show this afternoon, Cocky. Take off 15.30.'

'Yes, I know; take off 15.30.' Three hours ago, over Lille. It happened yesterday, and last week, and last month. It will happen again in exactly two and a half hours, and tomorrow, and next month.

The grass smelt sweet in the garden, and the shandy was good, and Robin's panting, and the gramophone playing, 'Momma may I go out dancing – yes, my darling daughter'.

It was hot at dispersal and the grass, what was left of it, brown and oil-stained. The Spitfires creaked and twanged in the sun.

'Everything under control, Hally?' [Flying Officer Hall was the squadron engineer officer.]

'Yes, Cocky, everything under control. DB's not ready yet, but it will be.' [DB were the identification letters of Bader's plane.]

'Well, for Christ's sake see that it is, or there'll be some laughing off to do.'

'It will be ready, Cocky.'

'OK, Hally.'

Inside is as hot as outside. The pilots, dressed almost as they like, lie about sweating.

'Chalk please, Durham.'

They all watch as I chalk initials under the diagram of twelve aircraft in three sections of four. Nobody moves much until I have finished and written the time of take-off.

'Smith, you'll be with DB. Nip, you and I on his right. Johnnie, you with the CO and two of 'B' Flight. OK?'

'OK, Cocky.'

Here comes DB.

'Why the bloody hell isn't my aircraft ready? Cocky, my bloody aeroplane's not ready. We take off in twenty minutes. Where's that prick Hally?'

'It's OK DB, it'll be ready. I've seen Hally.'

'Well, look at the bloody thing. They haven't even got the cowlings on yet. Oi, Hally, come here!'

Christ, I wish we could get going.

'Chewing gum, Johnnie, please. Thanks, pal.'

'OK, DB?'

'Yes, Cocky, it's going to be OK.'

'We walk together again, as far as the road.'

'Well, good luck, Cocky. And watch my tail, you old bastard.' 'I'll do that, DB. Good luck.'

Just time for two or three more puffs before climbing into A for Apple.

'Everything OK, Goodlad?' [the fitter who looked after my plane.]

'OK, sir.'

'Good show. Bloody hot.'

Climbing in, the hottest thing of all. The old girl shimmers like an oven, twangs and creaks.

'Good luck, sir.'

'Thanks.'

Up the line DB's motor starts. 610 have formed up and are beginning to move off across the airfield as we taxi out – DB, myself, Smithie, Nip, then two composite sections from both flights.

Straggle over the grandstand at Goodwood in a right-hand turn and set course east in a steady climb, Ken's twelve a little above and behind to the left, Stan's out to the right.

Ten thousand feet over Shoreham. The old familiar, nostalgic taste in the mouth. Brighton – Maxim's last Saturday night; dancing with Diana in the Norfolk. Beachy, once a soft summer playground, now gaunt buttress sticking its chin bluntly out towards our enemies. Spread out now into wide semi-independent fours. Glint of perspex way out and above to the south shows Stan and his boys nicely placed between us and the sun. Dungeness slides slowly past to port and we still climb steadily, straight on, way out in front.

Twenty-five thousand.

'Levelling out.'

Puffs of black ten thousand feet below show where the bombers are crossing between Boulogne and Le Touquet.

Six big cigars with tiers of protective fighters milling above them.

'Hello Douglas, Woody calling. There are fifty plus gaining height to the east.'

'OK, Woody.'

'Put your corks in, boys.' Stan.

Over the coast at Hardelot we nose ahead without altering course. 'DB, there's some stuff at three o'clock, climbing round to the southwest.'

'OK, I see it. Stan, you deal with them if necessary.'

'OK, OK. Don't get excited.'

Usual remarks. Usual shouts of warning. Usual bad language. Usual bloody Huns climbing round the usual bloody way.

St Omer on the left. We fly on, straight and steady in our fours, towards Lille. Stan's voice: 'They're behind us, Walker squadron. Stand by to break.'

Then, 'Look out, Walker. Breaking starboard.'

Looking over my shoulder to the right and above, I see the specks and glints which are Stan's planes break up into the fight, a quick impression of machines diving, climbing, gyrating. Stan, Ian, Tony, Derek and the rest of them are fighting for their lives up there.

Close to the target area now. More black puffs below show where the bombers are running in through the flak.

'Billy here, DB. There's a lot of stuff coming round at three o'clock, slightly above.'

Quick look to the right. Where the hell? Christ, yes! There they are, the sods. A typical long, fast, climbing straggle of 109s.

'More below, DB, to port.'

'OK, going down. Ken, watch those buggers behind.'

'OK, DB.'

'Come on, Cocky.'

Down after DB. The Huns are climbing fast to the south. Have to get in quick before those sods up above get at us. Turn right, open up slightly. We are diving to two or three hundred feet below their level. DB goes for the one on the left. Nipple is on my right. Johnnie slides across beyond him. Getting in range now. Wait for it, wait for DB and open up all together. 250 yards . . . 200 . . . wish to Christ I felt *safer* behind . . . 150. DB opens up. I pull my nose up slightly to put the dot a little ahead of his orange spinner. Hold it and squeeze, cannon and machine guns together . . . correct slightly . . . you're hitting the bastard . . . wisp of smoke.

'BREAK, Rusty squadron, for Christ's sake BREAK!'

Stick hard over and back into tummy, peak revs and haul her round. Tracers curl past . . . orange nose impression not forty yards off . . . slacken turn for a second . . . hell of a melee . . . better keep turning, keep turning, keep turning.

There's a chance, now. Ease off, nose up, give her two lengths' lead and fire. Now break, don't hang around, break! Tracers again . . . a huge orange spinner and three little tongues of flame spitting at me for a second in a semi-head-on attack. Round, round, so that she judders and nearly spins. Then they're all gone, gone as usual as suddenly as they came.

'Cocky, where the hell are you? Are you with me, Cocky?'

There he is, I think. Lucky to find him after that shambles. 'OK, DB, coming up on your starboard now.'

'Right behind you, Cocky.' That's Johnnie calling.

'OK, Johnnie, I see you.'

Good show; the old firm's still together.

It was cooler on the lawn, and still. The shadows from the tall trees stretched out to the east. Robin lay beside me pressing his muzzle into the grass, huffing at insects. The pint pot of Pimms was cool in my hands and the ice clinked when I moved. The cucumber out of the drink was good and cold and sharp when I sucked it.

'Hullo, Cocky.'

'What-ho, Johnnie.'

'Tough about Derek.'

'Yes Johnnie; and Mab.'

The croquet balls sounded loud to my ear, pressed in the grass. The distant gramophone started again on 'Momma, may I go out dancing'.

'Come on you old bastard, let's drink up and get out of here.'

The tide washed up the creek to Bosham and splashed against the balcony of the Old Ship. We sat and sipped our good, warm, heartening brandy and watched the red sun dip through the western haze, watched the stars light one by one, watched the two swans gliding past like ghost ships.

'Cocky.'

'Yes, Johnnie.'

'Readiness at four a.m.'

'OK, let's go.'

The consummate war-leader, Bader was also the consummate stunt flyer. But once, to the amazement of everyone at Tangmere, not least Bader himself, there arrived on the airfield an airman whose acrobatic skills eclipsed those of 'DB' himself. Johnson recalled:

Bader's frequent, almost daily displays were the delight of the ground crews, and we all strolled on to the tarmac to watch the wing commander.

His favourite manoeuvre was to climb swiftly to a height of about 3,000 feet over the centre of the airfield. Then he would aileron-turn into a steep dive and, just above our heads, reef the Spitfire into a series of upward rolls before regaining level flight with a roll off the top of the loop. The display was faultless whenever he carried out two upward Charlies [pilot jargon for rolls], but after a few days at Tangmere he attempted to introduce a third roll into the drill. The evolution was now seldom achieved with its former polish and often our wing commander stalled his Spitfire and spun ignominiously before the assembly. But his aerobatics revealed the pattern of his approach to life, he would not give up and tried, without marked success, to perfect the manoeuvre.

Some time later there was posted to the squadron a somewhat elderly, pedantic and heavily mustachioed flight lieutenant who, although possessing no combat experience, proved to be an aerobatic pilot of exceptional ability.

One hot day in the early summer, Bader had given the troops his usual breezy performance and was now lounging in his under shirt, cooling off after his exertions in the warm cockpit and chatting to Billy Burton and Ken Holden.

'Y'know, Billy, the Spit's not built to do more than two upward Charlies before the roll off the top. It's just not got the speed. I've pulled it off once or twice, but she's very slow at the top. Uncomfortable.' And the wing commander sucked his pipe reflectively. He continued:

'We ought to start some formation aerobatics here. The ground troops would love it. Ken could lead. I'll fly on the starboard and Billy on the port. And if the Huns won't come up, we'll put on a show over St Omer!'

But any further conversation was interrupted by the shattering roar of a Spitfire that retracted its wheels a few feet above our heads. It was our new flight lieutenant. Bader looked displeased and grunted:

'I say, Billy! Who's that chap? Can't have that sort of thing. Bad flying discipline.' We turned away to hide our grins.

All eyes were now glued on the newcomer, who stall-turned and streaked down towards our little group. Overhead he pulled the Spitfire into a steep climb and straight as an arrow, he commenced a series of beautiful climbing rolls. It was as if he had thrown the gauntlet at the wing commander's feet. Fascinated we watched and counted the evolutions.

'One.'

'Two,' we chanted out aloud.

'He'll never do the roll-off,' said Bader.

'Three,' we chorused and the Spitfire, now quite vertical, arced directly above.

'He'll never make it. No speed. I could've told him,' commented Bader.

Very slowly but with perfect timing the Spitfire half-rolled off the top of the loop and resumed level flight. The whole manoeuvre was carried out with exquisite skill, and to demonstrate that it was no fluke the pilot repeated the performance and side-slipped his Spitfire to a perfect three-point landing. And so he became the aerobatic king of Tangmere.

The acrobat of the air was Flight Lieutenant E.P.P. 'Patrick' Gibbs, shortly to be shot up over France; he escaped his aerial pursuers, however, by faking an inverted crash-dive only to flip the Spitfire over at the last moment and perform a textbook landing. He then eluded police and army pursuers by running off, and not stopping until he reached Spain.

Others were not as fortunate as 'Gibbo'. The Rhubarbs, Ramrods and Circuses took a deadly toll on the Spitfire boys. Pilot Officer Wilfrid Duncan Smith flew with 611 Squadron out of Hornchurch:

As the last sweltering days of June reached new heights in temperatures we seemed to get as many as four offensive sorties a day. One afternoon, with the sun scorching through the canopy of my Spitfire, I flew with 'Polly' Pollard as the Squadron climbed steadily for North Foreland. Our task was to act as high cover to bombers whose targets were the marshalling yards at Hazebrouck. We crossed the French coast at 28,000 ft, the sun glinting on the perspex of our cockpit hoods and long vapour trails streaming behind us. Below, I could see the stepped formations of the lower escort squadrons stretching down to the neatly packed group of twelve Blenheims with their close escort of Hurricanes, at about 12,000 ft. We called it the 'Beehive' because with individual aircraft weaving and jinking, the whole affair looked like a swarm of bees.

As we approached Hazebrouck, a formation of ten Me 109s, slightly below, came towards us. Eric Stapleton turned into them and started to dive; immediately the enemy formation rolled on to their backs and disappeared past the tail of the 'Beehive'. Almost on top of the target another formation of fifteen Me 109s appeared below and we promptly dived for them. They saw us coming and broke into our attack. I stuck close to 'Polly' as we waltzed around trying to get on to their tails. One group of 109s then broke right with two sections after them, while 'Polly' and I with two others latched on to four Me 109s circling across our left front. Swiftly we turned inside them and got into range. 'Polly' called me: 'Take the right 109 Charlie Two, I'll get the other.'

We were now well placed and the 109s stayed with us in a tight circle. They were staggered, the one on the right slightly above and behind the left-hand one with ourselves in a commanding position behind and a couple of hundred feet above.

I swung my nose across closing fast and as the 109 filled the width of my windscreen, I blasted into the side of his cockpit and engine. Bits flew off and thick smoke gushed; the 109 rolled slowly over and plunged vertically down. As I prepared to follow, tracers streaked past my cockpit and over the top of my propeller. I broke sharply in a right-hand climbing turn. 'Polly's' voice hit my earphones: 'Good boy, Charlie Two. Climb. I'm above.'

Wildly I looked round for 'Polly'. Turning, I saw two Me 109s flash past behind me, then above them the unmistakable wing pattern of a Spitfire. Giving my aircraft every pound of boost I had I rocketed upwards in a tight spiral. 'Polly' saw me coming and nosed towards me.

'Did you get one Charlie Leader?' I called him.

'Think so, can't tell – had to break – attacked by six bastards.' His reply snapped and crackled as other voices cut in.

We searched for the rest of the Squadron but could not see them. Below and above Spitfires wheeled. We were somewhere near the tail end of the 'Beehive'. I glanced at my altimeter and saw we had lost a lot of height. Smoke and dust clouds were rising from the target area below, and away to our right the bombers were flying homewards, angry black puffs of AA shell bursts following them.

'Let's get right into the "Beehive" and climb up.' 'Polly's' voice was flat. Experience had taught me never to fly straight and level, but to search the sky continually. Now as I searched behind my heart leapt into my mouth. Streaking straight at us in a loose line-abreast formation were – I couldn't believe it – nine Me 109s and they were too damned close for comfort.

'Charlie Leader, break.'

Close together we swung into a tight climbing turn to face the enemy.

It was no good. Three more 109s came at us from ahead. I saw the guns of the leading 109 wink at me and tracers flew past – there was a loud bang somewhere along my fuselage. The next second I was fighting for my life.

Again I heard 'Polly's' voice as I turned my Spitfire in a tight circle, wings shuddering, vision clouded in a grey mist as the blood drained from my head.

'Look out behind – dive for the deck.' My radio was terribly noisy.

I slewed round in my harness and looked behind. I saw a Me 109 slightly above with 'Polly' on his tail firing. I heaved my Spitfire round trying desperately to get behind 'Polly's' machine. Suddenly the 109 at which 'Polly' was firing at broke into a red glow; black smoke gushed and it hurtled down. More tracer whizzed past and once again I was corkscrewing out of the way. I caught a glimpse of 'Polly' as he rolled on his back and dived for the ground in a tight spiral, and immediately lost sight of him against the dark pattern of fields and woodland below. Just then the 109 that had fired at me shot past my port wing tip terribly close and I got a glimpse of a black helmeted head peering out as the enemy dived below me.

I rocketed down after the 109. He was out of range, losing height in a gentle dive. I glanced round behind, above, below – the sky was clear. Fairly close now and over on my left I could see the French coast. Slowly I gained on the enemy still diving and keeping just below his slipstream. Then at last the 109 began to loom large in my windscreen. I held my fire, a quick look behind; I had no intention of fouling it up. I was determined not to open fire until I was sure I could not miss. Now, I was ready to make the kill. I eased the stick forward a little and at close range pulled the nose of my Spitfire up sharply, lined up my sight and opened fire, pouring cannon shells into the enemy's belly. There was a sheet of flame, the 109 flicked over on to its back and dived straight into the ground. It crashed close to the corner of a wood, near a whitewashed and neat-looking farmhouse. I circled once clipping the tops of the trees with my wing tip, watching the column of black smoke belching into the air from the wreck. I felt elated and terribly pleased with myself.

I scrambled somehow back to Manston, hugging first the grey-green fields of France at treetop height, then the uninviting and hostile waters of the Channel. I didn't have much fuel to spare; I got down with about two sherry glasses left, and by now in a thoroughly filthy frame of mind, upset and frightened.

Later, back at Hornchurch, I discovered that between us we had destroyed seven Me 109s and probably destroyed or damaged a further five. As far as I was concerned there was nothing to celebrate, for tragically, 'Polly' had not returned. I hung about dispersal till late in the evening, then paced up and down in my room in a whirlpool of emotions. Operations had tried all the airfields, air/sea rescue units, the Navy. Nothing.

We had flown together many times and I had learned that by sticking together even when separated from the rest of the Squadron we could engage the enemy with success. The strength of the enemy attack this time had forced us apart because, as 'Polly' dived away I could not follow, since I was under attack myself. By then I had the bit between my teeth, against all advice and the known hazards of following a Me 109 diving back into France. But I had done it before and got away with it so why not this time? A cannon shell had hit my radio set and wrecked it. We were no longer in touch – no longer a fighting partnership – and in a matter of seconds lost touch for ever.

The loss of a close friend in war stirs a deeper feeling of personal sorrow because of its abrupt and harsh reality. Though there is no reason to brood on the tragedy, the chances are that if his name is mentioned it will recall the happy moments of laughter shared, and never any of darkness. Though it makes one aware of the uncertainty of life, it also hardens the will to survive and in a strange way the thought of death as the final enemy transforms it instead into an honourable escape.

F/O Pollard was seen by Charlie 2 to open fire on a Me 109E, which burst into flames and is therefore claimed as destroyed. F/O Pollard did not return from this sortie, and this report and claim are therefore submitted on his behalf.

Then one of 611's greatest aces fell to German guns. On 3 August 1941 the following note was entered in the Squadron Operations Record Book:

Slightly cloudy morning turned to lovely sunny afternoon. Six pairs of the squadron indulged in Rhubarbs, one in the morning and five pairs in the afternoon, but there was insufficient cloud cover over France so everyone came back except 'Lockie' (F/Lt E.S. Lock DSO, DFC) who went with F/Lt Cathels (403 Squadron) at D'Hardelot and was last seen streaking down a road at the back of Boulogne, brassing off soldiers on bicycles and whooping over the R/T, 'Ha-ha, look at the bastards running.' It seems a ruddy awful waste to lose so great a pilot on so trivial an expedition. It is anticipated that the German press will make much of Lock's capture or death. His aircraft was a Spitfire Vb W3257.

Lock, victor of twenty-six aerial encounters, was twenty-two at the time of his death.

Fighter Command was once again bleeding pilots; in six weeks from mid-June to the end of August 1941 the Command lost

194 pilots and planes on cross-Channel excursions. At Tangmere, 616 Squadron lost half of its full establishment of twenty-four pilots. The Tangmere Wing's casualties included its leader and talisman, Douglas Bader, on 8 August. Bader, of course, was too big for death; he survived baling out and landing in France on just one of his tin legs. Captured, he proved to be an object of interest to his Luftwaffe opposite numbers, among them Adolf Galland, who invited the British ace to tea:

An officer, a sergeant major and the driver fetched Bader in style. Some of our commanders and several other officers had tea with their British guest at the Group Staff Headquarters, and he was obviously surprised and impressed by the lavishness of the reception. Only after some time did he overcome the distrust he could not hide, in spite of his charming and winning manners.

Bader was on his guard against giving the slightest hint of any military information, and in any case we were strictly forbidden to interrogate prisoners; this was left entirely to specialists at the interrogation centres. Nevertheless, I had given instructions that nothing should be said which could even resemble a question. He did not even admit how many enemy planes he had to his credit.

'Oh, not many,' he said. He did not know how many had been recognised, and confirmations were still outstanding. 'Well, you must know approximately how many,' I urged him. 'No,' he replied, avoiding the issue defensively. 'Compared with Molders and your bag, they are so few that it's hardly worth talking about them.' Actually he had some twenty to his credit. Perhaps it really was only modesty that he did not want to talk about it with us.

Bader loosened up during the course of this free and easy conversation, so I proposed a little tour of our installations, which he accepted with pleasure and obvious interest. The leg which had been salvaged from the wreckage, squeaked and rattled like a small armoured car. Bader asked me if we could not drop a message over England to tell his boys and his wife that he was well and to get him his spare legs, a better uniform than his battledress, tobacco, and a new pipe to replace the broken one he had stuck together with adhesive tape. His wife would know what to do. The spare legs were on the left in the wardrobe. I offered him some tobacco and one of my pipes, but he refused. Naturally, it was outside my province to give him a definite promise to fulfil this request, which was certainly of considerable originality, but I promised I would do my best.

The masterly way in which our airfield was camouflaged attracted his attention as an expert, and a long conversation about technical details followed, during which he praised the better points of the Messerschmitt while we praised the Spitfire. Would I allow him to sit in the cockpit of my plane? 'Why not!' Everything had to be explained to him in the smallest detail. I enjoyed the interest and understanding this great pilot showed. He would have fitted splendidly into our 'Club'.

Bader bent down to me from the cockpit of my plane, in which he was sitting, and said, 'Will you do me a great favour?'

'With pleasure, if it is in my power,' I answered.

'At least once in my life I would like to fly a Messerschmitt. Let me do just one circle over the airfield.' He said it with a smile and looked me straight in the eyes. I nearly weakened, but replied:

'If I grant your wish, I'm afraid you'll escape and I should be forced to chase after you. Now we have met, we don't want to shoot at each other again, do we?' He laughed and we changed the subject. After a hearty goodbye, he went back to the hospital.

I immediately got in touch with Göring, reported my admiration for the legless Wing Commander and asked permission to have the spare legs sent. Göring agreed at once, maintaining that Bader's was the same spirit as they had shared during the First World War. They had extended any possible service they could to their shot down opponents, even though they had been enemies. We were to make radio contact with the RAF on international SOS wavelengths, offering free conduct to a British plane which could land on an airfield near the coast and unload all the things Bader wanted.

Radio contact was made, and our message about Bader's capture and his wishes was confirmed by the British. I was pleased that here, in the middle of the war, an action was about to be performed which would rise above the national bitterness of the fighting on both sides.

Some time later Bader vanished: during the night he had let himself down from a top window of the hospital by sheets knotted together and had escaped. This was very unpleasant for me and the persons responsible, and Command made a most embarrassing enquiry into his escape. Even his visit to our air base, for which I had not asked permission, came up in the course of a stern investigation.

The whole affair became even more unpleasant on account of Bader's spare leg. The British did not wait for our detailed suggestions. Soon after our aerodrome and other targets around St. Omer had been heavily raided, we received a radio message over the same wavelength; it had not been only bombs they dropped, but also the requested spare legs for Bader. A large box was duly found with a red cross painted on it and the words in German, 'This box contains artificial legs for Wing Commander Bader, Prisoner of War.'

Bader never encountered the Focke-Wulf 190, the new fighter introduced into service by the Luftwaffe in summer 1941. The Focke-Wulf, despite its incongruous, old-fashioned radial design was a highly effective foe, capable of 389mph. An official RAF report comparing the Spitfire VB with a captured Focke-Wulf 190 found that the enemy aircraft was 'superior in speed at all heights', and could outclimb and outdive the VB.

In manoeuvrability the 190 had the best of the Spitfire VB, 'except in turning circles, when the Spitfire can quite easily out-turn it'. Flight Lieutenant Johnnie Johnson was 'bounced' by FW 190s in November 1941:

12 Group always provided a duty wing of Spitfires which could be sent to the south at short notice. Early in November we refuelled at West Malling, and with two Canadian squadrons above us we patrolled just inside Dunkirk, to provide withdrawal cover for the 'beehive' returning from Lille.

The Canadians were heavily engaged, and Roy Marples, flying next to our inexperienced wing leader, quietly reported a dozen Messerschmitts well above us. When they slanted down to attack us, Roy called the break and Nip and I, leading our finger fours on either flank, drove our

Spitfires round in steep turns to meet the threat. But Roy was horrified to see the wing leader still flying straight and level, quite unaware of the danger. Roy yelled over the radio and as the cannon shells streamed at them, all except the wing leader took desperate evading action.

We were puzzled by the unfamiliar silhouettes of some of the enemy fighters, which seemed to have squarer wing tips and more tapering fuselages than the Messerschmitts we usually encountered. Later Nip swore that one of the enemy aircraft which fastened on to him had a radial engine, and another pilot said he had distinctly seen a mixed armament of cannons and machine guns, all firing from wing positions.

Whatever these strange fighters were, they gave us a hard time of it. They seemed to be faster in a zoom climb than a 109, far more stable in a vertical dive, and they turned better than the Messerschmitt, for we had all our work cut out to shake them off. One of our Canadian sergeants, Sanderson, who was in the leading section, was set upon by two or three of these enemy fighters, was chased and harried all the way across the Channel and barely managed to crash land his Spitfire on the east coast near Southend. We never saw the wing leader again, and later we heard that he had been shot down and killed.

Our own troubles were not over, for we returned to find the southeast corner of England covered by a thin fog which persisted to a thousand feet and reduced forward visibility to less than a few hundred yards. More than two hundred Spitfires, all of which had only enough petrol for another few minutes flying, were trying to find an airfield, and the radio homing channels were jammed with requests for assistance. I headed my section down sun, where the visibility was a little better, and by a sheer stroke of luck found what appeared to be an abandoned airfield. It was very small and we brought our Spitfires carefully over the boundary for precautionary landings, with plenty of power and the nose well up so that we should stop in the shortest possible space. We had in fact, landed on a disused, bomb-cratered airfield near Chatham, and it was only after a long delay that we were refuelled. Even then our misfortunes were not over, for Alan Smith nosed his Spitfire into a crater when we took off at last light.

Back at Kirton, and encouraged by Gibbs, we drew up our chairs and sketched plan and side views of the strange aircraft. Nip thought the wing tips were very similar to those of a Miles Master and Jeff West said he thought the fuselage was slender because of the bulk of the radial engine. We were all agreed that it was superior to the Messerschmitt 109F and completely outclassed our Spitfire 5S. Our sketches disappeared into mysterious intelligence channels and we heard no more of the matter, but fighter pilots reported increasing numbers of these outstanding fighters over northern France.

Later we were given the novel explanation that the new enemy fighters were probably some of a batch of Curtis[s] Hawk aeroplanes which the French had bought from the United States shortly before the war. It was suggested to us that the Luftwaffe had taken over the Curtis Hawks and were using them operationally. This was an absurd theory, for no pre-war aircraft had a performance to compare with these brutes, and it was not for some months that our intelligence admitted the introduction of a completely new fighter, the redoubtable Focke-Wulf 190, designed by Kurt Tank.

Wilfrid Duncan Smith, who 'never lost confidence in the Spitfire as a fighting lady', used the Spit's tight turn to bring down an FW 190 on one of his first missions as the new commander of 64 Squadron. But Duncan Smith was an exceptional fighter pilot and leader. Most other pilots struggled with the FW 190, and struggled with Leigh-Mallory's endless sweeps. Returning to ops after an extended leave, Al Deere was told, 'it is no longer a question of how many we shoot down; the reverse is true and the cry is, How many did we lose today'. Some pilots became deeply superstitious. American William Ash, flying out of Hornchurch with 152 Squadron, remembered:

> Like most of my colleagues, I became a bit superstitious. I always believed in the scientific efficacy of knocking on wood, but the cockpit of my beloved Spit, though brilliantly designed, was a bit short on mahogany. I solved this small design oversight by fixing a little wooden matchbox under the reflector sight of my gun.

Some of those who survived, thanks to their skill or their luck, sank into depression and exhaustion. Hugh Dundas at Tangmere found:

> I subconsciously shrank from battle. The instinct for survival, the inner urge to rest on my laurels, was very strong. I know there were a couple of occasions during the weeks that followed [Bader's capture] when I shirked the clash of combat at the critical moment. Looking back on it later, I recognized that this was a time of extreme danger for me and also to some extent for the men I was leading. It was the stage of fatigue which many experienced fighter pilots

have fallen as a result of misjudgement or a momentary holding back from combat.

An antidote to the FW 190 was clearly essential, and the Spitfire was thrown back into the melting pot. In the autumn of 1941 Supermarine began flight testing an experimental Spitfire fitted with a Merlin two stage supercharger. This new Spitfire would emerge as the Mk IX in summer 1942, but in the meantime the FW 190 flew amok. Fortunately for Fighter Command, the Luftwaffe was heavily committed to supporting the campaign in Russia, and the FW 190 fleet in the West was always small.

It was non-existent in Malta. There an older, more familiar foe, hunted. By spring 1942 Malta had been under siege for two years. Fixed in the blue Mediterranean just below Sicily, the island lay across the Axis' watery supply lines to North Africa. Determined to prevent the RAF's use of the island as a terrestrial 'aircraft carrier', the Luftwaffe pounded Malta in almost daily air raids, borne so stoically by the Maltese that King George VI awarded the island the George Cross. The island's continued survival depended on her air defences, which at first were Gloster Gladiators, then Hurricanes. Neither was a match for the Me 109F.

The only fighter in Fighter Command's armoury that could engage the Me 109F 'Friedrich' on superior terms was the Spitfire V. How, though, to get the Spitfire V to the island? The predatory, circling naval and air forces of Italy and Germany precluded large scale deliveries by ship. The British possession of Gibraltar was beyond the Spit's ferry range. There was only one answer; to take the Spitfires by aircraft carrier to a point off the Algerian coast, where they would be launched to fly the rest of the way. From the launch point to Malta was 660 long miles over the sea. For the flight each Spitfire carried a ninety gallon slipper tank. The Malta campaign was the first time that the Spitfire was posted abroad.

Between 7 March and 24 October 1942, 385 Spitfires were launched off aircraft carriers for Malta, of which 367 reached the island, and 18 failed to do so. Flying Officer Jack Rae, a New Zealander with 603 Squadron, flew off the loaned USS aircraft carrier *Wasp*. Hearing rumours of shortages of food, soap and cigarettes, he had taken care to stash a hoard of these treasures in the wings of his plane:

Dawn on 20 April was our planned time for take-off. Twelve Spitfires had been moved up on to the flight deck. At 4.15 a.m. we were up and having breakfast aware there had been a major problem, which could have been very serious. Up until this moment the fuel tanks of the Spitfires had been kept empty for safety reasons. However, now that they were being filled, some of the auxiliary tanks had shown leaks. In spite of the very real hazards crewmembers managed to repair them, which was a remarkable feat.

There was one sudden change that gave me a twinge of conscience at the time, although I could do little about it. Squadron Leader David Douglas-Hamilton came up to me at the last moment to advise that as I had to lead a section. My aircraft, which was still up on a sling, would have to be flown by a Canadian sergeant pilot and I was to take his plane. There would be no time to transfer our personal gear, which had to be left in the aircraft.

On inspecting what was now my aircraft, I found this poor man's very carefully parcelled and obviously exact 10lb of gear. Dare I tell him about those extras in the wings? I was now unable to remove them. He was a very nervous person so all I could say was that there was some extra weight in the plane and to give her all the power he could. That was a pretty stupid thing to say really because every one of us would be doing just that.

We boarded our aircraft in the hangar deck and one by one were pushed backwards on to the lift, then up on to the flight deck and moved off the lift for the next one. Aircraft engines then had to be started. We'd been warned that if an aircraft engine didn't start or showed any problem then it was likely the Spit would be pushed over the side, as time was critical. The Wasp's own fighters had taken off and were circling above. The sooner we departed the ship, the safer this convoy would be.

I heard later that the Spit I should have been flying did have quite a struggle taking off and the poor Canadian flew for miles just above the sea. How about my own take-off? The engine started without a problem and minimum time was taken to bring the temperatures up to safety. Then a quick cockpit check – boy, it had to be quick – and I was guided into take-off position. True to his word, the captain had that ship at maximum knots into a very welcome head wind. Sitting there with brakes hard on, the rev up signal was given and I opened the throttle steadily until I felt the tailplane trying to rise. The aircraft was straining to go. We all knew the drill by heart: snap off brakes, move forward gaining speed rapidly, the amount of deck in front disappearing, then airborne long before reaching the bow.

The skipper had been quite right; I had plenty of deck to spare, although it no doubt helped having only the

Canadian's correctly weighted personal baggage. Once aloft, came the anxious moment of switching to the auxiliary tanks. None of us had any problems so off we set in various formations for the long flight to Malta. The crew of the Wasp operated with maximum efficiency that day and had the forty-seven of us airborne in twenty minutes.

Pilot Officer Michael Le Bas of 601 Squadron (by then led by John Bisdee) had a 'hairier' take-off that morning:

The deck officer began rotating his checkered flag and I pushed forwards my throttle until I had maximum rpm. His flag then fell and I released the brakes and pushed the throttle to emergency override to get the last ounce of power out of my Merlin. The Spitfire picked up speed rapidly in its headlong charge down the deck, but not rapidly enough. The ship's bows got closer and closer and still I had insufficient airspeed and suddenly – I was off the end. With only 60 feet to play with before I hit the water, I immediately retracted the undercarriage and eased forward on the stick to build up my speed. Down and down with the Spitfire until, about fifteen feet above the waves, it reached flying speed and I was able to level out.

Once airborne, 601 and 603 Squadrons flew in loose formation to Malta at a sedate 200mph to conserve fuel, taking care to avoid the Luftwaffe base at Pantelleria. The Canadian sergeant pilot detailed to fly Rae's plane made the journey safely. The one loss on the three-and-a-half-hour journey was an American who deserted by flying his Spitfire to Algeria. Landing on Malta, Rae found 'the devastation . . . almost beyond description. The drome itself looked of reasonable size but there were bomb craters all over the place. Buildings that might have been dispersal huts were just shells and the windsocks, riddled with holes, hung limply on their poles, useless for indicating wind direction.'

The Spitfires were immediately put into blast pens and refuelled by the ground crew by hand with four-gallon petrol tins because there were no bowsers. Conditions on Malta were as bad as Rae had been led to believe. 'Malta Dog' – diarrhoea – was virulent and Rae suspected his 'bully beef' of being horse flesh. One Spitfire aircraftsman, George Howes, found that his five shilling black market pancake was fried in the hydraulic oil of the selfsame aircraft. The only alcohol to be commonly obtained was a coarse local wine, Ambete, known to all in the RAF as 'Stuka Juice'.

But all these hardships paled in comparison to the intensity of the Luftwaffe's attacks. Within three days of 601 and 603's arrival, all of their planes had been put out of action, either in combat or by bombing of the airfields. Still more Spitfires flew in. So did a man who would become the greatest Malta air ace, George 'Screwball' Beurling, a lone wolf Canadian with 249 Squadron. Squadron Leader P.B. 'Laddie' Lucas, Beurling's commanding officer, later wrote of him:

> George Beurling, by any test, was exceptional. He was exceptionally untidy. A combination of attributes placed Beurling in front of the rest. He was an outstanding shot, getting the very most out of his Spitfire as a superbly steady gun platform. It was an art which he had perfected with practice and infinite patience, after intense technical study.

I used to wonder sometimes how good he would have been at driven partridges in November.

Beyond that, his reflexes were like quicksilver and he had a pair of strikingly blue eyes, beneath a shock of fair, tousled hair, which penetrated the Mediterranean glare and the haze of the upper air as no other pilot's did. Screwball had the best eyesight of any man I have ever known.

'Tiger Leader, 109s at 2 o'clock same level; 88s a couple of thousand feet below . . . There are a helluva lot of the goddam screwballs . . .'

And then the rest of us would spot them. The seconds his wonderful eyes gained him gave him a priceless advantage in combat. His commanding control over his Spitfire and his precision shooting did the rest. But strangely, it was his meticulous honesty in reporting his numerous claims which left the most indelible impression.

I remember one day in July the squadron had had a brush with some 109s sweeping in high over the island after a bombing raid. Beurling had sent one down flaming into the sea off St Paul's Bay. Then way down below, his eye fastened on an Italian Macchi 202 heading north for Sicily on its own. Screwball attacked with machine guns alone, having used up all his cannon ammunition. Then he broke away and landed.

To the waiting Intelligence Officer he reported the destruction of a 109, having seen it crash into the sea. After that he had attacked a Macchi, seeing strikes behind the cockpit, in the engine and along the port wing. But he could only claim 'one damaged' as he had had to break away and had not seen what had happened to the aircraft.

Some while later, a Macchi 202 was reported to have force-landed on Gozo, a small island, just north of Malta. It had been hit behind the cockpit and in the port wing, but not in the engine. When they gave Screwball the news and told him his claim had been updated to 'one destroyed', his face showed no emotion whatever. 'Darnnit,' he muttered, dead pan, 'I was certain I hit that goddam screwball in the engine!'

Beurling's eventual score was twenty-six aircraft, but it wasn't only Beurling making kills in Malta. The island quickly became known in the RAF as 'the fighter pilots' paradise' because of the opportunities it presented for combat. 'It all makes the Battle of Britain and fighter sweeps seem likes child's play', thought Flying Officer R.A. Mitchell. The Spitfire boys may have been outnumbered but they did not lack courage. Squadron Leader Lord David Douglas-Hamilton of 603 Squadron wrote home to his wife:

> You will have gathered from the Press and News that we have raids every day and pretty heavy ones at that, but this place still holds out and it will continue to hold out . . .
>
> For the first time I have heard the whistle and explosion of a bomb, so clearly that I will never forget it! The boys here are simply marvellous – they have shot down masses of Huns . . . it is a real honour to be with such chaps.
>
> We too are lacing into them and one of the squadron, Bill Douglas, got a Hun today. My respect for the German pilots has gone down considerably – they are scared stiff of Spitfires!

The pendulum of the battle started hesitantly to swing in Allied favour; it was pushed there for good by the arrival in July 1942 of Air Vice-Marshal Park, former controller of No. 11 Fighter Group in the Battle of Britain, as the new head of the island's air defence. No sooner had Park landed than he reorganized fighter tactics along the lines adopted in the 'Spitfire Summer' of 1940. Like Douglas-Hamilton he had complete faith in the Spitfire and the Spitfire pilot's ability to instil fear in heart of the Germans. Park's special order of the day, issued on his arrival stated:

> Our day fighter strength has during June and July been greatly increased and the enemy's superiority in numbers has long since dwindled. The time has now arrived for our Spitfire squadrons to put an end to the bombing of our airfields by daylight. We have the best fighter aircraft in the world and our Spitfire pilots will again show their comrades on the ground that they are the best fighter pilots in the world.

Within weeks, the island's Spitfire contingent had gone from lame ducks to eagles. Mark Vs, equipped with a 250lb bomb, swooped on the airfields of the Luftwaffe and Regia Aeronautica (Italian Royal Air Force) to give them a taste of their own explosive medicine. It was the first time that the Spitfire had been used as a dive-bomber.

By October 1942 the Battle of Malta was over. The peril had been beaten back, but only just. Axis losses have since been estimated at 309 aircraft destroyed, compared to the RAF's 293 (both Hurricanes and Spitfires), but the figures dapple-shade the important truth. Once again, the Spitfire boys and Mr Mitchell's fighter had triumphed over the Luftwaffe and bought Britain a strategic victory.

The spring of 1942 saw another turning point in the air war in Europe.

One fine day at Hornchurch, Jeffrey Quill, back testing aircraft for Supermarine, arrived at the airfield with a prototype Spitfire, codenamed R6700. The Air Ministry confessed to few hopes for R6700, acknowledging that it was 'lash-up', the sole purpose of which was to give Fighter Command anything to tackle the Focke-Wulf 190 on equal terms. Quill however, was so impressed with R6700 that he decided, without official sanction, to show it to his friend Group Captain Harry Broadhurst. Hence Quill's visit to Hornchurch:

So I rang Broady, arranged to have lunch with him at Hornchurch, and flew there in R6700. I told him I had a Spitfire with a new engine and thought he might like to fly it and I kept things as casual as possible, because I did not want to enthuse over the aeroplane before he had flown it. We arranged that he would fly it after lunch. The Hornchurch Wing, which was led by Pete Powell, was due to take off on a sweep that afternoon and Broady and I saw them off, sitting in his staff car. I then saw him into R6700 and as he climbed aboard he said, 'I've told my driver to take you to the Ops Room. You can sit with the Controller and watch the Wing in action.' The underground Operations Room at Hornchurch was a little way from the airfield and by the time I arrived and sat beside the Controller, Ronald Adams, whom I remembered from 65 Squadron days, I could see from the plots on the table that the Wing was over the Channel heading for the French coast. Adam told me they were going to sweep round behind Lille at about 25,000 ft and return. As the Wing was approaching the coast at Boulogne, I noticed that behind them there was a single aircraft plot. I watched this for a bit, without thinking much about it, and then at a suitable opportunity I said to Adam: 'What's that plot there?'

'Oh,' he said, 'that's the Station Commander.'

'Goddammit,' I said, 'he's in my aeroplane! Do you realise that's the most important prototype fighter in the country right now – and what's more the guns aren't loaded!'

'Well – there's nothing I can do about it,' Adam replied, 'but right now he seems to be well over 35,000 feet.'

'Thank God for that,' I said and resigned myself to a very anxious wait, for there was a great deal of reaction from the Luftwaffe that day and the Wing was quite heavily engaged. I began to consider how I would explain away the circumstance; that I took off from Worthy Down in the morning in the trial installation Merlin 61 aircraft belonging to CRD [the RAF's Controller of Research and Development] and before the day was out it had been shot down in France.

Fortunately Broady returned safely, duly impressed with the aeroplane, and as I had expected, it was not long before the word spread into the upper reaches of Group and Command Headquarters.

One Spitfire pilot, seeing Broadhurst's R6700 above him, declared, 'That's no aircraft, that's a bleeding angel'.

Officially designated the Supermarine Spitfire Mark IX, the new Spit may have looked like the old warhorse the Spitfire V, but inside the marginally elongated body (9 inches) there beat a new engine, the Merlin 61, with a two stage supercharger (in which output from the first blower fed into the second to further compress the charge of air before it entered the carburettor). The difference in performance between the two models was a staggering 300hp. The Mark IX could also operate at a higher ceiling. Wilfrid Duncan Smith recalled:

> One of the greatest thrills was having twelve Spitfire Mk IXs in battle formation at 43,000 feet, in the knowledge that no German fighter could touch us. In fact the limiting factor rested in the flying equipment available to do the job because existing oxygen and ventilation systems could no longer be considered entirely efficient to meet the exacting conditions. Without pressurisation at such great altitudes, the physical discomfort from fatigue and pain from 'bends' limited the flight time we could endure to barely five minutes or so.

Wilfrid Duncan Smith's 64 Squadron was the first to be receive the Mark IX, but it was not fully re-equipped and gun tested until the end of July 1942. In the meantime, the shoot 'em up sweeps over France went on endlessly. William Ash, despite his lucky wooden matchbox, was shot down at the end of March after a skirmish with FW 190s and Me 109s in which he ran out of ammunition and was reduced to shouting 'Bang! Bang!' at his tormentors. After crash-landing, Ash was taken in by the French Resistance and hidden in an apartment in Paris belonging to a couple called Josef and Giselle. Somehow his presence was discovered by the Gestapo:

One night, in early June 1942, about a month after I had arrived in Paris, the front door of the apartment was kicked in, cracking and splintering under the weight of many jackboots. All three of us were dragged from our beds and forced to dress hastily at gunpoint, then held in the living room while a group of German soldiers ransacked the apartment and demanded our papers.

Knowing that the game was up, I tried talking to the one who seemed to be in charge, attempting to explain that I had just arrived and that these people did not know who I really was. They had just taken me in off the streets and should not be blamed for harbouring me.

I had only got halfway through my admittedly threadbare excuses, when I was cut short by a rifle butt in the face. We were dragged into waiting vehicles and brought straight to one of the most feared buildings in the world – the Gestapo headquarters in Paris, near the Opera. Josef and Giselle were dragged off in one direction, I in another. I never saw either of them again.

After a short spell in a basement cell, I was brought by two guards up to an office. There, behind a large and highly polished desk, sat a grey haired man in well tailored civilian clothes, with a face that I hated on sight. He motioned politely for me to take a small seat positioned in front of the large desk, while the guards hovered by the wall behind me. I sat down and immediately began gabbling my series of excuses about my hosts. My French must have still been pretty terrible, since the grey haired man stopped me in full flood with a terse request for me to speak English.

I started again from the beginning in English, but if anything my story sounded even lamer. Once again my interrogator cut me short. He told me to stop worrying about my former hosts and start worrying about myself. I responded that I was a prisoner of war and expected to be treated as one. The man leaned over towards me confidentially, 'There is only one way I will believe you are a prisoner of war,' he told me. He produced a pen and paper and I had a sinking feeling about where this little civilized chat was leading. 'You can prove you are really a pilot by giving me the names of every person who helped you since you crash-landed. Then we can check your story.'

I gave him the date and location of my crash, but he just sneered. Knowing the location of a downed plane did not prove I was the pilot and I had been captured in Paris in civilian clothes. It was my turn to sneer – I pointed out that with my terrible French and no German, I would not make much of a spy. He countered that I probably spoke such bad French to make my pilot story more plausible. He was beginning to get impatient. He wanted the names of every person who had helped me from my crash to my capture.

For once I was able to use the truth. Ever since I was a boy I've had a terrible memory for remembering names on demand. I leant over as he had done, as if about to divulge a secret. 'To tell you the truth, I'm terrible with names,' I confided.

This did not seem to have the desired effect. He turned purple and hissed at me, 'You do not seem to be taking your situation seriously enough. Perhaps we can help you.' With that, he tidied his desk and left the room.

He had hardly closed the door when one of the guards hauled me to my feet and grabbed my arms behind my back. The other hit me a vicious punch in the face. I turned my head away and the next blow crashed into my stomach. I tried to clench my muscles but a third crashing blow to my solar plexus left me gasping for breath as he returned to beating me around the face.

He stopped for a second, as if some shred of humanity had been rekindled somewhere inside him, but in reality he had merely stopped to fastidiously take a handkerchief from his pocket, wrap it carefully around his knuckles and then start over again, landing blow after vicious blow on my cheeks, jaw, neck and eyes.

As I came close to passing out, the guards shoved me back in the chair, where I cradled my head in my arms. One of the guards yanked my head up by the hair. As it rose, I saw that the sleeves of my shirt were covered in blood. He jerked my head back until I was once again staring at the grey haired Gestapo man, who had re-entered the room as silently as he had left.

He waved a piece of paper at me. One of my eyes was so swollen that it was practically shut, and the other one was swimming with blood. I struggled to focus.

'It's in German. I told you, I don't speak German.'

He seemed delighted to translate it for me. It was an order from the *Kommandantura*. It said that if the prisoner calling himself Bill Ash failed to provide satisfactory proof of identity, he was to be shot as a spy on 4 June 1942. Just as I've never been great with names, I am not much better with dates. I asked him to remind me what today's date was.

He leant over and whispered, 'June the third,' with obvious enjoyment.

TALLY-HO!

After a week of beatings and torture, Ash heard shouting outside his cell door:

My captors loved shouting – shouting at me, shouting orders at each other and shouting at anyone who did not do as they were ordered – but the tone of such shouting always had the same ring to it, of a superior bawling out some unfortunate *Untermensch*. This was different. A blazing row outside my cell was being fought out by two equals. I recognized one of the voices as that of my interrogator, and even though he was no slouch in the screaming department, he was gradually getting the worst of it from whoever was on the other side of this argument. A final bark by his adversary was accompanied by an insistent thump on my cell door, rapidly followed by the reluctant clank and shuffle of the loser unlocking it.

By the time the door opened, my interrogator had left already and I was faced by the stern but relatively friendly figure of a Luftwaffe officer and several soldiers. He seemed taken aback by my condition, but he saluted.

'We must leave now. You are now in the custody of the Luftwaffe as a prisoner of war and will be treated as such. But we must hurry. The Gestapo still dispute that you are a pilot and we should leave before they get a chance to have our orders countermanded. Come!'

I needed no further encouragement, but I was in such bad shape after the endless beatings that I needed some help from the Luftwaffe subordinates, as I limped my way out of that hellish place, which was something few of its unfortunate inmates ever lived to do.

As the heavy gates of the Gestapo headquarters closed behind me, I could almost hear the sigh of relief from my new captors. The fight between the Luftwaffe and the Gestapo for custody of prisoners was a recurring theme of their war, and a battle that the Gestapo would gradually win. But for now, the Luftwaffe had the upper hand, which was fine by me. In general they wanted to abide by the Geneva Convention, and on a less noble note, they knew that there were hundreds of Luftwaffe prisoners of war being held in camps in England and Canada. If word got out that the Gestapo were beating and shooting their counterparts, who knew what might start happening to German prisoners.

Ash was sent to Stalag Luft III where he met the inimitable Douglas Bader. Once, in conversation with Bader, Ash asked him for his views on the Battle of Britain. Bader's reply was concise, 'We couldn't have the bastards flying over England, attacking our own land and people, now could we?' Bader continued his personal war against 'the bastards' in Stalag Luft III by persistent escape attempts which he hoped at the very least, would tie down German soldiers. Eventually the Stalag Luft III commandant tired of Bader, who was forwarded to Colditz in August 1942. To roars of admiration from the Stalag Luft III prisoners, Bader, as he was being marched out of the camp, stopped and insolently lined up his escort for inspection.

While Ash was becoming acquainted with life as a 'Krigie' (short for *Kriegsgefangene* – prisoner of war) in Stalag Luft III, the Wing at Hornchurch suffered a devastating loss when Wing Commander Brian 'Paddy' Finucane, a fighter ace whose public veneration bordered on mania, was shot by machine gun fire on a low-level operation against a German camp at Etaples. 'Paddy' Finucane, victor in thirty-two aerial contests, was twenty-one. Pilot Officer F.A. Aikman was Finucane's 'No. 2' on that fateful 15th of July:

I remember that we were flying at zero feet right down on the deck. And as we flew over the beach, I saw a small machine gun post perched about 20 feet above the beach on a ridge of sand.

We were almost on the post before Paddy realized it was there, and the soldiers opened up at point-blank range. The fire burst went through Paddy's starboard wing and radiator.

I was flying behind him and to the right, and as I went in I took a crack at the gun post. When the dust had settled down a little, there was nothing to be seen on the sand, and I guessed my fire blew that post to blazes.

But Paddy did not know he had been hit, for he pulled up a little to fly over the post. I called him up on the radio, 'You have had it sir, in your radiator.'

He then called out, 'I shall have to get out of this. Hello, Wing Commander calling. I have had it. Am turning out.'

He went into a turn and then flew out on a reciprocal course. I was flying close to him and I could see him clearly in the cockpit. He opened his sliding hood and just before he crashed, I saw him take off his helmet. He was doing something else in the cockpit. Releasing his parachute harness I should say.

When the Spitfire hit the deck, I thought it might stay afloat for a few seconds. Long enough for him to get out.

But it sank like a stone, carrying Paddy with it. The impact must have knocked him unconscious.

We circled the sea for a long time after that. But all we saw was a slowly widening streak of oil which floated on the dark waters of the Channel.

Two weeks later the Hornchurch Wing had its revenge when, on the afternoon of 30 July 1942, Flight Lieutenant Donald Kingaby from 64 Squadron scored his 16th aerial victory:

I sighted approximately twelve FW 190s 2,000 ft below us at 12,000, just off Boulogne proceeding towards French coast. We dived down on them and I attacked an FW 190 from astern and below giving a very short burst, about half a second, from 300yd. I was forced to break away as I was crowded out by other Spits. I broke down and right and caught another FW as he commenced to dive away. At approx 14,000 feet I gave a burst of cannon and M/G, 400 yd range, hitting E/A along fuselage. Pieces fell off and E/A continued in straight dive nearly vertical. I followed E/A down to 5000 feet over Boulogne and saw him hit the deck just outside the town of Boulogne and explode and burn up. Returned to base at 0ft.

For all its laconic, matter-of-fact tone, Kingaby's report records an historic happenstance. It was the first time that the Mk IX and the Focke-Wulf 190 had met. And the Spitfire had triumphed.

Even so the commander of 64 Squadron, Wilfrid Duncan Smith, was disappointed because most of his unit – himself included – had pulled out of the attack on the FW 190s after a radio warning that the aircraft might be friendly. Duncan Smith's men redeemed themselves in the afternoon:

About halfway between the coast and St Omer we caught up with fifteen FW 190s 5,000 ft below us. I led the Squadron down again in much the same manner as the morning show, and got a 190 from slightly above and dead astern. No doubt this time; he burst into flames, spiralling down in a cloud of smoke. Stewart and Michel Donnet also destroyed one apiece, while two others got probables. Don Findlay, who was doing a staff job at Group at the time, in the Engineering branch, came on the trip with us, and claimed a damaged 190. We got separated as a result of the engagement, so Arne Austeen, my number two, a Norwegian and I flew home together on our own. A few miles off Calais, we found an FW 190 attacking a Spitfire, and since we had plenty of height, went after him. We caught him easily, each attacking in turn and sending the enemy into the sea in flames.

Duncan Smith ('Smithy') ended the war with twenty confirmed victories. He had handled firearms since childhood – as a boy he had been out shooting with a .22 rifle when, as previously mentioned, he saw a soaring golden eagle that inspired him to master flying – and many aces either had game shooting experience or were born with an eye for a moving target. Group Captain Bobby Oxspring of 66 Squadron later remarked:

Perhaps it would be overstating the obvious to remark that the really great fighter aces were supreme marksmen. Most pilots could be taught with practice to shoot tolerably well, but the select few had a natural reaction to a moving target, and whatever the target's speed and position, they could instantly and accurately assess the deflection required for a hit. The ability in the air was almost always reflected on the ground, and such pilots were excellent shots with a twelve bore against game birds or clay pigeons.

R.R. 'Bob' Stanford Tuck of 92 Squadron was the proof positive of Oxspring's observation. Stanford Tuck's thirty victories in the air were matched by his reputation on the ground for shooting clay pigeons. 'What an eye he had!' recalled one of his squadron's engineers. For Stanford Tuck shooting enemy aircraft was 'a precision business'. Johnnie Johnson, who would eventually become the RAF's greatest fighter ace of the war with thirty-six confirmed victories, made the same connection between game shooting and plane shooting:

> Personally, I found my own game and wild fowling experiences to be of the greatest value. The fighter pilot who could hit a curling, downwind pheasant, or a jinking head-on partridge, or who could kill a widgeon cleanly in a darkening sky, had little trouble in bringing his guns to bear against the 109s.

Johnson modestly thought that the New Zealander Edward Preston 'Hawk-Eye' Wells (a multiple winner of clay pigeon competitions in his homeland), to be the finest Allied shot in the air, followed by 'Screwball' Beurling, who made his name in Malta. Conversely, Johnson noted, a man who was bad with a shotgun was a poor shot with a Spitfire and cited his friend Hugh 'Cocky' Dundas as a prime example:

Cocky never became a good shot, either when poking a twelve bore at driven game or lining up the multiple guns of his Spitfire, but he was always a determined and courageous pilot and he possessed a rare ability to lead, either in the air or on the ground. The keystones of his simple creed were honour and duty and to enjoy life to the full at the same time.

Dundas did indeed possess the right stuff as a leader. In 1944, at the age of twenty-four, he was made a Group Captain, the youngest ever in the RAF.

Enjoying life to the full was the Spitfire's pilots' mantra when off duty. They flew hard, they partied hard. For tomorrow they might die. Of his social life before his shooting down and capture, William Ash wrote:

I had a lovely young WAAF officer riding on the pillion as we raced from room to room before finally roaring out of the front door and taking off down some steps. I can't remember landing, but I found out that she got engaged to one of the Czech pilots a week later.

Many of us were very keen on motorbikes and sports cars at the time, particularly if they were filled with high-octane aviation fuel, which made them go like rockets. The aviation fuel was dyed bright green to prevent such wicked misuse, but our youthful wartime perspective on life and death meant that we were not overly bothered by such regulations. Some of our cars and bikes had dummy fuel tanks with just enough of the legal fuel to pass the spot checks by the stern men from the Special Investigations Branch, who sometimes paid us unexpected visits, waving their dipsticks menacingly.

When not attempting to break speed records, we were avid players of demented communal games, which were usually somewhere between a team sport and a riot. Near the heart of virtually every such venture was a superb flyer called Wilfrid Duncan Smith, known to one and all as Drunken Duncan. When he was not leading the inebriated festivities, he was one of the most skilled and deadly fighter pilots I ever met. He taught me tactics for surviving and winning a dogfight that were not to be found in any training manual and almost certainly saved my life. When he was in party mood he was just as unstoppable.

One of his performances that was in greatest demand was his impersonation of a Heinkel 111 German bomber on a daring daylight raid over London. With no props but a few chairs and a very bad Hitler impression, he would launch his bombing raid, using anything that was handy as projectiles, and would stop only when the rest of us had shot him down and sent him crashing to the floor.

Other games were based on the losers buying the winners drinks, which inevitably led to more games in which the winners had to reciprocate, until no one could remember if they had won or lost. A favourite one was Prisoners, with no discernible rules, other than the objective to capture as many of the other team as possible and sit on them at your side of the room, until eventually everyone was on the same side of the room, either being sat on or perched on top of a heap of prisoners. While it was funny at the time, my later experiences in prisoner-of-war camps across Europe made me realize what it was like to be sat on for several years in a row.

Usually the authorities turned a blind eye to such boisterous behaviour. Occasionally they tried to rein the flyboys in, as William Ash found, and divert them to more refined pleasures:

> Probably in an effort to curtail the worst excesses of marauding amorous pilots, the 'powers that be' attempted to regulate our social life by staging tea dances at Grosvenor House, where well brought up young ladies would risk life and limb dancing with foreign pilots. In order to get on the social register, we pilots had to turn up at an imposing house near Cadogan Square for a sort of upper-class interview. I think we were given points for polite chit-chat and not slurping our tea. The winners were invited to dances or to weekends in stately country mansions that looked like the setting for Agatha Christie murders. I seem to remember that the person in charge of such things was called Lady Frances Haggard. She was probably even more haggard because of the behaviour of some of her adopted pilots.
>
> After my teatime interview, I was curious to know how I had scored. I got to know one of the girls who worked there and persuaded her – probably at the risk of a firing squad for supplying information to the enemy – to retrieve my notes from the files. The report read, 'Nice American manners . . . can go most places'. I felt as if I had been mentioned in dispatches.

Ash loved visiting London, where he was overcome by the affection of the population towards the flyboys who had fought for them in the Battle of Britain:

If I went to the cinema and bought a ticket for the cheap seats for the princely sum of one shilling and threepence, I was immediately herded to the best, more expensive seats, the 'two-and-nines', by some patriotic usherette. Londoners particularly loved their fighter pilots, wherever they were from. They knew, without ever saying so, that for some of the young men enjoying themselves in London that night, depending on their fortunes in the air war the next morning, this might be their last visit.

Everyone adored the Spitfire Mark IX, because it divinely balanced power with manoeuvrability, unlike some of the later Spitfires, which were so heavy they barely deserved the hallowed name. Everyone loved the Mk IX – except German pilots, who were unsure whether the Spitfire before them was a Mk V or a Mk IX (they were virtually impossible to tell apart in the air) and suddenly they became decidedly cautious. Fighter Command's losses dropped almost overnight.

Group Captain Harry 'Broady' Broadhurst, now legitimately in the cockpit of a Mark IX, clinically demonstrated the Mark IX's ability as an FW 90 killer, on the morning of 19 August 1942, the day of Operation Jubilee; the Anglo-Canadian landings at the French port of Dieppe. According to the Biggin Hill Intelligence report:

G/Capt Broadhurst took off from Northolt at 06.00 hrs on a lone observation patrol over Dieppe. At 25,000 feet he noticed odd lots of pairs of enemy aircraft coming out apparently 5 miles northeast of Le Preport, then swooping down towards Dieppe, making passes at our patrols and ships on the way. The Group Captain having observed this repeated movement, picked on the No. 2 of a pair of FW 190s carrying out similar tactics. While sitting up sun at 5,000 feet above them, he started to dive and fire. With the hand of the clock at beyond dial reading point and the boost more than ordinarily pulled, he rather cruelly closed in to close range of 50 yards and let the enemy have some 160 cannon shells. The Hun very naturally turned on its back and went down in a vertical spin.

The Group Captain then fired a small amount of demoralising machine gun fire at the No.1 aircraft, which followed the original victim for a little way. It soon did the correct thing by bursting into all sorts of coloured smoke and dived to its doom into the sea. The enemy aircraft seemed to be working in pairs and starting their dives down sun from 15,000–20,000 feet. Weather over the target was perfect.

The main tasks of the Spitfires on the Dieppe raid were to defensive cover for the ground troops and escorts for the bombers. The American Eagle Squadron set off for Dieppe before dawn. An anonymous pilot remembered:

When we started the Merlin engines of our Spitfires, some cloud patches had piled up in the east, making it very dark. We pointed our Spits into the breeze in tight formation of fours, and took off into the night, then we quickly shifted to line astern. We flew low over Kent on our way out, and, still flying almost on the deck, we arrived at our departure point on the English coast. Then we set our course for Dieppe, flying very low and close to the sea. Each of us watched his instruments carefully, for in the dark there was no horizon and the sea was flat.

It was still dark when we arrived to cover the dawn landing. Our troops were already ashore and were fighting hard. And the heavy guns of both forces were firing steadily; they were feeling for their targets. Whenever one of the big guns on shore hit one of our boats, we could see the flames leap up and sometimes there would be an explosion. From where we were up above, we could spot the shrapnel burst and the almost continuous streaks of red Bofors projectiles, rising and converging toward our Hurricane bombers that were ahead of us and flying low, making absolutely point-blank attacks against the German gun posts, trying to knock them out so they could not operate against our troops that had already landed and those that were coming in to land.

Just as the first light of day was breaking and the protective cover of darkness was disappearing, a bomber from our side skimmed in with his belly almost touching the water, and laid a smoke screen across the harbour. A very light wind drifted it towards the cliffs and into the eyes of the German gunners who were firing from there.

From the sea hundreds of our corvettes, transports, destroyers, troop and tank transports, minesweepers, trawlers and rescue boats were deployed. Those nearest shore were advancing doggedly through the Hun minefields and a strong artillery barrage. From time to time one of them was hit and exploded. Whenever there was an explosion, the boat disappeared below the water under a cloud of spray and foam, leaving an oil slick. Over the whole of the battle area there hung a thickening pall of smoke from the cordite, the smoke screens, distress flares, and exploding shells.

Our naval artillery action was having a particularly good

effect. This barrage was gradually silencing enemy positions. High up above we could sit in the cockpits of our Spitfires and look down, and we noticed a slackening in the numbers of huge geysers that had been rising among our numerous sea craft. The enemy's primary resistance was slowly being overcome by our naval guns and by the attack of the Commandos themselves, who were capturing a number of positions in hand-to-hand fighting. As darkness changed into daylight, we could see that our fellows were advancing against the harbour's fortifications. We could also see that our troops were filtering throughout the town by means of hard street fighting. I can tell you it made us feel mighty good as we stooped around upstairs looking down and watching those troops advance into the teeth of all the Germans could throw at them. It was pretty darn exciting, and I reckon I was seeing one of the best shows any man has ever seen; it was mighty spectacular.

Curiously, our squadron did not encounter strong fighter opposition on that first sortie, and this lack of fighter resistance over the principal landing area surprised us a lot; we had expected the Germans to come up immediately and give strong opposition as soon as they realized the size of the combined attack we were launching. But in this initial stage of the battle, the enemy fighters which did rise were few in number, and they attacked in a very half-hearted manner. Only one of our chaps – it was Strickland – got a shot at a Focke-Wulf 190. He damaged it, and the other Huns near by were so jittery they promptly whipped about and fled.

It was well after sunrise when this first sortie drew to its close and we turned toward the sea, headed for home. We made our landfall, then steered for base, flying low over the beautiful hills and fields of Kent. The country lanes around Canterbury and Tunbridge Wells, winding among valleys, were filling with ground fog. We were glad that our drome was on a hilltop.

Before our propellers stopped turning, our splendid ground crew went into action, quickly refuelling, rearming and inspecting our craft. We learned that Morgan had crash-landed with a glycol leak near Beachy Head, coming down alongside a burning Blenheim.

We pilots agreed that while enemy coastal resistance at Dieppe might be lessened when next we went over, we knew that air resistance would be increased. We knew that Jerry would simply have to come and give us fight. He could not sit at home on his duff, while a show like this was going on. Hence we gulped our coffee and prepared for the second sortie.

As we were going out the second time, when we were about 20 miles off shore, we passed some of our sea craft returning with the first batch of the wounded.

When we approached Dieppe this time, we saw great fires and high columns of smoke rising, the harbour, the Casino and some of the hotels that once were so famous at this resort were now blazing, while ammunition dumps were blowing up here and there. It was quickly apparent that our main forces had landed effectively, and had spread far afield. The work of the demolition squads was particularly apparent; they had blasted a number of buildings and from time to time another would rise up into the air, shudder for an instant, then splatter. It was great fun to watch the demolition boys do their work.

As we were flying over Dieppe we were informed in the

air that the Canadians had captured the racetrack, and that it was available as an emergency field if any of us had to crash-land.

This time when we arrived there were plenty of enemy aircraft in the air. As we approached the battle area we could see an absolute swirl of twisting aeroplanes. One hell of a big battle was going on in the air as well as on the ground.

Many of the Spitfire pilots flew four sorties on that grim, exhausting day, which saw forty-eight Spitfire squadrons in action. Unfortunately, only four of the squadrons were equipped with the new variant Spitfire. These did not include Squadron Leader Johnnie Johnson's 610 Squadron. On his first sortie of the day Johnson tangled with an FW 190:

I spotted a solitary aircraft over the town. I eased towards him and recognized the enemy as a Focke-Wulf 190. For once I was harried and I yawed my Spitfire to cover the blind spot behind me. But these movements attracted the attention of the enemy pilot and he snaked towards me, almost head on, and then we both turned hard to the left and whirled round on opposite sides of what seemed to be an ever decreasing circle.

The 190 bore strange markings on the side of its fuselage just below the cockpit. This painted crest looked very similar to the markings of the Italian Air Force, and I thought, This pilot is an Italian! We had not seen them since they had received some severe treatment over the Thames Estuary towards the end of the Battle of Britain. We had been looking for them ever since, for we had little regard for their fighting qualities in the air. He's mine, I thought.

He's mine, and I forgot the vulnerability of a lone Spitfire and tightened my turn to get on his tail.

With wide open throttle I held the Spitfire in the tightest of shuddering vertical turns. I was greying-out, and where was this Italian, who should, according to my reckoning, be filling my gunsight? I couldn't see him, and little wonder, for the brute was gaining on me and in another couple of turns would have me in his sights. The overconfidence of but a few seconds before, had already given way to irritation at losing my opponent, and this was replaced by a sickening apprehension. I asked the Spitfire for all she'd got in the turn, but the 190 hung behind like a leech and it could only be a question of time, and not much of that!

Stick over and well forward and I plunged into a near-vertical dive – a dangerous manoeuvre, for the 190 was more stable and faster than my Spitfire in such a descent, but I had decided on a possible method of escape. At ground level I pulled into another steep turn, and as I gauged the height and watched the roof tops I caught a glimpse of the promenade, of stationary tanks, of the white casino and a deserted beach. The 190 was still behind and for a few seconds we dodged round the spires and columns or smoke. Then I made my bid to throw him off.

A short distance off shore I could see a destroyer surrounded by a clutter of smaller ships. We had been carefully briefed not to fly below 4,000 feet over the shipping, otherwise they would open fire. I rammed the throttle into the emergency position, broke off my turn and at sea level headed straight at the destroyer. Flak and tracer came straight at me from the destroyer, and more, slower tracer from the 190 passed over the top of the cockpit. At the last

moment I pulled over the destroyer, then slammed the nose
down and eased out a few feet above the sea. I broke hard
to the left and searched for the 190, but he was no longer
with me. Either the flak had put him off, or better still, had
nailed him. I made off at high speed to West Malling.

Johnson thought that the Luftwaffe at Dieppe, 'bested us in the
air fighting and shot down more than two of our aircraft for
everyone lost to them, a fair indication of their all-round
superiority of the Focke-Wulfs over our Spitfire 5s'. It was an
accurate assessment of the air battle in which the RAF lost 100
aircraft. The ground raid fared even worse; the attacking forces
suffered heavy casualties, with half of the 5,000 men becoming
casualties.

The good news for Fighter Command was that the production
lines at Castle Bromwich, where the Mark IX was built, were
humming along. Eventually 5,665 Mark IXs entered service,
making it the most numerous Spitfire after the Mark V. One of
these Mark IXs, souped-up, earned a footnote in the history of
aviation for taking part in the highest aerial combat of the Second
World War.

With Bomber Command's raids on Germany beginning to
hurt, there came insistent demands from the Nazi top circle for
retaliatory air attacks on Britain. The Luftwaffe, committed to
the war in Russia, did not have the wherewithal for another
Blitz, so it formed a new unit, the *Hohenkampfkommando* (High
Altitude Bomber Detachment), to carry out stratospheric
bombing raids on the enemy's homeland. The *Hohenkampfkommando*, its grandiose title aside, had only two aircraft; its real
purpose was propagandistic and psychological. By flying far
above the operating level of the RAF's fighters, the

Hohenkampfkommando would show that the Luftwaffe could make daylight raids on Britain with Teutonic morale breaking impunity.

On the morning of 24 August 1942, a specially converted Ju 86R bomber belonging to the *Hohenkampfkommando* took off from Beauvais in northern France to begin the unit's operation against Britain. Over the next fortnight the *Hohenkampfkommando* mounted almost daily raids, its crews watching amused as Spitfire V squadron upon squadron tried to climb up to intercept them, but could not.

Fortuitously for Fighter Command, the two stage supercharger on the newly delivered Spitfire Mark IX enabled the plane to operate at great height. Even in the stratosphere.

Hurriedly, a Special Service Flight of six pilots was formed from men medically selected for high altitude work. They were to fly modified Mark IXs (lightened by about 450lbs, principally by the removal of all armour). Among the pilots picked for the Special Service Flight was Pilot Officer Prince Emanuel Galitzine, a White Russian brought to England as a child in 1918. To Galitzine's delight, Special Service Flight pilots were put on a special diet 'which included plenty of sweets, chocolate, eggs and bacon, fresh orange juice and other things at that time that were either strictly rationed or unobtainable'. (Spitfire pilots were generally fed, the American volunteer William Ash had found, 'like prize geese'.)

On 10 September, Galitzine flew the modified Mk IX for the first time and found it 'absolutely delightful to handle' and far and away the best Spitfire he flew during the war, reaching 43,000 feet without difficulty.

Two days later he scrambled to meet an aircraft heading in from France. In his subsequent combat report Galitzine refers to the intercepted aircraft as a Junkers 86P. The 'R' sub-design was unknown to the RAF at the time, so was always but erroneously referred to as the Ju 86P.

SECRET FORM 'F'
PERSONAL COMBAT REPORT.
'S.S. FLIGHT NORTHOLT'
Defensive Patrol
P/O GALITZINE
A. DATE 12/9/42
B. UNIT s.s. Flight Northolt
C. TYPE OF OUR A/C Spitfire IX
D. TIME OF ATTACK 1005/45 (approx)
E. PLACE OF ATTACK Southampton area
F. WEATHER Patches of wispy cloud
G. OUR CASUALTIES, A/C Nil
H.   „   „   pilots Nil
J. ENEMY CASUALTIES in air combat 1 Ju 86 P.1.
damaged
GENERAL REPORT
I took off from Northolt at 0930 hours to intercept raid 5 and climbed to 15,000 over the aerodrome. I was then given a vector 240 degs and told to climb to 30,000 ft. I was next told to fly 130 degs. (35,000 ft.) and then 190 degs and told that E/A was to port at 40,000 ft. my height at that time being 32,000 ft. No Hun could be seen. The next course given was 245 degs. And I was told that the E/A was to port at 42,000 ft. my own height then being 38,000 ft. Almost immediately I saw black trails but to starboard, and made off in that direction, quickly overhauling the a/c but I saw still below at 41,000 ft. I turned to starboard to maintain

climbing speed and avoid overshooting and came level at 42,000 ft. with the a/c – which I recognised as a Ju 86P. I was then about 1/2 mile to port. The E/A jettisoned a medium bomb (in the Southampton) area and I jettisoned my reserve fuel tank so that I could gain height. Both of us climbed again and became level at 43,000 feet. I got slightly to starboard and 2-300 ft above and came in to within 600 yds. I dived down on him out of the sun and from 200 yds, dead astern I opened fire with a 3 sec. burst closing to 150 yds, observing that his starboard wing outside the engine nacelle was hit. My port gun then jammed and I flew into his slipstream, my windscreen becoming completely obscured. I broke away to port and climbed to 43,700 ft. When my screen had cleared, I picked up the E/A again and getting into position for attack, dived fairly steeply on him from astern with an A.S.I. of 165. When within 100 yards the Ju 86 did a surprising 45 degs. turn to starboard. I turned outside him and began to lose height, so I straightened out and climbed again to 44,000 ft. I again dived on the E/A, who was now flying but he shook me off by steering through a patch of thin mist which had the appearance of expanded smoke trails. My windscreen became obscured again. Climbing again, I waited until he was in sight and dived on him, closing to 100 yds and opened fire with the starboard cannon only. This pulled my a/c round and caused me to drop into his slipstream again with the usual result – my windscreen became clouded. I had by now lost distance somewhat but I picked up the E/A again. I lost him, however, in another patch of mist and he was not seen again. I was now about 25 miles from the French Coast (Cherbourg area). On instructions I landed at Tangmere at 1100.

The pilot only was seen in the Ju 86P and no return fire was experienced. The wing root of the E/A was so wide that it appeared to have no fuselage. I estimate that its A.S.I. was between 100 and 110, it was very economical in its use of full throttle. I never found difficulty in overtaking it. In the Southampton area, when I was at 35,000 ft. one burst of A.A. burst 600 yards ahead of me and 500 ft. below, and after crossing the English Coast intense A.A. was seen below both of us and ahead.

My A.S.I. was 130 climbing, 145 on the level above 40,000 ft. and 165 diving.

Rounds fired:– Cannon port

Galitzine's high-flying Mark IX was far from being Fighter Command's only specialist Spitfire. At the outset of the war, Dowding had released two of his precious Spitfires to 'No. 2 Camouflage Unit', later the 'Heston Special Flight', but properly the Photo Reconnaissance Unit (PRU), and headed by Wing Commander Sydney Cotton. Each Spitfire was fitted with wing mounted 5-inch cameras, but then stripped of all unneeded weight – guns, radio, armour-plating. All joints in the skin were carefully filled with plaster of Paris, before the aircraft was painted sky blue (later, a fetching evening pink) and coated with polish to give a gloss finish. With these changes the top speed of the Spitfire PR1A was 12mph faster than the fighter Mark I version. Pilot Officer Gordon Green recalled:

During the early [PRU] missions there was no such thing as cockpit heating in our Spitfires. For the high altitude missions we wore thick suits with electrical heating . . .

A big worry over enemy territory was that one might start leaving a condensation trail without knowing it, thus pointing out one's position to the enemy. To avoid that we had small mirrors fitted in the blisters on each side of the canopy, so that one could see the trail as soon as it started to form.

The early missions of the PRU Spitfires over Germany in 1939–40 were a conspicuous success, and Dowding released a dozen more Spitfires for the reconnaissance role. 'Long range' and 'extra long range' versions were developed, with Supermarine redesigning the wing to take up a huge additional fuel tank along the leading edge. The fuel load of the PR1D, nicknamed 'The Bowser', made the plane so ungainly, commented a later PRU commander, Gordon Tuttle, that, 'You could not fly it straight and level for the first half hour after take-off.' The 'extra long range' PRs however, were capable of covering formidable distances in the five-and-half hours they could remain airborne, reaching Trondheim in Norway and the Ruhr Valley in Germany. It was the Spitfire PR XI that brought back the famous photographs showing the dams breached by Guy Gibson's 617 Squadron of Lancasters on 12 May 1943.

PRU Spitfires flew low, as well as high. In Malta, Wilfrid Duncan Smith seized the chance to fly 'photo recce' missions with 683 Squadron, equipped with the Spitfire PR XI. The unit was commanded by the dashing Squadron Leader Adrian Warburton, whose exploits dazzled his friends and dismayed his foes alike. (He once managed to take photographs of an Italian admiral's personal washing on his flagship, as well as highly secret Axis facilities.) Duncan Smith later wrote:

In the next four weeks I escorted Warburton on several photo recce missions in connection with the forthcoming invasion of Sicily . . . We usually ran into trouble. Once 'Warbie' decided to take pictures of Syracuse and without wavering I found myself following him into the harbour at zero feet to me by the strongest ack-ack fire. We flew up, down and out with everything shooting at us and the only reason we escaped was because the enemy could not depress their medium guns sufficiently – we were so low.

PRU Spitfires flew fast, too. On 27 April 1944, a reconnaissance version of the Mark IX, flown by Flight Lieutenant Eric 'Marty' Martindale, reached a record-breaking 606mph in a 45 degree dive. (After the war, in 1951, a reconnaissance Spitfire, a PR XIX, powered with a Rolls-Royce Griffon engine, registered 690mph, or Mach 0.94, a shade under the sound barrier.)

The agile, speedy Spitfire remained the RAF's principle spy plane for the course of the War, operating in every theatre.

The PRU's heroes tended to be unknown outside the RAF, with the exception of Warburton who, remembered Duncan Smith, was a walking institution, 'immediately recognized . . . and greeted affectionately by civilians and servicemen alike'. (Warburton died flying a photo recce mission in Italy in 1944.) One, anonymous, PRU pilot felt moved to tell the world of his travails in verse:

> This is the tale of the Gremlins
> Told by the P.R.U.
> At Benson and Wick and St. Eval –
> And believe me, you slobs, it's true.
> When you're seven miles up in the heavens,

TALLY-HO

(That's a hell of a lonely spot)
And it's fifty degrees below zero
Which isn't exactly hot.
When you're frozen blue like your Spitfire
And you're scared a mosquito pink
When you're thousands of miles from nowhere
And there's nothing below but the drink.
It's then you will see the Gremlins,
Green and gamboge and gold,
Male and female and neuter,
Gremlins both young and old.
It's no good trying to dodge them,
The lessons you learnt on the Link
Won't help you evade a Gremlin
Though you boost and you dive and you jink.
White ones will wiggle your wingtips,
Male ones will muddle your maps,
Green ones will guzzle your Glycol,
Females will flutter your flaps.
Pink ones will perch on your perspex,
And dance pirouettes on your prop;
There's a spherical middle-aged Gremlin
Who'll spin on your stick like a top.
They'll freeze up your camera shutters,
They'll bite through your aileron wires,
They'll bend and they'll break and they'll batter,
They'll insert toasting forks in your tyres.
That is the tale of the Gremlins,
Told by the P.R.U.,
(P)retty (R)uddy (U)nlikely to many,
But fact, none the less, to the few.

★

Meanwhile, there was always someone in training to be a Spitfire pilot. The demand never lessened. Malta alone claimed the lives of 120 British and Commonwealth pilots. Losses from Leigh-Mallory's sweeps and Circuses over France were running at more than ten a week during 1942–3. And so Pierre Clostermann, a Sergeant Pilot with the Free French Air Force, having done his initial pilot training at RAF Cranwell, found himself heading for an Operational Training Unit (OTU) in Wales. And his first flight in a Spitfire:

1942

The high Welsh hills, half drowned in mist, glided to left and right of the railway line. We had passed Birmingham, Wolverhampton and Shrewsbury buried in greasy soot. Without exchanging a word, Jacques and I gazed indifferently at the depressing landscape, washed by an incessant drizzle, the dirty enervating mining towns crawling up the valleys, each one crushed by a pall of grey smoke anchored to the housetops, so dense that the wind, blowing in icy gusts, could not move it.

Our fellow passengers gazed curiously at our navy blue, gold buttoned French uniforms. The pilot's brevet of the 'Armee de l'Air' gleamed proudly on our breasts, with the wings of the RAF over our left pockets.

Barely a fortnight before we had still been pilots under training at the RAF college at Cranwell, dragging round manuals on navigation and armaments and thick books full of notes.

All that was only a memory now. In a few hours, perhaps, we would be flying a Spitfire, thus clearing the last hurdle that separated us from the great arena.

A few minutes more and we reached Rednal, No. 6i OTU – for a conversion course on Spitfires before a squadron posting.

Suddenly Jacques pressed his face to the window: 'Look Pierre, there are our Spitfires!'

Sure enough, as the train slowed down alongside an airfield, a damp ray of sunshine succeeded in piercing the fog, revealing twenty or so aircraft lined up along a strip of tarmac . . .

The great day had come! It had snowed all night and the airfield was dazzling white beneath the blue sky. Heavens, how good to be alive! I filled my lungs with the icy air and felt the snow crunch under my feet, soft and yielding like an oriental carpet. It brought back many memories. The first snow I had seen for so long . . .

At the door of the flight hut, where you shelter between flights, my instructor was waiting for me, smiling.

'How do you feel?'

'OK, Sir,' I replied, trying to hide my emotion.

All my life I shall remember my first contact with a Spitfire.

The one I was going to fly bore the markings TO-S. Before putting on my parachute I stopped a moment to gaze at it – the clean lines of the fuselage, the beautifully streamlined Rolls-Royce engine: a real thoroughbred.

'You've got her for one hour. Good luck!'

This thunderbolt was mine for an hour, sixty intoxicating minutes! I tried to remember my instructor's advice. Everything seemed so confused. I strapped myself in, trembling, adjusted my helmet, and still dazed by the mass of instruments, dials, contacts, levers, which crowded on one another, all vital, and which one's finger must not fail to touch at the psychological moment, I got ready for the decisive test.

Carefully I went through the cockpit drill, murmuring the ritual phrase, BTFCPPUR – Brakes, Trim, Flaps, Contacts, Pressure (in the pneumatic system), Petrol, Undercarriage and Radiator.

Everything was all set. The mechanic closed the door behind me and there I was, imprisoned in this metal monster which I had got to control. A last glance.

'All clear? Contact!'

I manipulated the hand pumps and the starter buttons. The airscrew began to revolve slowly, and suddenly, with a sound like thunder, the engine fired. The exhausts vomited long blue flames enveloped in black smoke, while the aircraft began to shudder like a boiler under pressure.

When the chocks were removed I opened the radiator wide, for these liquid cooled engines overheat very rapidly, and I taxied very carefully over to the runway, cleared by snowploughs, jet black and dead straight in the white landscape.

'Tudor 26, you may scramble now, you may scramble now!' Over the radio the control tower authorised me to take-off.

My heart was thumping in my ribs. I swallowed the lump in my throat, lowered my seat and with a clammy hand I slowly opened the throttle. At once I felt myself swept up by a cyclone.

Snatches of advice came back to me.

'Don't stick the nose too far forward!'

In front of me there was only a slight clearance between the ground and the tips of the enormous airscrew, which was going to absorb all the power from the engine.

Timidly I eased the stick forward, and with a jolt that glued me to the back of my seat, the Spitfire started forward, then moved faster and faster while the airfield swept by on either side with increasing speed.

'Keep her straight!'

I ruddered frantically to check incipient swings.

Suddenly, holding my breath, and as if by magic, I found myself airborne.

By 1943 the Spitfire was operating far outside its original British habitat. Planes had been shipped to the USSR for use by the Soviet Air Force (143 Mk Vbs, followed by 1,200 Mk IXs), and three squadrons of Spitfire VCs were dispatched to Australia, where they easily outclassed anything the Japanese sent over the Northern Territory, including the feared Zero. When Spitfire met Zero for the first time on 2 March 1943, the Spits knocked down two Zeros, despite the Australian pilots' lack of combat experience. Despite too, the fact that the Spitfire VCs sent to Australia had suffered from heavy use back in Britain and were close to being scrapped. (Later, Churchill sent the rather better Mark VIII which, numerals aside, was actually an improved Merlin 61 Mark IX.) Down Under the Royal Australian Air Forces' Spitfires continued to score heavily, and their success over Chittagong in 1943–4 caused Tokyo to postpone its invasion of Australia, in much the same way that Hitler had found his mind changed by the combativeness of the Spitfire in the Battle of Britain.

On the Arakhan front in Burma, the Japanese had the misfortune to run into the Spitfire again. In the jungle Battle of

TALLY-HO!

Kohima, the Thermopylae of the war in Burma, the RAF's Spitfire took a small yet crucial role, strafing Japanese positions and supply lines, at the same time as denying the Japanese air superiority over the battleground. Brigadier M.R. Roberts gave a ground level view of the air battle between Spitfires and Zeros:

> On 10 February 1944, about eighty plus Zeros and other came over and stooged around and then started to peel off by squadrons. I put on my tin hat and made for my command post, but as I was entering the slit I heard the high whine of hotted up Spitfires. The battle took place right above my head and in twenty minutes I saw fifteen Japs go down. These were all that the air force actually claimed destroyed, but they put in fourteen as probable and twenty-three damaged.
>
> I saw one Jap Zero swoop down and I thought he was going to shoot us up, then he shot up again practically perpendicular, towering like a pheasant hit in the lungs – then he fell backwards and crashed.
>
> In view of the fact that after the battle I never saw more than three Jap aircraft at any one time, my view is that both the probables and the damaged were in fact destroyed.

In the Far East the weather was as much an enemy as the Japanese. On 10 August 1944, Flying Officer Hank Costain of 615 Squadron, was tootling back from the Nagaland front to RAF Baigachi, Calcutta, when the sky was swallowed by a thick, black monsoon. Costain recalled:

> Within seconds, I was completely out of control and with the artificial horizon toppled, I had not the faintest idea

254

which way was 'up'. Outside it was so dark that I could not even see my wing tips, and the pounding of the walnut-sized hailstones on the fuselage drowned even the noise of the engine.

Costain's Spitfire was hauled violently upwards by a current of air, only to be dropped like a stone. At 1,000 feet he bailed out, landing in a paddy field with a broken leg. Three of his squadron's twelve pilots died in the storm.

In North Africa too, where the RAF stepped up operations following the lifting of the siege of Malta, the weather was perfidious and hostile. Bobby Oxspring of 72 Squadron flew into Tunisia in the wake of Operation Torch; the amphibious Allied landings of 8 November 1942, to spend Christmas in a tent in the rain:

All day long the rain pelted down and no flying was possible. Squelching through the mud we prepared to make the best of it. David Cox had bartered an enormous turkey from a local Arab with which to celebrate the great day. Since it was still alive, he kept it tied to his camp bed until the day of execution, but when eventually cooked for our feast we felt this splendid bird might not have been sacrificed. We couldn't get our teeth into the meat which must have seen twenty summers. A bounty arrived from the Ordnance Corps of one bottle of gin per head. In the absence of any suitable alternative, the potency of this overseas proof liquor was diluted with tangerine juice. To ensure continuity of the festive celebration, Derek Forde persuaded the Foreign Legion to part with a quantity of so-called *vin ordinaire* which, there being no other containers available, had to be transported in petrol tins. A mouthful of this pernicious gut rot, flavoured with the fumes of 100 octane gasoline, was sufficient to recede the hairline untold inches. We huddled in our dripping tents, knocking back the witch's brew and toasted the health of faraway kin.

Next day the rain stopped, and Oxspring and his squadron, 'strapped on our mud smeared Spits and staggered aloft to resume the war'. Arriving in Tunisia two months later, Wing Commander Hugh Dundas was 'amazed and alarmed' by the conditions before him:

> The Spitfires were operating off strips of wire matting, laid on top of rushes which in turn had been laid on the mud. The strips were between eight hundred and a thousand yards long and only twenty-five yards wide. They were connected with the squadron dispersal areas by more strips of matting, laid down in narrow lanes. A pilot who put a wheel off the runway while landing – and it was all too easy to do so when coming down in a gusty crosswind – was certain to capsize his plane. If you ran off the narrow taxi track, your plane had to be manhandled back again. For the worst winter experienced in Algeria and Tunisia for many years had turned every square yard of ground into a quagmire.
>
> Alongside these makeshift airfields the squadron officers and ground crews lived and ate in tents. The conditions in these cold, windswept, waterlogged camp sites certainly provided a brutal contrast with the comfortable and solid quarters, mostly built in the middle and late thirties, in which all ranks of the RAF had been accustomed to live at

home. Yet morale was high and it was obvious that everyone really took a secret pride in making the best of the foul conditions.

The Spitfire squadrons in North Africa were flying the tropicalized Spitfire Vb equipped with a Vokes engine intake dust filter. The bulbous filter did nothing for the Spitfire's looks and many complained that it 'knocked a bit off the speed'. Nevertheless, Bobby Oxspring thought the variant performed 'very creditably'. Certainly the tropicalized Vb was more than a match for the Italian aircraft in the theatre, which included Savoia-Marchetti 79, a lumbering tri motored torpedo bomber. Yet there were enough Luftwaffe Me 109Fs and FW 190s to make life interesting. 'Almost every mission,' recalled Bobby Oxspring, 'resulted in a clash of opposing fighters. In this environment 72 had a ball.' Over five months, 72 Squadron claimed fifty-three enemy aircraft destroyed; three 72 Squadron pilots were killed in action, three posted missing, four were wounded and two were killed in a mid-air collision. Oxspring himself survived shooting down by ground fire, to land his Spitfire in no-man's-land between the British and German lines. Covering fifty yards in record time he dived into a British slit trench and safety.

As the North African campaign ended with attempted escape of German troops from Cap Bon, the eager Spitfire boys found some unusual targets upon which to practice:

1st May 1943
To the Mess President of No. 244 Wing
Sir,
    It has been observed by various individuals of unimpeachable

character that Spitfires are making use of valuable clan buoys as targets.

These Bans, which mark the way through a minefield, have been laid at enormous expense and with great skill and daring in order to safeguard the shipping bringing you your bully, biscuits, pickles and booze Repeat booze. Should the unlikely event occur of one of these buoys being sunk or damaged by your planes, no booze will be forthcoming. Calamity!!!!

For a fee we could lay a very large sized beacon for you to practise on and perhaps hit.

Should this pernicious habit of buoy strafing not cease, no further pennies will be contributed to buy you new Spitfires.

GEOFFREY R. PRICE LT RNVR ROBIN BELL LT RNVR C. W. PEARCE LT RNVR

It was at the outset of the 1942–3 Tunisian campaign that the Seafire, the Royal Navy's long awaited version of the Spitfire, made its debut in violence. The Seafire differed nothing from the conventional Spitfire, save for an arrester hook and attachment for a catapult launch. On 8 November 1942 Sub-Lieutenant G.C. Baldwin of 801 Squadron, flying off HMS *Furious*, shot down a Vichy French Dewoitine 520. As Baldwin noted the Seafire had 'excellent air-to-air combat qualities', but 'it was really very unsuitable for the rugged type of flying where none too experienced pilots threw it on to the flight deck'. His point was proven in the following year, 1943, when the Seafires covered the Allied invasion at Salerno in Italy; more Seafires were lost in landing accidents than lost to enemy action. Out of 121 Seafires embarked for Salerno a total of forty-two

Seafires were written off in accidents and a further forty-one damaged.

The Fleet Air Arm co-opted Jeffrey Quill as an advisor. After many hours landing Seafires on aircraft carrier decks, he suggested some improvements, principally, 'an improved undercarriage design having higher energy absorption and reduced rebound ratio, the incorporation of a "sting" hook with its thrust lines passing more nearly through the aircraft's centre of gravity, the incorporation of a hydraulic damper to eliminate hook bounce . . .'

There was not much to be done, concluded Quill, about the perennial Spitfire landing problem – the poor view from pilot's cockpit – except for the pilot to 'approach the ship in a gently surviving left hand turn with a thoroughly well controlled rate of sink, sneaking in, as it were, just in front of the Seafire's blind area astern of the ship'. Fitted out with Quill's recommendations, the Seafire went from strength to strength. The last of the long line of wartime Seafires, the Mark XV had a 2,000hp Griffon engine and weighed almost as twice as much as the Spitfire Mark I. Fittingly, it was a Seafire which, on 15 August 1945, in Tokyo Bay, was the last aircraft to make an aerial kill in the Second World War. Afterwards, fighter operations against Japan were halted due to a competing operation; the atomic bombing of Hiroshima and Nagasaki.

Patrolling the Allied invasion beaches of Sicily on the morning of 10 July 1943, Wilfrid Duncan Smith saw a 'magnificent sight' below him:

The shallow waters were packed with amphibious craft and infantrymen wading ashore, while further out a grey shield of warships formed a protective arc, the red flashes of their guns stark against the dawn sky. Our Spitfires were stepped in layers from 10,000–20,000 feet, waiting to pounce on any enemy formations that dared to interfere with the operations on land and sea.

Few enemy aircraft did take to the sky. Only at the end of the day did Duncan Smith 'get any joy' when, leading 1435 Squadron, he broke up a formation of Macchi 202s and FW 190s attempting to bomb the ships. On the following day, he had better luck:

Soon after getting on patrol, I spotted four Macchi 202s immediately below and realised they had not seen us. I went down after them with my number two, and was about to open fire on the lead Macchi when they saw us and broke into our attack, still keeping immaculate formation. Thereafter a hectic dogfight took place. This Italian pilot really knew what he was doing; apart from giving a splendid aerobatic display, I found that each time he stayed and turned he gained on me in the turn. I looked frantically about for help but there was no sign of my number two. Knowing my Spitfire's capabilities so well, I pulled her up sharply in corkscrew turns into the sun as steeply as I could. I expected to hear and feel the unwelcome bangs of exploding shells in my fuselage but nothing happened, until suddenly I felt my Spitfire shake violently and the next instant we were spinning – I caught her after a couple of turns, and getting control again looked for the Macchi. Sure enough there he was, slightly to one side and below me asking to be shot down. My first burst caught him in the cockpit area and wing root and he went up in flames, shedding bits as he winged over and dived into the high ground overlooking Noto. He must have thought he had got me when he saw me spin.

I had followed him down, so I climbed up searching for the rest of my patrol. At 15,000 ft I joined up with a group of Spitfires from one of the other Wings and almost at once got mixed up with a formation of eight FW 190s. During the dogfight I chased after a solitary and managed to damage him, when once more I had to turn hard, on being attacked from behind. To this day I am not sure if the aircraft that attacked me was a Me 109 or a Spitfire. Anyway, it was extremely hostile, and as I was nearly out of ammunition, I decided I had had enough; spiralling down towards the coast, I streaked back to Malta well satisfied with life. Later, after the Italian surrender, I found when I visited Lecce that the Macchi I destroyed that day had been piloted by one of Italy's fighter aces, credited with a large number of our scalps. In general the standard of flying of the Italian pilots was very high indeed, and in encounters with Macchi 205s particularly, we were up against aircraft that could turn and dogfight with our Spitfires extremely well.

Wilfrid Duncan Smith thought the Macchi a good plane and the general standard of Italian flying 'very high'. He already knew the capabilities of the Luftwaffe, which were underscored a few days later when the grey nose of a Me 109 opened fire at him head-on:

There were two enormous bangs behind my back and the Spitfire seemed to double up with pain as the stick was wrenched out of my hand. I heard a high-pitched whine in my earphones and my radio went dead. The Spitfire then pitched into a steep, nose up attitude and the next thing I remember was that I was spinning. Collecting my wits, I struggled with the controls, and using brute force finally got the Spitfire out of the spin and level again.

Saying a prayer for his Spitfire, knowing that if he had to bale out over the sea he had no radio to send a Mayday call, Duncan Smith crawled back to Malta. On landing he found:

My Spitfire was in a mess. Cannon shells had blasted a couple of large holes in the side. One had burst against the radio and armour behind my seat. Another, having made a hole the size of a football, had torn the control wires to shreds. The elevator was hanging by one thread of frayed wire and my rigger neatly snapped this with a sharp blow from his fingers. 'You'll not be needing that any more,' he grinned at me . . . Another cannon shell had torn big pieces out of the elevator and rudder surfaces.

Duncan Smith's escape was testament, once again, to the durability of the Spitfire. The damage inflicted upon Duncan Smith's Spitfire was proof that the Luftwaffe could still 'mix it'. As the Sicilian campaign sped by, however, Duncan Smith found that enemy pilots were increasingly reluctant to come to combat. As Johannes Steinhoff, a Luftwaffe fighter commander in Sicily, explained this absence of combativeness had good cause, for, 'we lacked everything necessary to a fighter unit's operations – skilled personnel, spares, ammunition, even petrol'. Crucially, Steinhoff lacked planes and pilots. He acknowledged too that the Allied fighters were 'in quality . . . our superiors'. The Luftwaffe in

Sicily suffered a body blow to their spirit when their Commander-in-Chief sent them an Order of the Day blaming their lack of success on their absence of courage:

> Together with the fighter pilots in France, Norway and Russia, I can only regard you with contempt. If an immediate improvement is not forthcoming, flying personnel, from the Kommodore downwards, must expect to be reduced to the ranks and transferred to the Eastern Front to serve on the ground.
>
> Signed, Reichsmarschall Hermann Göring.

Deflated morale, attrition and withdrawals to other fronts meant that by spring 1944 the Luftwaffe in Italy was capable of little more than patchy resistance. Deprived of aerial prey, the Spitfire turned from fighter to grounder strafer and fighter bomber ('bombfire'). Normally the 'bombed up' Spitfire carried two 250lb bombs under the wings or a 500- pounder under the fuselage. This new role for the Spitfire, thought Hugh Dundas, was 'unexciting and un-spectacular'. It was also effective and dangerous.

Wing Commander Dundas joined 244 Wing on 31 May 1944. The Wing Operations Book recorded that he, 'arrived on posting – just in time for the party, naturally' which was held in an abandoned farmhouse with five bars and drinks so potent, 'one felt the only thing to do was call out the fire tender'. The work allocated to the Wing sobered everyone up:

> Our attention was directed entirely to ground targets. We flew out in sections of four or six aircraft, to look for enemy transport moving on the roads and when we found it we dived down to strafe with our two cannons and four

machine guns. It was not a very profitable or efficient way in which to make use of a whole Wing of Spitfires. There was a limit to the damage which could be done with guns alone against ground targets but of course, the risks were just as great as if we had been using more powerful weapons. Indeed they were greater, for you had to get down very low in order to inflict damage, and even then some targets were impervious to mere gunfire. On 7 June we had nearly lost Squadron Leader Nevil Duke, the CO of 92 Squadron and one of the finest fighter pilots in the RAF, when he was hit by ground fire and forced to bale out behind the lines. Luckily he was rescued by Italian patriots. On 15 and 16 June four aircraft and pilots were lost.

In these circumstances, and in the light of the intelligence information available to air headquarters, which showed that the enemy fighter forces had been reduced to token numbers, it was not surprising when a load of bomb racks was dumped on our doorstep on 20 June and we received the order to prepare to make use of them without delay. There thus began for me what was, I think, the most wearing and certainly the most frightening period of the whole war, ending only when the Germans finally surrendered ten and a half months later. But the first thing was to learn how to drop our bombs with reasonable accuracy. For this purpose we were allowed one week.

There were no bomb ranges available, so we practised by dropping fluorescent markers into the sea and aiming our bombs at these. Spitfires used for bombing were fitted with no special devices. We had to use the ring-and-bead reflector sight intended for air fighting. But it was extraordinary how accurate a good pilot could become with experimentation and experience.

We each had to develop and try to perfect our own technique for achieving accuracy. In due course I found that if I flew so that the target passed under my wing, just outside the cannon mounting, then held my course until it reappeared aft of my wing, I would be in about the right position to begin my dive. The target would thus be a little to one side and very slightly behind. It was then necessary to turn the Spitfire over on to its back and let the nose drop through the vertical, using ailerons and elevators to position the red bead of the reflector sight on the target and hold it there. The angle of dive would be about twenty degrees off the vertical and this would be held from the starting height of about eight thousand feet to something under two thousand feet. At this point I would decrease the angle slightly to bring the bead ahead of the target, at the same time counting 'One-and-two-and-three', then press the button. No doubt the whole procedure sounds thoroughly Heath Robinson, but it worked. In due course I reached the stage where I was most dissatisfied if my bomb burst more than fifty yards from target – and a five hundred pound bomb exploding only fifty yards away can be rather more than an irritant. Usually I succeeded in doing much better than that.

For months on end Dundas dive-bombed and strafed German targets in support of the Allied armies as they battered their bloody way north up Italy. His Spitfire sustained serious flak damage on two occasions, the second in an attack on the German's heavily fortified Gothic Line in late summer 1944:

There was a road bridge north of Rimini, a vitally important link in the enemy supply line, which we were ordered to destroy and keep out of action. It was a target we all hated, because around it the flak was particularly intense. One morning we were ordered to put a whole squadron on to it.

As I had to decide which squadron would do the job, it seemed only fair that I myself should lead it. We flew out through a clear sky, no cloud to hide our coming. I followed the coast, flying a few miles out to sea. North of Rimini I turned and led the way in. The black puffs burst all around us before we had even crossed the coast, with the target still four or five miles ahead. The temptation to swerve away was almost overpowering. I felt naked and exposed and was sure that I was going to be hit. The target passed under my wing and I rolled over into a dive. Down through the black bursts, down headlong into the carpet of white, where the 40mm shells came up in their myriads to meet me, down further into the streaking tracer of machine gun fire. I dropped my bomb and kept on down – safer on the deck than climbing up again – and used the R/T to tell the others to do the same, everyone to make his own way back across the line. Just after I had transmitted there was a thudding explosion and my Spitfire juddered. Bloody hell! A great hole had been ripped in my port wing, halfway between cockpit and wing tip. But she kept on flying and I held my course and speed, gaining height as soon as I had crossed the line.

I flew home without difficulty. My wheels and flaps came down all right so I went in for a normal landing. But one of my tyres had been punctured. As soon as the weight came down on it the plane slewed round and I could not hold it. The undercarriage leg collapsed and I ended up with one wing tip on the ground.

I went to the caravan where Brian Kingcombe and I had our living quarters. He was entertaining Duncan Smith, who had flown over to see us. They both treated my adventure as a huge joke – quite rightly, too. But for once I was not feeling jokey. I told them to go to hell and lay down on my bunk and thought, 'Oh Christ, Oh Christ, I can't go on like this.'

But of course Dundas had to go on. And did.

The Italian campaign, which later branched into southern France, sapped the soul of the Spitfire boys. Aside from trying to survive the odds – Douglas Bader, wearing his air historian's hat, estimated that three months was the life expectancy for a Spitfire boy in Italy – the pilots found that strafing brought the nature of killing into sharp relief. Wilfrid Duncan Smith, in autumn 1944, found a German soldier tried to ward off his strafing by firing an automatic pistol. 'A few seconds later,' recalled Duncan Smith, 'he disintegrated in a cloud of dust . . . The carnage on the roads was awful.'

The non-human carnage caused by 324 Wing's ground attacks in a three week period was 156 motor vehicles, 1 tank, 14 locomotives, 182 horse-drawn vehicles, and a tracked howitzer gun. The Spitfire had been conceived as a fighter. It was yet another tribute to Mr Mitchell's design that it could also be conjured into a ground attack airplane. It was a workhorse as well as a thoroughbred.

For one Spitfire pilot somewhere, it was always the day for his first big show. Sergeant Pilot Pierre Clostermann of the 'Alsace Squadron' commanded by Battle of Britain veteran Al Deere, participated in his first sweep over France in Spring 1943:

13.15 hours. I was already installed, firmly fixed to my Spitfire NL–B by the straps of my safety harness. I had tested the radio, the sight, and the camera gun. I had carefully adjusted the oxygen mask and verified the pressure in the bottles. I had armed the cannon and the machine guns and adjusted the rear vision. Tommy was wandering round the aircraft with a screwdriver, getting the detachable panels firmly fastened. My stomach seemed curiously empty and I was beginning to regret my scanty lunch. People were busy all round the field. In the distance Deere's car stopped by his aircraft, under the control tower. He was wearing a white flying suit and he slipped quickly into his cockpit. The fire crew took up their positions on the running boards of the tender, and the medical orderlies in the ambulance. The hour was approaching.

13.19 hours. Deep silence over the airfield. Not a movement anywhere. The pilots had their eyes glued on Mouchotte who was consulting his watch. By each aircraft a fitter stood motionless; his finger on the switch of the auxiliary starter batteries. Another stood guard by the fire extinguishers lying on the grass at the ready. My parachute buckle was badly placed and was torturing me, but it was too late to adjust it.

13.20 hours. Mouchotte glanced round the twelve Spitfires, then began to manipulate his pumps. A rasping rattle from the starter, then his propeller began to turn. Feverishly I switched on.

'All clear? – switches ON!'

Kept in perfect trim, my Rolls–Royce engine started first shot. The fitters rushed round, removing chocks, dragging batteries away, hanging on to the wing tips to help the aircraft pivot. Mouchotte's NL-L was already taxiing to the northern end of the field.

13.22 hours. The engines of 611 were turning and the twelve Spitfires beginning to line up on either side of Deere's in a cloud of dust. We lined up behind them in combat formation. I took up my position, my wing tip almost touching Martell's. I was sweating.

13.24 hours. The twenty-six aircraft were all ready, engines ticking over, wings glinting in the sun. The pilots adjusted their goggles and tightened their harness.

13.25 hours. A white rocket rose from the control tower. Deere raised his arm and the thirteen aircraft of 611 Squadron started forward. In his turn Mouchotte raised his gloved hand and slowly opened the throttle. Eyes fixed on Martell's wing tip, and my hands moist, I followed. The tails went up, the Spitfires began to bounce clumsily on their narrow undercarriages, the wheels left the ground – we were airborne.

I raised the undercart and locked it, throttled back and adjusted the airscrew pitch. We swept like a whirlwind over the road outside the airfield. A bus had stopped, its passengers crowding the windows. I switched over to the auxiliary tanks and shut the main tank cocks. Handling the controls clumsily and jerkily, I contrived to keep formation. The Spitfires slipped southward at tree and roof-top level in a thunderous roar which halted people in the streets in their tracks. We jumped a wooded hill, then suddenly we were over the sea, its dirty waves edged with foam and dominated on the left by Beachy Head. A blue hazy line on the horizon must be France. We hurtled forward, a few feet above the water.

Some disconnected impressions remain vividly impressed on my memory – a British coastguard vessel with its crew waving to us; an Air Sea Rescue launch gently rocking with the swell and surrounded by a swarm of seagulls.

Out of the corner of my eye I watched the pressure and temperature – normal. I switched on my reflector sight. One of the 611 aircraft waggled its wings, turned and came back towards England, gaining height. Engine trouble, probably.

13.49 hours. Over the radio we could hear in the far distance shouts and calls coming from the close escort squadrons – and suddenly, very distinctly, a triumphant, 'I got him!' I realised with a tightening of the heart that over there they were already fighting.

13.50 hours. As one, the twenty-four Spitfires rose and climbed towards the sky, hanging on their propellers, 3,300 feet a minute.

France! A row of white cliffs emerged from the mist and as we gained height the horizon gradually receded – the estuary of the Somme, the narrow strip of sand at the foot of the tree crowned cliffs, the first meadows, and the first village nestling by a wood in a valley.

Fifteen thousand feet. My engine suddenly cut and the nose dropped violently. With my heart in my mouth and unable to draw breath, I reacted instinctively and at once changed to my main petrol tanks. My auxiliary was empty. Feeling weak about the knees I realised that through my lack of experience I had used too much power to keep my position, and that my engine had used proportionately more fuel. A second's glide, a splutter, and the engine picked up again. At full throttle I closed up with my section.

'Brutus aircraft, drop your babies!' sounded Deere's clear voice in the earphones. Still considerably shaken, I pulled the handle, hoping to God that the thing would work . . . a jerk, a swishing sound, and all our twenty-four tanks fell, fluttering downwards.

'Hullo, Brutus, Zona calling, go over Channel C Charlie.'

'Hullo, Zona, Brutus answering. Channel C. Over!'

'Hullo, Brutus. Zona out!'

I pressed button C on the VHF [very high frequency] panel. A crackling sound, then the voice of Squadron Leader Holmes, the famous controller of Grass Seed, 'Hullo, Brutus leader, Grass Seed calling. There is plenty going on over target. Steer o96°-zero, nine, six. There are forty plus bandits fifteen miles ahead, angels thirty-five, over to you!'

'Hullo, Grass Seed. Brutus answering. Steering o96°. Roger out.'

Mouchotte put us in combat formation:

'Hullo, Turban, combat formation, go!'

The three sections of four Spitfires drew apart. Below to my right the Gimlets did the same.

'Brutus aircraft, keep your eyes open!'

We were at 27,000 feet. Five minutes passed. The cloudless sky was so vast and limpid that you felt stunned. You knew that France was there, under the translucent

271

layer of dry mist, which was slightly more opaque over the towns. The cold was painful and breathing difficult. You could feel the sun, but I could not make out whether I was being burnt or frozen by its rays. To rouse myself I turned the oxygen full on. The strident roar of the engine increased the curious sensation of being isolated that one gets in a single seater fighter. It gradually becomes a sort of noisy but neutral background that ends up by merging into a queer kind of thick, heavy silence.

Still nothing new. I felt both disappointed and relieved. Time seemed to pass very slowly. I felt I was dreaming with my eyes open, lulled by the slow rhythmical rocking movement up and down of the Spitfires in echelon, by the gentle rotation of the propellers through the rarefied and numbing air. Everything seemed so unreal and remote. Was this war?

'Look out, Brutus leader, Grass Seed calling. Three gaggles of twenty plus converging towards you, above!'

Holmes's voice had made me jump. Martell now chimed in:

'Look out, Brutus, Yellow One calling, smoke trails coming three o'clock!'

I stared round and suddenly I spotted the telltale condensation trails of the Jerries beginning to converge on us from south and east. Christ, how fast they were coming! I released the safety catch of the guns.

'Brutus calling. Keep your eyes open, chaps. Climb like hell!'

I opened the throttle and changed to fine pitch, and instinctively edged closer to Martell's Spitfire. I felt very alone in a suddenly hostile sky.

'Brutus calling. Open your eyes and prepare to break port. The bastards are right above!'

Three thousand feet above our heads a filigree pattern began to form and you could already distinguish the glint of the slender cross shaped silhouettes of the German fighters.

'Here they come!' I said to myself, hypnotised. My throat contracted, my toes curled in my boots. I felt as if I were stifling in a strait jacket, swaddled in all those belts, braces and buckles.

'Turban, break starboard!' yelled Boudier. In a flash I saw the roundels of Martell's Spitfire surge up before me. I banked my aircraft with all my strength, opened the throttle wide, and there I was in his slipstream! Where were the Huns? I dared not look behind me, and I turned desperately, glued to my seat by the centrifugal force, eyes riveted on Martell turning a hundred yards in front of me.

'Gimlet, attack port!'

I felt lost in the melee.

'Turban Yellow Two, break!'

Yellow Two? Why, that was me! With a furious kick on the rudder bar, I broke away, my gorge rising from sheer fear. Red tracers danced past my windshield . . . and suddenly I saw my first Hun ! I identified it at once – it was a Focke-Wulf 190. I had not studied the photos and recognition charts so often for nothing.

After firing a burst of tracer at me, he bore down on Martell. Yes, it certainly was one – the short wings, the radial engine, the long transparent hood; the square cut tailplane all in one piece! But what had been missing from the photos was the lively colouring – the pale yellow body, the greyish green back, the big black crosses outlined in white. The photos gave no hint of the quivering of the wings, the outline elongated and fined down by the speed, the curious nose down flying attitude.

The sky, which had been filled with hurtling Spitfires, seemed suddenly empty – my No. One had disappeared. Never mind, I was not going to lose my Focke-Wulf. I was no longer afraid.

Incoherent pictures are superimposed on my memory – three Focke-Wulfs waggling their wings; tracers criss-crossing; a parachute floating like a puff of smoke in the blue sky.

I huddled up, with the stick hugged to my stomach in both hands, thrown into an endless ascending spiral at full throttle.

'Look out! . . . Attention! . . . Break!' – a medley of shouts in the earphones. I would have liked to recognise a definite order somewhere, or some advice.

Another Focke-Wulf, wings lit up by the blinding flashes of its cannon firing – dirty grey trails from exhausts – white trails from square wing tips. I couldn't make out who or what he was firing at. He flicked – yellow belly, black crosses. He dived and fell like a bullet. Far below he merged into the blurred landscape.

Another one, on a level with me. He turned towards me. Careful now! I must face him!

A quick half roll, and without quite knowing how, I found myself on my back, finger on firing button, shaken to the marrow of my bones by the roar of my flame-spitting cannon. All my faculties, all my being, were focused on one single thought; I MUST KEEP HIM IN MY SIGHTS.

What about deflection? – not enough. I must tighten my

turn ! More . . . more still . . . more still ! No good. He had gone, but my finger was still convulsively pressed on the button. I was firing at emptiness.

Where was he? I began to panic. Beware, 'the Hun you haven't seen is the one who gets you!' I could feel the disordered thumping of my heart right down in my stomach, in my clammy temples, in my knees.

There he was again – but a long way away. He dived, I fired again – missed him! Out of range. Ranging, I persisted . . . one last burst . . . my Spitfire quivered, but the Focke-Wulf was faster and disappeared unscathed into the mist.

The sky had emptied as if by magic. Not one plane left. I was absolutely alone.

A glance at the petrol – thirty-five gallons. Time to get back. It was scarcely a quarter past two.

'Hullo, Turban, Yellow Two. Yellow One calling. Are you all right?'

It was Martell's voice from very far away.

'Hullo, Yellow One, Turban Yellow Two answering. Am OK and going home.'

I set course 320° for England, in a shallow dive. A quarter of an hour later I was flying over the yellow sands of Dungeness. I joined Biggin Hill circuit. Spitfires everywhere, with wheels down. I wormed my way in between two sections and landed.

As I taxied towards Dispersal I saw Tommy, with arms raised, signalling and showing me where to park.

I gave a burst of throttle to clear my engine and switched off. The sudden silence dazed me. How odd to hear voices again undistorted by the radio.

Tommy helped me out of my harness. I jumped to the ground, my legs feeling weak and stiff.

Martell came striding towards me, and caught me round the neck.

'Good old Clo-Clo! We really thought you had had it!'

We went over to join the group by the door round Mouchotte.

'Hey, Clo-Clo, seen anything of Beraud?'

Beraud, it appeared, must have been shot down.

Bouguen's aircraft had been hit by two 20 mm shells. 485 Squadron had brought down two Focke-Wulfs. Mouchotte and Boucher had severely damaged one each.

I was now voluble and excited. I told my tale, I felt lighthearted, as if a great weight had been lifted from me. I had done my first big sweep over France and I had come back!

That evening, in the mess, I felt on top of the world.

Clostermann, who would also fly Typhoons, ended the war as one of the Allies' top scoring aces, with thirty-six aircraft confirmed destroyed.

The liberation of Clostermann's homeland, France, was the centrepiece of the Allies' strategy for defeating Germany in the West. In preparation for D-Day; the Allied invasion of Normandy on 6 June 1944, Fighter Command (temporarily renamed Air Defence Great Britain) was tasked with achieving air superiority over France and 'softening' up German defences. The former had already largely been achieved with the introduction of the Spitfire Mark IX; the latter took weeks of dive-bombing and strafing. From 19 May to 1 June 3,400, fighter sorties were flown against railway locomotives and marshalling yards alone. As in Italy, strafing and dive-bombing turned out to be lethal work, but in the catchphrase of the time, the Spitfire boys 'pressed on regardless'. On 19 May 1944 the commanding officer of 411 (RCAF) Squadron was blown to bits when the bomb he was carrying took a direct hit from flak at Hazebrouck.

So effective was the work of the Spitfire in the pre-invasion period, that the Luftwaffe was unable to turn up for the big day. Flying over the invasion beaches at midday, Clostermann was almost disappointed by the, 'astonishing absence of reaction on the part of the Luftwaffe'. Some overly keen USA Air Force pilots in Mustangs were the biggest menace to the Alsace Squadron:

> The sky was full of American fighters, in pairs. They were wandering about rather haphazard, and showed a tendency to come and sniff at us from very close to. When they seemed too aggressive we showed our teeth and faced them. One Mustang coming out of a cloud actually fired a burst at Graham. Graham, whose shooting was as good as his temper was bad, opened fire on him, but luckily for the Mustang, he missed.

Wing Commander Johnnie Johnson, now leading the Canadian Wing, considered that the air space above the beaches was so crowded with Allied craft that, 'the danger was not from the Luftwaffe, but from a mid-air collision.'

Just as British troops at Dunkirk had asked, 'Where is the RAF?' German troops on the ground in Normandy asked the question, 'Where is the Luftwaffe?' The answer was uncomplicated and painful; it barely existed in Normandy. According to Adolf Galland, the Luftwaffe's fighter supremo, the Luftwaffe had 319 serviceable fighters in theatre, a ratio of 1:20. Over the next month a transfer of fighters from the Reich built up the Luftwaffe's pool of fighters on the invasion front to 1,000. 'Now we fought and met the Luftwaffe daily over the Normandy countryside,' recalled Johnson, as both sides went on search-and-destroy sweeps. One such mission by 222 Squadron pounced on a German staff car scuttling along a Normandy back lane. Among the wounded was one Field Marshal Erwin Rommel.

For all the guts of the Luftwaffe's fighter pilots ('These boys are staying to fight,' Johnson would call out his R/T), they could not dent the Allies' air superiority; partly because of Allied numbers, partly because of the superiority of the Spitfire Mark IX, and partly because the Allies were now able to fly off strips and bases in France itself, thereby giving their planes more time in the air than before. It was over Normandy that Johnson topped Sailor Malan's record of thirty-two confirmed kills:

Our skirmish had drawn us away from the scene of the original melee and now we found ourselves over a layer of white cloud. A perfect backcloth on which to spot enemy aircraft, and I climbed our small section still higher. A 109 sprang out of the cloud, climbed and levelled out 2,000 feet below. We were ideally poised for a surprise attack, well hidden in the strong sun. Bill had not seen the 109. Nor should he, for it was his job to guard our tails, mine to search and strike.

'One 109 at ten o'clock, Bill. Going down. All clear?'

'All clear, Greycap. I'm covering you.'

This was perfect teamwork. I could pay undivided attention to the Hun below and I hit his ugly yellow nose with a long, steady burst. Thick black smoke poured from the Messerschmitt, but he continued to fly and darted for the protection of the cloud. We tore after him and I reflected on the wisdom of this move. I did not know the depth of this layer of cumulus cloud and it could reach to the ground. My blind flying instruments had toppled in the dive and I was losing height very rapidly. If the cloud was very deep, then perhaps there wouldn't be sufficient height to recover when we rocketed out of its base. But I was committed to the chase and we plunged into the swirling white, blanket. For a second of time, which seemed an eternity, the cloud held and imprisoned my bucking Spitfire. The glaring whiteness blinded me, but my fears were groundless, as the layer was very thin and I dropped into a safer world, bounded by wide horizons of green and gold patchwork fields. The 109, conspicuous by its trailing banner of smoke, was some 800 yards ahead and I closed in for the kill. But the Messerschmitt was out of control, and at a shallow angle struck the ground. For a moment I had thought the enemy pilot was trying to pull off a crash landing. If so he was far too fast, for the aircraft hit the ground at well over 200 miles an hour. For a short distance it careered across the uneven surface of a meadow. Then it hit a dyke, tore into a stout hedge and pitched into the air once again. The wings and tail were torn apart. The fuselage twisted as it fell to the earth, where it disintegrated into a thousand pieces.

We flew back to St Croix at low level, only varying our height when we had to climb to 6,000 feet to clear the enemy's efficient flak belt west of Caen. I felt exhausted and was anxious to get down, so that I could stretch out on my bed and relax. We had pursued the enemy and had been hunted ourselves. During the last short encounter with the Messerschmitt, all my energy and impulses had been geared high in the scale of violence; I had taken a deliberate and calculated risk when I dived through the cloud, and now the reaction set in. On the last few miles of the flight back to the airfield, with the ever vigilant Draper guarding my flank down sun, I felt drained and fatigued. It was the first time this had occurred in the air.

Back at St Croix, there was a good deal of handshaking and backslapping since the Messerschmitt brought my total of victories to thirty-three. The news soon spread, and within an hour a batch of Allied press and radio correspondents arrived on the scene for their stories. I tried to explain to the correspondents that it was my job to see that the Canadians brought down the maximum number of enemy aircraft. In carrying out this job I had topped Sailor Malan's score of thirty-two confirmed, but otherwise there was little similarity between our two tasks. Malan had fought with great distinction when the odds were against him. He had matched his handful of Spitfires against greatly superior numbers of Luftwaffe fighters and bombers. He had been forced to fight a defensive battle over southern England and often had to launch his attacks at a tactical disadvantage when the top cover Messerschmitts were high in the sun.

The Spitfire Mark IXs in Johnson's Wing were fitted with the latest gyroscopic gun-sight which automatically computed the amount of deflection needed when attacking a German aeroplane. Johnson himself preferred the old-fashioned reflector gun-sight and ensured that his personal Spitfire kept it. However,

Johnson's Canadians did come up with one engineering novelty he wholly approved of; some ingenious mind modified the Spit's bomb racks to carry small barrels of beer over from England.

The Germans, no slouches at technological innovation themselves, at dawn on 13 June 1944, launched the first FXG-76 or V1 flying bomb against London. It fell short, hitting the village of Swanscombe, Kent. Nine others were fired off that morning, three of them hitting London. Then the V1s – the V stood for *Vergeltungswaffen* or 'vengeance weapon' – started dropped out of the sky with alarming and deadly regularity. On 18 June, 500 V1s were launched, one of which fell of the Guard's Chapel at Wellington Barrack's, St James, killing 121 people.

Londoners knew the 2 ton rocket as the 'doodlebug'. Once again, Spitfire boys were called on to save London from a 'Blitz'. All available Spitfire squadrons flying the new Mark XIV (which was fitted with a Griffon 61 series engine, with a two-stage supercharger) were deployed to Kent to combat the menace. In all, Spitfire and Typhoon pilots shot down 1,999 of the missiles. The redoubtable Bobby Oxspring, from 91 Squadron, was among them:

Until we gained a little experience, the art of destroying Doodlebugs caused us much chagrin and sometimes grief. The average speed of the targets was 400mph which was around the low limits of the Spit XIVs and Tempests. It was necessary to maintain a high cruising speed and superior altitude to be able to drop on the Divers [as the RAF called the V1s] as they streaked across Kent towards London. My first encounter occurred at Maidstone, and as I curved after my target I underestimated its speed and found myself in a stern chase. Very slowly I reduced the range until able to fire, and as I did so bits flew off the rear end and the craft plummeted down. Concentrating on the action, I had not kept track of my position until I saw to my consternation my target explode on a Nissen hut in the bounds of Battersea power station. The hut disintegrated but I afterwards heard to my relief that there were no casualties . . . We found the ideal tactics for destroying these menacing missiles to be crucially governed by the range at which we fired. Over 250 yards usually hit the flying control system of the craft, which would dive to the ground with an active warhead. Often a range of 250 yards or less almost always clobbered the warhead which could severely damage the attacking fighter. The ultimate lay in accurate shooting between 200 and 250 yards, which provided a reasonable certainty of exploding the warhead in the air without undue danger to the fighter.

Or the Spitfire pilot could flip the V1 off balance using the plane's wing. In tackling the V1 the Spitfire boys, as ever, showed uncommon valour. None more so than Oxspring's fellow pilot in 91 Squadron, Frenchman Jean Maridor, who, after blasting a V1 into a dive, realized that it would crash into a field hospital. At this, Maridor deliberately rammed his Spitfire into the rocket and blew it up midair, killing himself in the process.

The pugnacious Spitfire XIV was a brute to master, as Flight Sergeant Ronnie Ashman found on climbing into the cockpit on a familiarization course:

I knew I had an audience as the instructor went over the details as I climbed in the cockpit, which made me more nervous than ever. I could see my mates watching at the flight hut. The starting procedure differed and when the engine fired it sounded very rough, different again to the smooth Merlin, but it was obvious to me that much more power was harnessed under that huge nose. Taxiing to the runway it was clumsy, forward vision was virtually nil, necessitating constant swinging left and right, and sticking one's head out from one side to the other. With butterflies in my tummy I lined her up on the runway and asked permission of control to take-off.

The take-off was a nightmare; to an onlooker it would appear I was a complete novice. This engine rotated the propeller the opposite way to any other Spitfire and I'd taken note of it when I read the handbook. Pilots on all aircraft have to trim the rudder for take-off, to counter the torque of the propeller shaft which swings the aircraft to one side, otherwise he hasn't the strength in the opposite leg to keep it straight on the runway and the aircraft will swing off it before becoming airborne, as the power builds up. Properly trimmed, the rudder will respond to the slightest pressure of the pilot's feet. I don't know why – nerves, a hangover or whatever – but I trimmed her for the Merlin engine as usual, the opposite to this Griffon, and opened the throttle far too wide for take-off, and too soon. I could feel the terrific thrust in my back as the speed built up much too fast; with my left foot hard down to keep her straight it was of no avail. She veered off the runway sideways, but luckily she became airborne at the wide intersection of the runways 45 degrees off course.

These Spitfires had been known to turn over on their back when too much power was applied on take-off, killing the pilot immediately. However, once airborne and climbing, I pulled myself together quickly and got her under control. The power of the aircraft was fantastic. She scared me to death, she was a real handful, but I was determined to master her. Fortunately the landing was good and when I taxied back to the dispersal I got a right going over by the flight lieutenant; he said I was very lucky not have burst a tyre on take-off. Inspection of the undercarriage showed severe tyre scrub necessitating the fitting of new tyres and the oleo legs had to be checked for stress.

When mastered, however, Ashman found the Mark XIV had all the Spitfire hallmarks:

She required more skill than a lighter Spitfire to fly at low speed, but she more than made up for it when she was in full song, as all the characteristics of the earlier Spitfires made themselves apparent. Aerobatics at speed were easy if one carried them out correctly. She was so sensitive that she flicked into a spin without much warning, if one was ham-handed. Once one was used to the high speed needed for the heavy all-up weight, she was a lovely, stable machine.

Not even a 439mph Spitfire Mark XIV could catch Hitler's next terror weapon sent against London the V2 rocket, first launched against London from sites in Holland in September 1944. Designed by Wernher von Braun, the V2 reached 5,000mph. (Braun, after the war, supervised the NASA programme that led eventually to the Moon landing.) All that could be done against the V2 was to destroy its launch sites in Holland. Flight Lieutenant Raymond Baxter of 602 Squadron explained the dive-bombing procedure used against the sites:

> If you were leading you flew over the target so that it passed under your wing, just inboard of the roundel. You would then count, 'One and a thousand, two and a thousand,' roll on your back and come down like that, with every aeroplane following doing the same thing. So ideally, it was a stream of four aeroplanes together. We bombed individually but obviously did not drop bombs until the leader had pulled away. And that was the trick. It all depended on how good the leader was because if he was too far away, and his dive wasn't steep enough, the other dives would tend to be flatter and flatter which made the bombing inaccurate and was also dangerous. The desires angle of the dive was 70 to 75 degrees, which feels vertical. Ideally we would start at 8,000 feet, drop the bombs at 3,000 feet and then pull out, maintaining low level to clear the area. We never bombed at random, only when we were sure we had identified the pinpoint target.

On one such diving-bombing mission, 602 Squadron earned themselves a footnote in aeronautical history. Baxter recalled:

> During our attacks on a launching site we must have caught the V2 firing crew well into countdown. After we had released our bombs and we going back for a low-level 'strafe' with our cannon, one of the flame belching monsters began to climb slowly out of a clump of trees. Flight Sergeant 'Cupid' Love, one of my pilots, actually

fired a long burst at it with his cannon – which must have been the first ever attempt to bring down a ballistic missile in flight.

Baxter's 602 Squadron flew the brand new Spitfire XVI, introduced in September 1944, which was effectively a low-level interceptor Mark IX powered by a Merlin engine produced under by the American Packard Company. Later versions were fitted with a bubble or teardrop canopy. Baxter declared the XVI as, 'easily the most offensively optimized Spitfire I ever flew', while some Spitfire pilots thought it merely the most offensive Spitfire they ever flew. A batch of Spitfire XVIs sent to Johnnie Johnson's Canadian Wing, now based in liberated Belgium, turned out to be faulty, the Americans having put the wrong sort of metal in the big ends. As a result these Spitfires seized up in mid-flight, causing a number of casualties.

To make matters still more dismal for Johnson's Wing, the re-equipment with Spitfire Mark XVIs coincided with the appearance over the Western Front of the first German jet planes, principally the 540mph Me 262. Johnson recalled his first aerial encounter with a Me 262:

Suddenly, without warning, an enemy jet appeared about hundred yards ahead of our Spitfires. The pilot must have seen our formation, since he shot up from below and climbed away at high speed. Already he was out of cannon range, and the few rounds I sent after him were more an angry gesture at our impotence than anything else. As he soared into the darkening, eastern sky, he added insult to injury by carrying out a perfect, upward roll.

Yet even against jet power, the Spitfire still had a trick in its wings. The classic, time-honoured manoeuvrability of the Spitfire sometimes allowed an ascendancy over the Me 262. On 25 December 1944 Flight Lieutenant J.J. Boyle of 411 (RCAF) Squadron managed to despatch his second Me 262 jet, bagging himself a Christmas present envied by all in Fighter Command. In his subsequent combat report he recorded:

> While flying as yellow one with 411 Squadron I returned to Base after a sweep and was letting down over Base from 15,000ft. I sighted enemy a/c at 3,000ft. My air speed was 400 plus and range 300 yards when I opened fire. Angle of attack on first burst of two seconds was 30 degrees. Second burst of three seconds from line astern, range 500 yards, made port jet unit flame. I was then able to maintain my range; third and fourth burst of five seconds each, range 500, knocked pieces off enemy a/c. He tried a crash landing but hit trees and then the ground. He exploded and the a/c disintegrated. Red Leader (S/L) Newell witnessed the crash. G.G.S [Gyroscopic gunsight] and Cine Camera used.
>
> I claim one ME 262 DESTROYED.

Two months later, flying over Holland, Flight Lieutenant F.A.O. Gaze of 610 Squadron also downed a Me 262:

> I did an orbit at 13,000 feet to clear off the ice on the windscreen and sighted three Me 262s in vic formation passing below me at cloud top level. I dived down behind them and closed in, crossing behind the formation, and attacked the port aircraft, which was lagging slightly. I could not see my sight properly as we were flying straight into the

sun, but fired from dead astern at a range of 350 yards, hitting it in the starboard jet with the second burst, at which the other two aircraft immediately dived into cloud. It pulled up slowly and turned to starboard and I fired, obtaining more strikes on the fuselage and jet, which caught fire.

A more commonplace method of dealing with the Me 262s was to destroy them when they were at their most vulnerable; stationary on the ground. Thus the Me 262 airfields were added to the long list of patrolling, armed recce, strafing, dive-bombing and bomber escort duties of the Spitfire squadrons as the front edged closer to Germany. The supposed 'glamour boys' of the fighter squadrons found their job distinctly lacking in that quality. Sergeant E.A.W. Smith of 127 Squadron confided to his diary:

We came a gutser, day before yesterday. Our skipper Smik and Flying Officer Taymans (Belgian) both got the chop. We have been 'shook rigid' as the airmen say, ever since. There were eight of us NCO's on the show, and we could not even eat lunch after debriefing, we were so shaken. Why Smik took us down to bomb and strafe Zwolle marshalling yards, we certainly will never know.

We were out on a simple armed recce, patrolling Arnhem-Hengele-Zwolle. We had plenty of petrol, each of us carrying a sixty gallon belly tank. Why we didn't continue patrolling until we found some METs or even a railway train in a siding, is a good question – to which there will never be an answer. Even as Red Leader came in on r/t, I found myself saying, silently, 'No, shit, no, no, no! Not the marshalling yards, for Christ's sake!' What he said was,

'Monty Squadron, this is Monty Red Leader. Jettison tanks – arm bombs. We are going in. Count five, and in we go.'

I could feel my face freezing, as if from a dentist's hypodermic. Hell, we hadn't jettisoned half the drop tanks when the flak guns started firing. The heavies had our height and range immediately – twenty, thirty black mushroom puffs from 88s. Before half of us rolled over for the dive, the 37 and 20 mm tracers came arcing up from all around the yards.

I was fourth in, flying number two to Eckert, and even as I started diving I saw they had my range, too. I was following Eckert, making sure that I would not shoot him in the dive, then the tracers flashed below and above my wings, like fireworks. I was perhaps 300 feet, pressing the bomb tit, when I saw one gigantic red–yellow streak flash across the yard rails for perhaps two hundred yards, and I knew immediately that someone had bought it. Did I see – or imagine – out of the corner of my right goggle, a cart-wheeling mass of Spitfire wing, like a broken boomerang, at ten, twenty feet, crossing almost every shiny rail to the starboard side? Now I was down to the deck, very con-scious of the flak zipping past me, braced for the hit that would surely come. I suddenly realized that I was below the power wire pylons, and I had to pull up to clear them. To my quiet horror, I saw a Spitfire cross my beam from starboard, and I realized it was one of Yellow Section – and he hadn't even seen me. I watched him pull up, rudder pedals obviously kicking madly, and I saw the tracers literally snapping at his arse.

Then, stupidly, I stole a glance in my rear view mirror, and saw whatever was shooting at him was happening to me. Self-preservation was telling me, 'Pull up! Pull *uppp*!' and my logic said, 'Stay down!' I was flying across Zwolle, rooftops just beneath me, seemingly for a minute, but actually a matter of seconds.

It took us minutes to re-form at angels eight, far away from the gunfire. There were still traces of black (88) smoke as we climbed. I saw no bombs explode, though they must have done. Then, it was the clear, accented, calm voice of Peter Hillwood Blue Leader. 'Monty Squadron, call off by position, angels eight. This is Monty Blue Leader.' 'Monty Blue Two.' 'Blue Three.' 'Monty Blue Four.'

'Yellow Section?' 'Yellow Leader' – etcetera. 'Monty Red Leader – are you with us – *over*?'

There was just – silence. Peter Hillwood must have known. 'Monty Squadron. Form up on me.' He waggled his wings, steeply, left, right, left right. We know what to do. Leave the missing planes as holes in Red Section. 'Setting course. Longbow Control – this is Monty Squadron. Coming home. Over.'

'Roger, Monty – Can we help?'

'Actually, Longbow, no.'

I have never been as wet with sweat, or as shivering cold, as I was on the way back. When I jumped down from the wing's trailing edge – I thought that my legs were gone – had given out. I could barely stand.

Debriefing went on and on. Many questions, few answers. I wanted to make an emotional outburst. More importantly, I needed to relieve my bladder. The bladder won, in the circumstances.

Today, I flew on a show, low level bombing and strafing gun positions at Dunkirk. Though we did not see much flak, Griffin got a hit in the engine. He got back okay. In a way, it was a wizard show. We started fires, and the smoke covered the target even before we left. We got a 'blue ribbon' bulletin just before squadron release. It read, 'The following message has been received by 84 Group from SHAEF via TAF to be passed on to 132 Wing:

THE ARMY WAS MUCH IMPRESSED BY THE WING'S EFFORTS THIS MORNING'S TARGETS – KEJ I, KEJ2, AND KEJ3.

Commendations do not come every day. I have lifted a copy from the adj's office to stick in my flying log book.

I hope to God that we never go down again on a Zwolle. I will remember Zwolle.

September 6th, B.33, Camp Neuseville

We are here, and it is miserable. Cold, blustery winds, sudden showers. All of our gear is wet. The entire wing landed safely, all but for two 331 Squadron pilots, who landed on soft earth, two point, and nosed over. One of them nosed over right at the end of the field, and sat there as a mute warning to the rest of us who landed later. As each of us landed at the top of the hill, we were met by our airmen, who braced themselves under our wings, so that we could taxy to a tarpaulin. It was slow, maddening slow work – and arduous for our hard backed airmen. Food for lunch – M and V (meat and veg in cans) cold. The fires won't keep lighted in the wind and rain. The hard tack biscuits are all wet. Thank God for the new orange canvas beds with the steel struts! We carried them in the gun ports, separate to our two rolled blankets.

We ate the M and V, and immediately turned to the task of setting up the cots, and opening our kit bags, and shaving kits. It seemed only an hour before we were called to briefing. It was an immediate show, and a dangerous one. We were to strafe a radar station in the precincts of Boulogne, a major city. Two squadrons called for – 331 and 127. At the briefing they showed us two or three aerial recce photographs, showing us clearly what we had to strafe – to put out of action. The photos were taken from angels eight. Good pictures.

Following the briefing, Bradley briefed us separately, standing in the open field with rain falling steadily. Here is what he said, 'When we roll over, it will be out of cloud, and directly over target. We will dive as close to vertical as we can make it. You will push your throttle through the gate, if you can. We will be going as balls out as balls out can go. Pull out when you see me pull out – not a foot higher or a foot lower. Expect flak like you've never seen before. This is Boulogne, and I can promise you that they've got the flak, and the bastards will be ready for us. Throttle through the gate, so we can all have tea together! Good luck!'

We took the same arduous procedure to get into the air. Two airmen shoulder each wing. At the given call 'Two-six!' they brace their bodies and lift. Pilot guns the throttle, and the Spitfire trundles three or four yards. Brace again – 'Two six' – gun the throttle – and move forward three or four more yards. Finally, we are on the compressed soil, the take-off strip which the trucks have pounded, before we arrived. We do not turn 'in herringbone'; noses in to each other, because there is no room to take off in pairs. We must remember to hold the control column back, so that we don't hit a soft area with the tail up. Take-off is fraught with danger, and each aircraft staggers off the ground. Mercifully we are not carrying bombs, or 60 gallon belly tanks, as we would not get off the ground.

Once airborne, we had to circle base once, as the teams of three fours were slow getting off the ground. The target area was about six-tenths cloud covered, so we at least had some element of surprise. We flew in and out of cloud, with violent bouncing, and then Bradley spoke, 'Monty squadron sections – close up. Monty Red Section – in we go.' I was flying right behind Bradley, and I rolled over on my back, following him exactly. As he went into a vertical dive, he flipped to r.t. switch again. 'Balls out! Here it comes!' I shoved the stick and throttle hard forward, and saw the flak tracers coming up, slow at first, then increasing to incredible speed. I made sure that Bradley was not in my gunsight, and depressed the centre of the gun button. I picked the centre building on the ground, depressing the stick even more. I saw the airspeed indicator winding up, as the altimeter was winding down – very fast.

Suddenly, in a split second, I felt my heart stop as the target was obliterated by the black explosion of an 88-millimetre flak burst! In that same instant, my eyes picked out the other three bursts, as eighty-eights are always in bursts of four. My propeller chewed straight through the black puff, as I fully expected to be ripped apart by shrapnel. Apparently I was half a second too late – the shrapnel was already outside my span. I continued firing cannons and point fives, and suddenly Bradley pulled out, and as I followed him I was almost too late. I could clearly see the black ring around his duck egg blue propeller, then he was way above me, and I surely felt the main span creak under

'G' forces that I had never deliberately caused before. Ahead and still above, Bradley dove for the deck once more, 20-millimetre tracers following him, like rain.

Clear of the target and the flak, Bradley spoke: 'Monty squadron, re-form angels eight, over river bend.'

My throat was very dry. My shoulders, my back, my buttocks, all were wet as though I had been soaked in a pool. My first thought was, 'Is it blood?' I slipped my left hand around my back. It was simply the sweat of fear. As we flew back to the wheatfield, my battle dress, tunic and trousers, became miserably – *cold*. We broke cloud, over the field, at under 1,000 feet. It was raining. The airmen were so soaked – you could have put them through a mangle. Their greasy blues could not have held any more rain. What men they are! *Two six! Two-six!*

It is raining into the night. Will this continue? Will we be able to fly out of here?

Smith loathed strafing, dive-bombing and armed recces. When he heard that the squadron was to escort B-25 Mitchells on 18 November, he 'could have jumped for joy'. The bombers duly drew all the flak ('a carpet of 37mm you could walk on') and the only discomfort he suffered was the cold, because at 'angels eighteen' the cockpit of his Spit was comparable to 'a tub of ice cold water'. Ronnie Ashman's beautiful fur-lined leather Irvin flying jacket, issued to him to keep such exigencies at bay, was stolen by a covetous soldier.

On 1 January 1945 the Luftwaffe mounted its last major attack of the war, when 800 fighter and fighter bombers crossed the Rhine to attack thirteen British and four American airfields as

part of Hitler's 'Autumn Mist' counter-offensive, better known
to the Allies as the Battle of the Bulge. In this desperate role of
the dice, 144 Allied planes were destroyed, mostly on the
ground, including eleven Spitfires of Johnnie Johnson's Canadian
Wing at Evere, where normal patrolling had been delayed
because of ice on the runway:

> From our reasonably safe position on the ground Bill and I
> took stock of the attack. The enemy fighters strafed singly
> and in pairs. Our few light ack-ack guns had already ceased
> firing; later we found that the gunners had run out of
> ammunition. The enemy completed dominated the scene,
> and there was little we could do except shout with rage as
> our Spitfires burst into flames before our eyes.

In the mayhem Johnson noticed, with the eye of the seasoned
veteran, that the German pilots' shooting was atrocious and their
flying reminiscent of training school novices.

A tactical success from the Luftwaffe, the New Year's Day raid
could not offset the sheer numbers of aircraft being produced by
the US and Great Britain. Or stem the Allied drive into the skies
of the Reich. The Operations Record Book of E.A.W. 'Ted'
Smith's 127 Squadron, RAF 132 (Norwegian) Wing, shows the
ceaseless, varied destructions the Spitfire took to the to the Reich
in winter and spring 1945:

> 6 January: After being recalled from a false start 127 and 322
> Squadrons, led by S/Ldr Sampson, got away at 12.55 hours
> as area cover to Marauders bombing P.870777. They swept
> the target area uneventfully. Owing to 10/10ths cloud, the
> ground could not be seen. One aircraft returned early with

R/T trouble and another Spitfire provided escort. The squadron landed at 1445 hours. F/Lt CR Birbeck arrived on posting from 84 GSU.

22 January: Dive bomb V2 oxygen factory at Alblasser-dam. 66, 127, and 332 Squadrons were detailed for the aforementioned mission. Twelve aircraft of 127 Squadron took off at 10.25 hours and followed 332 Squadron in a dive from 8,000 to 4,000 feet. Nine 500lb and twenty-four 250lb MC .025 seconds delay were dropped with only a fair result obtained. Five hits were scored in the target area and several near misses were observed. Of three 500lb bombs which hung up, two were jettisoned in the target area and one fell off at D.8538. There was meagre, accurate, heavy flak from the target area and it is believed that F/Lt Richardson, who is not yet reported, was hit. He was last seen weaving low in an easterly direction away from the target area. The squadron landed back at base at 11.05 hours.

127 and 322 Squadrons were detailed to carry out a Fighter Sweep in the Osnabruck area, which was designed to catch enemy aircraft returning back to their bases after attacking Allied bombers.

Twelve aircraft of 127 Squadron led by F/Lt Lea were airborne at 14.10 hours and patrolled the area uneventfully, returning to base at 15.45 hours.

4 February: Six Spitfires of 127 Squadron led by F/Lt Fyfe were detailed to escort Mitchells bombing target at Deventer. They were airborne at 14.25 hours and proceeded to rendezvous but owing to 10/10ths cloud contact was not made and Mitchells were actually found returning from the target, and were escorted back to our lines. The section landed at 15.55.

10 February: Twelve aircraft led by F/Lt Fyfe took-off at 13.15 hours to Blind Bomb an Ammunition Dump at Xanten. They proceeded to rendezvous north-east of Arnhem where, at 10,000 feet, they were taken over by MRCP control. Twelve 500 and twenty-two 250lb MC 025 seconds were dropped and all fell closely concentrated in the centre of the target. Smoke was seen but there was no abnormal explosion. Two 250lb bombs hung up and were jettisoned. One aircraft returned early due to losing formation in cloud. The squadron landed at 14.25 hours.

66 and 127 Squadrons were detailed to dive-bomb German Military headquarters at Kasteel Biyenbeek. Twelve aircraft of 127 Squadron led by F/Lt Fyfe were airborne at 16.25 hours. Nine 500 and twenty-two 250lb MC 025 seconds bombs were dropped in a dive from 8,000 to 4,000 feet, scoring one direct hit on the most northerly building and the remainder in the target area. Three 500 and two 250lb bombs hung up of which one 500lb and two 250lb were brought back. One 500lb fell off on the runway whilst one 500lb was jettisoned. The squadron landed at 17.25 hours.

13 February: Armed recce area V. Ten aircraft operating in pairs at 15 minute intervals were airborne, commencing at 10.10 hours. Three MET [Mechanized Enemy Transport] moving north-west at A.0457 were attacked and one MET was damaged. Four trucks heading east at A.0457 were attacked and one MET was damaged. Four trucks heading at A.0457 were also attacked, two were left burning and the other two were damaged. A large covered lorry was destroyed at E.9973. There was intense, light flak from A.1560 and one Spitfire was damaged (Category AC) but

the pilot was unhurt. The section landed by 12.45 hours.

Operating in the same area, eight aircraft were airborne at 14.40 hours but were recalled due to poor weather and landed at 15.25 hours.

21 February: Fifteen aircraft with pilots arrived at Fairwood Common. What a break.

21 March: 66 and 127 Squadrons were detailed as escort to Mitchells bombing Borken. Eleven aircraft of 1276 Squadron were airborne at 10.30 hours and made rendezvous with the bombers according to plan. The escort was uneventful and the bombing appeared good; a big fire being seen in the target area. There was intense, inaccurate, heavy flak from the target area, and the north-east of Bocholt. The squadron landed at 11.45 hours.

66 and 127 Squadrons again operated as escort to Mitchells. Eleven aircraft of 127 Squadron were airborne at 16.10 hours. Rendezvous as planned and escort uneventful. Then bombing appeared good. There was moderate, accurate, heavy flak from the target area and Borken. The squadron landed at 17.35 hours

22 March: Eight aircraft, led by F/O James, were airborne at 10.00 hours on rail interdiction in the Amersfoort-Zwolle area. Two cuts were observed on the line at Z.5108 and Z,5209. One hit was scored on the railway embankment at Z.9924. All aircraft landed at 11.20 hours.

The squadron was released from 12.00 hours until 12.00 hours on 23 March 1945.

24 March: The squadron was detailed to patrol Arnhem, Emmerich and Rees. Eleven aircraft under S/Ldr Lister were airborne at 09.15 hours and commenced patrolling at 09.30 hours at 12,000 feet. No enemy aircraft were sighted,

but one section went down and destroyed a motorcycle moving north at E.9473. One aircraft landed at B.89 due to tank trouble. Moderate, inaccurate, heavy flak was experienced east of Arnhem and intense, accurate flak from Woods (E.9475). The squadron landed at 10.50 hours.

The squadron was detailed to carry out an armed recce in the areas of Arnhem, Zwolle, Oldenburg and Emmerich. They operated in two sections of four, the first section being airborne at 1225 hours. One MET moving south-west at V.1102 and one MET at A.1398 were destroyed.

Whilst two MET moving south at A.1084 and one MET moving east at V.0035 were damaged. There was intense, inaccurate, light flak from Doetinghem A.0175. The last section landed by 14.20 hours.

Twelve aircraft, led by S/Ldr Lister, were detailed to carry out a Fighter Patrol in the areas Arnhem, Emmerich and Rees. They took off at 16.20 hours and patrolled uneventfully at 5,000 feet. Moderate, inaccurate, heavy flak came up from Arnhem. The squadron landed at 17.45 hours.

25 March: Fighter Patrol – Arnhem-Emmerich and Rees. Twelve aircraft led by F/Lt Fyfe got away at 05.55 hours and whilst on the patrol line, were vectored on to a dogfight south-west of Bocholt. F/Lt Willis and P/O Smith got on the tail of a Me 109, knocking portions off the tail and causing glycol to stream from the engine. The enemy aircraft then went down in a spiral dive and was seen to crash to the ground. The pilot baled out. The destruction of the Me 109 is shared between two pilots, although nearly everyone claimed to have got a squirt at it. The squadron landed at 07.25.

TALLY-HO!

The newly promoted Pilot Officer Ted Smith was lucky to get half a kill in a dogfight at this stage of the war, because his wing rarely encountered the Luftwaffe in the air. Soon afterwards, Smith discovered that the German population called the Spitfire boys '*Terrorflieger*': 'Terror Flyers'. He thought the name deserved because his Spitfire Wing had virtually stopped the German army moving by day.

Group Captain Johnnie Johnson, now commanding 125 Wing, seemed to have an affinity for smoking out the few remaining 'Hun' fighters. As Flight Sergeant Ronnie Ashman, who flew occasionally as Johnson's Wingman in 125, wrote later, 'Johnnie Johnson was hard to contain when enemy fighters were sighted; he banged open his throttle through the gate and a slight delay in following suit left one miles behind especially if one flying an elderly hard flown plane.'

At the end of April Johnson issued a bulletin in celebration of the Wing downing 38 fighters during the month.

One day, finding no Luftwaffe to tidy up, Johnson decided to take his boys on a jolly to Berlin:

I led the wing on the Berlin show at the first opportunity. For this epic occasion our first team took to the air. George led a squadron and Tony Gaze flew with me again – the first time since we flew together in Bader's wing. We swept to Berlin at a couple of thousand feet above the ground, over a changing sunlit countryside of desolate heathland, small lakes and large forests, with the empty, double ribbon of the autobahn lying close on our starboard side.

We shall not easily forget our first sight of Berlin. Thick cloud covered the capital and forced us down to a lower level. The roads to the west were filled with a mass of refugees fleeing the city. We pressed over the wooded suburbs, and Berlin sprawled below us with gaping holes here and there. It was burning in a dozen different places and the Falaise smell suddenly hit us; the corrupting stench of death. The Russian artillery was hard at it; as we flew towards the east, we saw the flashes of their guns and the debris thrown up from the shells. Russian tanks and armour rumbled into the city from the east. Tony said, 'Fifty-plus at two o'clock, Greycap! Same level. More behind.'

'Are they Huns, Tony?' I asked, as I focused my eyes on the gaggle.

'Don't look like Huns to me, Greycap,' replied Tony. 'Probably Russians.'

'All right, chaps,' I said. 'Stick together. Don't make a move.' And to myself I thought: I'm for it if this mix-up gets out of hand!

The Yaks began a slow turn which would bring them behind our Spitfires. I could not allow this and I swung the wing to starboard and turned over the top of the Yaks. They numbered about a hundred all told.

'More above us,' calmly reported Tony.

'Tighten it up,' I ordered. 'Don't break formation.'

We circled each other for a couple of turns. Both sides were cautious and suspicious. I narrowed the gap between us as much as I dared. When I was opposite the Russian leader I rocked my wings and watched for him to do the same. He paid no regard, but soon after he straightened out of his turn and led his ragged collection back to the east.

We watched them fly away. There seemed to be no

pattern or discipline to their flying. The leader was in front and the pack followed behind. Rising and falling with the gaggle continually changing shape. They reminded me of a great, wheeling, tumbling pack of starlings which one sometimes sees on a winter day in England. They quartered the ground like buzzards, and every few moments a handful broke away from the pack, circled leisurely and then attacked something in the desert of brick and rubble. In this fashion they worked over the dying city.

And then came the end of the war in Europe. In the Operations Record Book 127 Squadron, RAF 132 (Norwegian) Wing the diarist wrote:

28 April: Nothing doing
29 April: Another quiet day.
30 April: Squadron – Disbanded.

A week later, on 7 May, the Germans signed the instrument of unconditional surrender at Eisenhower's headquarters. 'The next morning,' Johnson recalled, 'we were not awakened by the powerful song of our Spitfires being run-up on the pre-dawn checks. We realized then that the war was really over.'

It was time for the Spitfire boys to say goodbye to their faithful, beautiful, deadly planes. Group Captain Hugh Dundas:

I do not know exactly how many hundreds of hours I spent in a Spitfire's cockpit; over sea, desert and mountains, in storm and sunshine, in conditions of great heat and great cold, by day and by night, on the deadly business of war and in the pursuit of pleasure. I do know that the Spitfire never let me down and that on the occasions when we got into trouble together the fault was invariably mine.

Wing Commander Bobby Oxspring:

The day before VE Day I strapped on a Spitfire for a carefree sort of acrobatics . . . I could scarcely believe I was still in one piece after six years of war and still flying my faithful Spitfire . . . Thanks to the dedicated engineers at Supermarine and Rolls-Royce, the Spitfire remained Queen of the Sky. Circumstances had aligned my embattled survival with her ever increasing performance.

Wing Commander Wilfrid Duncan Smith:

The next morning I walked out to my Spitfire and climbed into the cockpit. A couple of slaps on my shoulder from the ground crew. The farewells were over. Waving away the chocks I taxied out, the familiar crackle and snarl of the Merlin dulling my senses. I opened up the power and, easing my Spitfire into the air, turned in a wide arc, setting course across the mountains for Rome and Naples.

I had time to reflect on my long partnership with this unique fighting lady. A joy to fly, a sureness of robust qualities, a challenge to risk all.

Epilogue

The Spitfire belonged to the Second World War. It served from first to last, and was the only Allied fighter manufactured throughout the entire six years of the conflict. The future – which the Spit had met in the *Götterdämmerung* final days of the Reich – belonged to the jet. Nevertheless, the Spitfire had a long, if dwindling, swan song.

On the day the Second World War concluded, the RAF had a fraction under 1,000 Spitfires in front-line units and continued, along with the Fleet Air Arm, to take delivery of the latest variants of Mitchell's fighter until February 1948, when the last Spitfire of the final mark, the XXIV, left the Supermarine factory at South Marston, near Swindon. Simultaneously, the Spitfire force was rapidly run-down as the RAF was reduced in strength and most of its squadrons converted to jet fighters.

This left an extravagant surplus of Spitfires, which the British government turned into hard cash by selling, without too many questions asked, to any foreign government with the necessary money. Thus Spitfires were shipped to, among other countries, Thailand, Belgium, Eire, China, the Soviet Union, Turkey, Greece,

France, India, Egypt and Czechoslovakia. The latter nation sold on thirteen Spitfires to Israel which led to the bizarre circumstance during the Israeli War of Independence, 1948–9, of Israeli Spitfires fighting the Spitfires of neighbouring Egypt and the Spitfires from the international overseer, Britain. Odder still, the Israelis also flew the Avia S-199 which, to all intents and military purposes, was the Spitfire's old nemesis, the Messerschmitt 109G, built under licence in Czechoslovakia. The Israeli War of Independence was the last war in which a Spitfire was downed in action.

It was not the last war in which the Spitfire fought. The Spit's naval sister, the Seafire, flew off HMS *Triumph* at the beginning of the Korean War in 1950, undertaking 245 offensive patrols and 115 ground attacks on Communist forces. Meanwhile, another Communist uprising, in Malaya, caused Britain to declare a state of emergency in the colony in 1948, and Spitfires from 81, 28 and 60 Squadrons RAF responded with rocket and bomb attacks on Malayan Communist Party targets. In all, Spitfires from the RAF flew 1,800 sorties over Malaya, the ultimate sortie coming on 1 January 1951, flown by 60 Squadron. Fittingly, leading the squadron that day was Wing Commander Wilfrid Duncan Smith, the former Second World War ace and the Spit's most ardent champion.

Never again would the RAF fly the Spitfire in anger. Mitchell's design to satisfy Specification F7/30 would find a job performing photo reconnaissance, meteorological and training tasks until 1957, but its days as a front-line fighter had ended. It hardly mattered, for the Spitfire had long since passed into legend. A pair of elliptical wings with RAF roundels, the steady beat of a Rolls-Royce engine and a fresh-faced boy man in blue in the cockpit, will forever be the sight and sound of Britain at war for her life. And the world's liberty.

Glossary

AA: Anti-aircraft fire
AASF: Advanced Air Striking Force
ACM: Air Chief Marshal
AEAF: Allied Expeditionary Air Force
AI: Airborne Interception (Radar)
ALG: Advanced Landing Ground, being a temporary airfield
AM: Air Marshal
AOP: Air Observation Post
ASI: Air Speed Indicator
ATA: Air Transport Auxiliary
AVM: Air Vice-Marshal
Beehive: Formation of bombers with close escort fighters
BEF: British Expeditionary Force
CAS: Chief of the Air Staff
Circus: Fighter escort for bombers
DR: Dead Reckoning
Erk: Airman
ETA: Estimated Time of Arrival
FAA: Fleet Air Arm

GLOSSARY

Flak: Anti-aircraft fire

Flg Off (F/O): Flying Officer

Flt Lt (F/Lt): Flight Lieutenant

Flt Sgt (F/Sgt): Flight Sergeant

Glycol: aircraft engine coolant

Gp Capt: Group Captain

IFF: Identification friend or foe (for radar)

OTU: Operational Training Unit, last stage before joining squadron

Plt Off (P/O): Pilot Officer

PRU: Photographic Reconnaissance Unit

RAuxAF: Royal Auxiliary Force

RCAF: Royal Canadian Air Force

Rhubarb: Low-level fighter sweeps

RNZAF: Royal New Zealand Air Force

R/T: Radio telephone (voice)

SASO: Senior Air Staff Officer

SHAEF: Supreme Headquarters Allied Expeditionary Force

U/S: Unserviceable

USAAF: United States Army Air Force

WAAF: Women's Auxiliary Air Force

Wg Cdr: Wing Commander (or 'Wingco', slang)

W/T: Wireless transmission (morse)

Sources and Acknowledgements

IWM: Imperial War Museum, London.

NA: National Archives, Kew, London.

'The Aeroplane', quoted in *The Spitfire Log*, compiled by Peter Haining, Souvenir Press, 1985

F.A. Aikman, BBC Sound Archive

Ronald Adams, BBC Sound Archive

Johnny Allen, BBC Sound Archive

Anonymous Pilot, American Eagle Squadron, BBC Sound Archive

William Ash, *Under the Wire*, Bantam Press, 2005. © William Ash and Brendan Foley 2005. Reprinted by permission of Random House

R.V. Ashman, *Spitfire Against the Odds*, Patrick Stephens Ltd., 1989. © Peter Ashman

Tony Bartley, *Smoke Trails in the Sky*, William Kimber, 1984

Raymond Baxter (with Tony Dron), *Tales of My Time*, Grub Street, 2005

John Bisdee, quoted in *The Battle of Britain* by Matthew Parker, Headline, 2000

J.J. Boyle, NA 50/142

Peter Brown, NA Air 50

Elsie Cawser, reprinted by permission of the Salamander Oasis Trust

Winston S. Churchill, *Into Battle: War Speeches*, Cassell, 1948; *The Second World War*, Volume II, Cassell, 1949. Copyright © W.S. Churchill, 1949. Reprinted by permission of Curtis Brown

Pierre Clostermann, *The Big Show*, Chatto & Windus, 1951

David Crook, *Spitfire Pilot*, Greenhill Books, 2006. © David M. Crook 1942

Lettice Curtis, *The Forgotten Pilots*, G.T. Foulis & Co., 1971

Alan Deere, *Nine Lives*, Hodder & Stoughton, 1959. © 1959 Alan C. Deere

David Douglas-Hamilton, *The Air Battle for Malta*, Mainstream, 1981

Wilfrid Duncan Smith, *Spitfire Into Battle*, Hamlyn, 1982. Reprinted by permission of the estate of W. Duncan Smith

Hugh Dundas, *Flying Start,* Penguin, 1990. © Hugh Dundas 1988

John Dundas (609 Squadron diary), quoted in *The Story of 609 Squadron* by Frank Ziegler, Macdonald & Co., 1971

B.J. Ellan (Brian Lane), *Spitfire, The Experiences of a Fighter Pilot*, John Murray, 1942

Desmond Flower, quoted in *The War 1939–45*, edited by Desmond Flower and James Reeve, Cassell, 1960

Emmanuel Galitzine, NA Air/2

Adolf Galland, *The First and the Last*, Methuen, 1955

Charles Gardner, BBC Sound Archive

F.A.O. Gaze, quoted in *Spitfire: The Biography* by Jonathan Glancey, Atlantic, 2006

SOURCES AND ACKNOWLEDGEMENTS

D.E. Gillam, quoted in *Air Battle for Dunkirk* by Norman Franks, Grub Street, 2006

Jim Goodson, quoted in *Spitfire Women of World War II* by Giles Whittell, Harper Press, 2007

Roger Hall, *Clouds of Fear*, Coronet, 1977. © 1975 R.M.D. Hall

R.F. Hamlyn, BBC Sound Archive

Richard Hillary, *The Last Enemy*, Macmillan, 1943. © R. Hillary 1942

Johnnie Johnson, *Wing Leader*, Chatto & Windus, 1956

Sandy Johnstone, *Spitfire into War*, William Kimber, 1986

Donald Kingaby, NA Air

Brian Kingcombe, IWM Sound 132–3

Sidney Leach, IWM Docs 19–20, 31–32

Michael Le Bas, IWM Docs

Eric Lock, NA Air/50

P.B. 'Laddie' Lucas, quoted in *Fight for the Sky: The Story of the Spitfire and Hurricane* by Douglas Bader, Fontana, 1978

J.E. McComb, quoted in *Air Battle for Dunkirk*, Norman Franks, Grub Street, 2006

John Gillespie Magee, 'High Flight', *The War in the Air: An Anthology of Personal Experience*, edited by Gavin Lyall, Hutchinson & Co, 1968

Eric Marrs, IWM Docs 127 Squadron, RAF 132 (Norwegian) Wing, Operations Record Book, NA Air

Bobby Oxspring, *Spitfire Command*, Grafton Books, 1987. © Group Captain Bobby Oxspring 1984

'Polly' Pollard, NA AIR 50/173

Jeffrey Quill, *Spitfire: A Test Pilot's Story*, John Murray, 1983. © Jeffrey Quill 1983

J.D. 'Jack' Rae, *Kiwi Spitfire Ace*, Grub Street, 2002

M.R. Roberts, quoted in *Fight for the Sky: The Story of the Spitfire and Hurricane* by Douglas Bader, Fontana, 1978

Beverley Shenstone, 'Shaping the Spitfire' in *Spitfire: A Documentary History* by Alfred Price, Macdonald and Jane's, 1977

E.A.W. Smith, *Spitfire Diary*, William Kimber & Co. Ltd., 1988. © E.A.W. Smith 1988

Ralph Sorley, 'Eight Guns for a Fighter' in *The Spitfire Log*, compiled by Peter Haining, Souvenir Press, 1985

Robert 'Bob' Stanford Tuck, IWM Docs 125–6

Ulrich Steinhilper (and Peter Osborne), *Spitfire on My Tail*, Independent Books, 1989

222 Squadron, Combat Report, NA AIR 50/177

George Unwin, IWM Sound 133, 134, 136

J. Van Schaik, NA AIR 50/171

Tim Vigors, *Life's Too Short to Cry*, Grub Street, 2006. © 2006 Tim and Diana Vigors

Geoffrey Wellum, *First Light*, Viking 2002. © Geoffrey Wellum 2002. Reprinted by permission of Penguin UK

Index

INDEX